LONDON ARCHITECTURE

by Marianne Butler

Photography by Stephen Millar

London Architecture

Written by Marianne Butler
Photography by Stephen Millar
Front cover Canary Wharf
Inside cover Imagination atrium © Imagination
Edited by Abigail Willis by Andrew Kershman
Design by Lesley Gilmour & Susi Koch
Illustrations by Lesley Gilmour

Published in 2012 by
Metro Publications Ltd, PO Box 6336, London, N1 6PY

Metro® is a registered trade mark of Associated Newspapers Limited.
The METRO mark is under licence from Associated Newspapers Limited.

Printed and bound in India.
This book is produced using paper from registered sustainable
and managed sources. Suppliers have provided both LEI and
MUTU certification.

ISBN 978-1-902910-38-3

For Kelvin, Tom and Lucy
with love

Acknowledgements

I would firstly like to thank those at Metro Publications: Andrew for giving me the opportunity to write this book, Susi for her help and advice and Lesley for her patience with my endless questions. I am also indebted to Abigail Willis for her thoughtful editing and to Stephen Millar for his superb photography. My thanks and apologies to my long-suffering friends and family all of whom have shared my enthusiasm for London's architecture, whether they wanted to or not. I would especially like to thank Maxwell Hutchinson, who taught me more about the subject than any course or book ever could, and for his immense help with the last chapter of this book.

About the Author

Marianne Butler has a Masters degree in ancient history from the University of London and works as a freelance researcher and writer. She has worked with the architect and broadcaster Maxwell Hutchinson on the book, published by Headline, of the much acclaimed Channel 4 series 'No 57 – The History of a House'. Marianne divides her time between her old house and garden in the Scottish borders and the architectural delights of London.

About the Photographer

Stephen Millar lived in the City of London for seven years, and was married in St Bartholomew the Great. He is the author of London's Hidden Walks and London's City Churches and has written and produced photographs for a number of magazines and books including The Independent on Saturday.

Contents

Foreword.. vii

Introduction 1

Area Maps...2

01 In the Beginning 10

02 London Before Wren...18

03 Wren and the Rebuilding of the City 56

04 From Restoration to Georgian.................................84

05 Victorian London.. 132

06 Edwardian London and the Rise of Modernism........ 166

07 1945 to the 21st Century 198

08 Walking London's Architecture:

    Bartholomew Walk... 257

    Fleet Street and Beyond Walk............................... 266

    Greenwich Walk 274

    John Nash Walk 284

    South Bank Walk... 298

    Strand Walk.. 312

    Whitehall Walk.. 320

09 Eat and Drink Architecture 332

10 Shopping and Architecture..................................... 354

11 Architecture with a View 364

Appendix (Timeline, Glossary, Bibliography, Websites) 372

Index 378

Darwin Centre, Natural History Museum, see p.248

Foreword

London can justly claim to be one of the world's most architecturally fascinating cities. Admittedly, Rome has its great antiquities, New York its soaring 1930's skyscrapers, Haussmann's plan gives Paris its unique spacious grace, and Athens is of another era. But where else in the world does mould-breaking contemporary architecture lie within a stone's throw of over 2,000 years of history?

Stand outside Richard Rogers 1980's Lloyd's building, which is still a most remarkable structure, turn through 180 degrees and Norman Foster's Swiss Re Insurance 'gherkin' tower points skywards in an architectural gesture undreamed of before the third millennium. A sprightly five-minute walk will take you to the last remains of the 2,000 year old Roman wall outside the Museum of London.

In a peculiarly British way these contrasting architectural styles cohabit peacefully. Britain, and London in particular, has its own idiosyncratic approach to architecture and architectural style. Admittedly, many of England's finest Gothic cathedrals are more French than British – no accident as most of them were built under Norman influence. From then on the British placed a pragmatic filter over the extreme swings of Continental architecture endeavour. The originality of Palladio's northern Italian villas was distilled into London's post-Fire churches by Wren, Gibbs and Hawksmoor. The exuberance of Italian Baroque spread north to become the elegance of Georgian Bath. Regency terraced houses made a miniature Versailles look-alike available to all with party walls at 17'6" intervals.

In the second half of the 19th century however it was a different story. Britain led the way in the Industrial Revolution and with it coined a myriad of new architectural types, the railway stations, bridges and viaducts, mills and factories which sprang up throughout the country's industrial heartlands. Economic housing for the new urban working class and offices for the administration of Empire coincided with the greatest period of church building since the Middle Ages, in a style which, with a typical English nod and a wink is just that, Medieval.

In more recent times London has taken the very best of Continental Modernism from Germany, France and Scandinavia and cooked up a pragmatic British Modernism which is as peculiarly individual as the cut of an English gentleman's suit.

Post-modernism spread north across the English Channel and east across the Atlantic. London has its fair share of buildings which are woeful examples of 1980's post-modernism. Thankfully, following the economic collapse of the early 1990's after John Major's withdrawal from the European Exchange Rate Mechanism, the architectural scene was rescued and reinvigorated by the introduction of the National

Lottery in 1994. Lottery millions gave London the Tate Modern, the Great Court at the British Museum and extensions to the Wallace Collection, the National Portrait Gallery and the Royal Opera House as well as creating… The Dome. London's Docklands, and particularly Canary Wharf, are an economic, if not an architectural, triumph. The barren wastelands of yesterday's docks have provided fertile soil for third millennium capitalism which regrettably seeks to express itself, in the main, in retro-Manhattan style skyscrapers. However, Foster's 'gherkin', quite literally, points the way to a different style and approach to London's high rise office buildings of the future.

London's current architecture owes a great deal to the impact of computer-aided design. Firstly, the form of buildings has been liberated from the dominance of the drawing board generated right angle. Norman Foster's GLA building and the Great Court at the British Museum would have been impossible without the flexible geometry of the microchip. Everywhere columns and beams have become deliciously slender with gravity-defying spans as the computer takes the drudgery and uncertainty out of the structural calculations. The third millennium affords the architect a whole new palate of materials to lighten and freshen the appearance of all buildings, large and small alike. And finally, the new computer-generated architecture is colourful. Plans can now be reproduced in accurate colours and conveyed through digital printing and photography – no watercolours or coloured pencils in sight.

Much of 19th-century architecture owes its genesis to cast iron and steel. Twentieth century architecture is dominated by the new freedoms and economies of reinforced concrete. So far, the 21st century is the architecture of transparency, of glass. Time alone will tell whether the world's aspirations for a low-carbon economy will cast doubt on the wisdom of lightweight enclosures and structures. Buildings are responsible for producing the largest proportion of carbon dioxide and also the vast proportion of embodied energy. Glass requires extensive heat for its production, is heavy and energy inefficient to transport and has less than admirable thermal characteristics. On the other hand new glass technology enables architects to dream new dreams and lighten the built environment with a delicate deftness of touch.

It is all too easy to see London's architecture simply in terms of the contemporary abundance of works by Norman Foster and Richard Rogers. Look back a decade or so and there are Terry Farrell's *grandes projets* with his English take on Post Modernism. Already, London's architecture can be seen as the work of a small number of forceful and opinionated architects. In the immediate post War period, assured young men like Leslie Martin, Philip Powell and Hidalgo Moya and the entire London County Council Architects Department did their best to rebuild Britain with energy and enthusiasm. Victorian London would not be what it is without the works of George Gilbert Scott; Regency London was created, in the main, by John Nash while Christopher Wren forged a new London out of the ashes of the Great Fire of 1666. Sad to say there is little left of pre-Fire London, the flames swept away the remains of the greatest Medieval city in Northern Europe taking with them the old Gothic St Paul's Cathedral, the largest structure of its kind in the world.

Marianne Butler's refreshing and tasteful guide to London's architecture shows us just how accessible are the capital's many architectural styles. On any one of her walks the architectural enthusiast or someone approaching the subject for the first time will be able to experience this variety within a few streets. Fortunately, London with its various 'villages' is a walking city. The square-mile that is the City of London can be absorbed in less than a day. The squares of Bloomsbury or Belgravia can be walked in an hour or so. John Nash's great urban plan from Regent's Park to Buckingham Palace is but an hour's walk with architectural variety at every twist and turn.

Regardless of the location there is one simple rule about enjoying London's architecture, avoid the shop-fronts, the enticing interiors of cafés and bars – always excepting London's fantastic collection of Victorian public houses – and, quite simply, look up. All travellers habitually look down, maybe because the pavements have a habit of being somewhat hazardous. Cast your eyes upward and you will often be surprised by the architectural details above the bland, contemporary shop fronts.

There is a lot to see in London's architectural landscape. It is not necessary to understand the subtle nuances of personality, style and function. With the help of this charming little book it is possible to take things, quite literally, at face value. Look and enjoy. On the other hand, read with care between the lines and wonderful stories tumble out of every door and window.

London's buildings are as human and entertaining as Londoners themselves. And don't forget that there are 28,000 architectural guides available to everyone in London – the drivers of the city's black taxi-cabs. By a strange process of osmosis the London cabby has become as knowledgeable and opinionated about architecture as anybody in the capital. Hail a cab from outside, say, the Royal Exchange in the heart of the City and ask the driver to take you to Buckingham Palace. Once underway just ask what they think about any building you care to mention. They will have an opinion and, in the main, it will be well informed.

London's architecture is for and about people. I am privileged to live in the very heart of what I consider to be the greatest architectural city in the world, and I can heartily recommend Marianne Butler's handy and accessible guide to anyone who wishes to explore London's unique architectural landscape.

Maxwell Hutchinson, Clerkenwell, London

German Gymnasium, see p.152

Introduction

Having been born and brought up in an architecturally soulless New Town, what I remember most about childhood was the annual visit to London. The visit was ostensibly to see Father Christmas at the splendid Selfridges store, but my imagination was captured by the buildings I encountered in the capital – a visit to Leicester Square cinema meant sitting in the largest, plushest interior I had ever encountered. Of course I didn't know it was 'Art Deco', or that it belonged to any particular era at all, I just knew the place oozed glamour as did the Lyon's Corner House where I was taken for tea afterwards. What I loved was the fact that a simple stroll down any London street could reveal buildings of startling contrast in age, form and function. I still find London and its architecture exciting and, fortunately, I am not alone in my enthusiasm.

These are exciting times with internationally renown architects making their mark on the capital – Renzo Piano with the soaring glass Shard transforming a once uninspiring corner of Southwark and his colourful addition to the area of St Giles, Will Alsop's arresting 'Palestra' on the Blackfriars Road, and Zaha Hadid's splendid Aquatics Centre at the Olympic Park. It is not just the sparkling new-builds that engage us. The wholesale revamping of areas such as Covent Garden, the Paddington Basin, and more recently St Pancras and Kings Cross, has transformed once rather forbidding places into vibrant public spaces, occasionally revealing architectural gems (such as the German Gymnasium opposite). Architecture buffs can also explore buildings normally closed to the public during the annual 'Open House Weekend' (see p.377), giving us the chance to see the interior of treasures such as the Lloyd's Building in the City of London and the Daily Express Building on Fleet Street.

This guide is essentially a hop, skip and jump through the history of London's built environment. Each chapter begins with a brief description of a particular period and offers a selection of buildings that are representative of that era. Those buildings that have been included will, I hope, give the reader an insight into the architectural forces that have shaped this great city.

The aim of this guide is to forge or further an interest in London's architecture. I have tried to avoid jargon – it is one thing to know a spandrel from a spangle, but a beautiful building can be admired and understood without recourse to technical language. With this book to hand, and some comfortable shoes – the best of London's architecture awaits you!

I have greatly appreciated the correspondence generated from the first edition of this book. Please e-mail your thoughts to londonarchitecture@yahoo.co.uk.

Marianne Butler

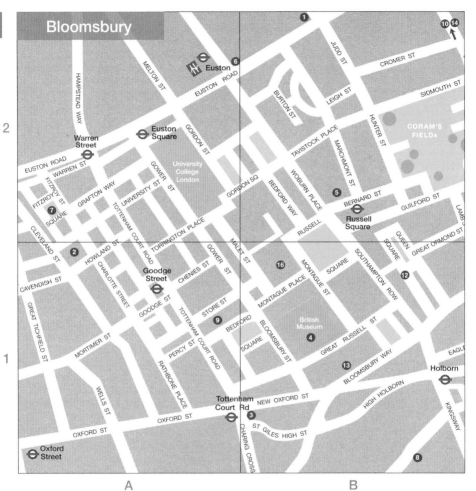

Bloomsbury

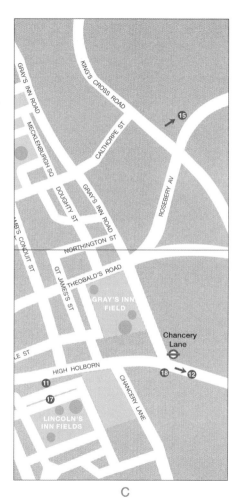

C

1) British Library B:2 *(p.226)*
2) B T Tower A:1 *(p.209)*
3) Centre Point B:1 *(p.210)*
4) British Museum B:1 *(p.125, 232)*
5) Daimler Car Hire Garage B:1 *(p.193)*
6) Euston Fire Station A:2 *(p.173)*
7) Fitzroy Square A:2 *(p.115)*
8) Freemasons' Hall B:1 *(p.187)*
9) Imagination A:1 *(p.220)*
10) The Midland Grand Hotel B:2 *(p.154)*
11) Renaissance London Chancery Court Hotel C:1 *(p.341)*
12 St Andrew, Holborn C:1 *(p.66)*
13) St George's, Bloomsbury B:1 *(p.95)*
14) St Pancras Station B:2 *(p.154)*
15) Sadler's Wells C:1 *(p.229)*
16) Senate House, University of London B:1 *(p.196)*
17) Sir John Soane's Museum C:1 *(p.122)*
18) Staple Inn, Holborn C:1 *(p.43)*

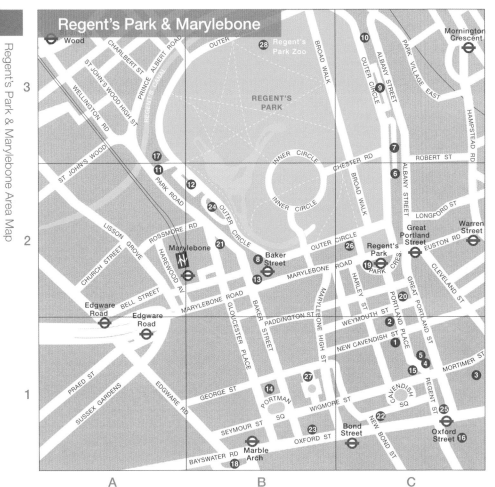

Regent's Park & Marylebone

Wood

St John's Wood

CHARLBERT ST

ST JOHN'S WOOD HIGH ST

WELLINGTON RD

PRINCE ALBERT ROAD

REGENT'S CANAL

OUTER

28 Regent's Park Zoo

BROAD WALK

REGENT'S PARK

10

ALBANY STREET

OUTER CIRCLE

PARK VILLAGE EAST

Mornington Crescent

HAMPSTEAD RD

9

7

ROBERT ST

6

INNER CIRCLE

CHESTER RD

ALBANY STREET

LONGFORD ST

Warren Street

17

11

PARK ROAD

12

24

OUTER CIRCLE

INNER CIRCLE

BROAD WALK

OUTER CIRCLE

26

Great Portland Street

Regent's Park

19

PARK CRES

EUSTON RD

CLEVELAND ST

ST JOHN'S WOOD

LISSON GROVE

ROSSMORE RD

HAREWOOD AV

21

Marylebone

8 Baker Street

13

MARYLEBONE ROAD

HARLEY ST

20

GREAT PORTLAND ST

CHURCH STREET

BELL STREET

Edgware Road

Edgware Road

MARYLEBONE ROAD

BAKER STREET

GLOUCESTER PLACE

PADDINGTON ST

MARYLEBONE HIGH ST

WEYMOUTH ST

PORTLAND PLACE

NEW CAVENDISH ST

2

1

5

4

15

3

MORTIMER ST

PRAED ST

EDGWARE RD

SUSSEX GARDENS

GEORGE ST

27

14

PORTMAN SQ

WIGMORE ST

CAVENDISH SQ

NEW BOND ST

22

REGENT ST

25

Oxford Street

16

SEYMOUR ST

23

OXFORD ST

Bond Street

BAYSWATER RD

Marble Arch

18

A   B   C

1   2   3

1) 17, 21 & 23 Portland Place C:1 *(p.290)*
2) 27-47 Portland Place C:1 *(p.290)*
3) All Saints Church, Margaret St C:1 *(p.144)*
4) All Souls Church C:1 *(p.293)*
5) BBC Broadcasting House C:1 *(p.292)*
6) Chester Gate C:2 *(p.289)*
7) Chester Terrace C:3 *(p.288)*
8) Cornwall Terrace B:2 *(p.289)*
9) Cumberland Terrace C:3 *(p.287, 288)*
10) Gloucester Lodge & Gloucester Gate C:3 *(p.286)*
11) Hanover Gate A:2 *(p.289)*
12) Hanover Terrace B:2 *(p.289)*
13) Holy Trinity Church, Marylebone B:2 *(p.122)*
14) Home House B:1 *(p.110)*
15) Langham Hotel C:1 *(p.292)*
16) Liberty's C:1
17) London Central Mosque A:3 *(p.289)*
18) Marble Arch B:1
19) Park Crescent C:2 *(p.290)*
20) Royal Institute of British Architects C:2 *(p.292)*
21) Rudolf Steiner House B:2 *(p.190)*
22) St Peter, Vere Street C:1 *(p.103)*
23) Selfridges B:1 *(p.360)*
24) Sussex Place B:2 *(p.289)*
25) Top Shop C:1
26) Ulster Place C:2 *(p.290)*
27) The Wallace Collection B:1 *(p.234)*
28) Regent's Park Zoo B:3 *(p.286)*

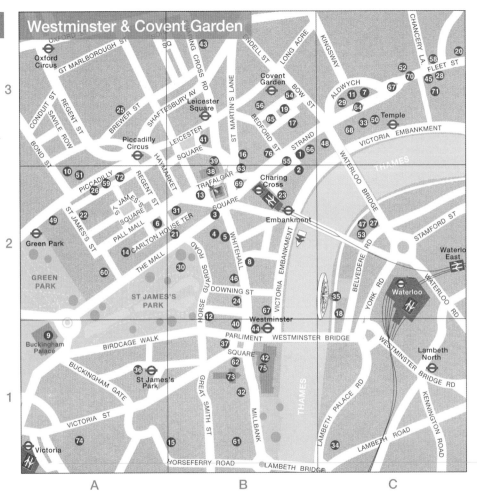

Westminster & Covent Garden

1) 6-10 Adam Street B:3 *(p.114, 318)*
2) Adelphi B:2 *(p.114)*
3) Admiralty Arch B:2 *(p.325)*
4) Admiralty House B:2 *(p.325)*
5) Admiralty Screen B:2 *(p.325)*
6) The Athenaeum A:2 *(p.294)*
7) Australia House C:3 *(p.317)*
8) Banqueting House B:2 *(p.47)*
9) Buckingham Palace A:1 *(p.295)*
10) Burlington Arcade A:2 *(p.357)*
11) Bush House C:3 *(p.317)*
12) Cabinet War Rooms B:2 *(p.331)*
13) Canada House B:2 (p.323)
14) Carlton House Terrace A:2 *(p.295)*
15) Channel 4 Headquarters B:1 *(p.225)*
16) Coliseum Theatre B:3 *(p.176)*
17) Country Life Offices (Former) B:3 *(p.177)*
18) County Hall (Former) C:2 *(p.182)*
19) The Piazza, Covent Garden B:3 *(p.48)*
20) Daily Telegraph building C:3 *(p.268)*
21) Duke of York's Column B:2 *(p.295)*
22) The Economist Building A:2 *(p.208)*
23) Embankment Place B:2 *(p.225)*
24) Foreign and Commonwealth Office B:2 *(p.328)*
25) Former Lex Garage A:3 *(p.190)*
26) Fortnum & Mason A:2 *(p.360)*
27) Hayward Gallery C:2 *(p.206)*
28) Hoare's Bank C:3 *(p.269)*
29) India House C:3 *(p.318)*
30) Inn the Park B:2 *(p.349)*
31) The Institute of Directors B:2 *(p.294)*
32) Jewel Tower B:1 *(p.32)*
33) King's College C:3 *(p.316)*
34) Lambeth Palace C:1 *(p.55)*
35) London Eye C:2 *(p.371)*
36) London Transport Headquarters A:1 *(p.189)*
37) Methodist Central Hall B:1 *(p.180)*
38) National Gallery B:2 *(p.322)*
39) National Portrait Gallery B:3 *(p.346)*
40) New Government Offices B:1 *(p.329)*
41) Odeon Cinema, Leicester Sq B:3 *(p.195)*
42) Palace of Westminster/ Houses of Parliament B:1 *(p.32, 141)*
43) Phoenix Theatre B:3 *(p.191)*
44) Portcullis House B:1 *(p.329)*
45) Prince Henry's Room C:3 *(p.270)*
46) Privy Council Chambers B:2 *(p.328)*
47) Queen Elizabeth Hall C:2 *(p.207)*
48) Queen's Chapel of Savoy C:3 *(p.318)*
49) The Ritz A:2 *(p.340)*
50) Roman Bath C:3 *(p.314)*
51) Royal Academy of Arts A:2 *(p.222)*
52) Royal Courts of Justice C:3 *(p.313)*
53) Royal Festival Hall C:2 *(p.205)*
54) Royal Opera House B:3 *(p.235)*
55) Royal Society of Arts B:3 *(p.114)*
56) Russell House, Covent Garden B:3 *(p.101)*
57) St Clement Danes C:3 *(p.314)*
58) St Dunstan in the West C:3 *(p.269)*
59) St James's, Piccadilly A:2 *(p.90)*
60) St James's Palace A:2 *(p.42)*
61) St John's, Smith Square B:1 *(p.336)*
62) St Margaret's, Westminster B:1 *(p.41)*
63) St Martin's-in-the-Fields B:2 *(p.323)*
64) St Mary-le-Strand C:3 *(p.102)*
65) St Paul's Church B:3 *(p.48)*
66) Savoy Hotel B:3
67) Scotland Yard House B:2 *(p.330)*
68) Somerset House C:3 *(p.316, 319)*
69) South Africa House B:2 *(p.325)*
70) The Temple Bar C:3 *(p.272)*
71) Temple Church C:3 *(p.52)*
72) Waterstone's, Piccadilly A:2 *(p.361)*
73) Westminster Abbey B:1 *(p.25)*
74) Westminster Cathedral A:1 *(p.174)*
75) Westminster Hall B:1 *(p.32, 141)*
76) Zimbabwe House B:3 *(p.179)*

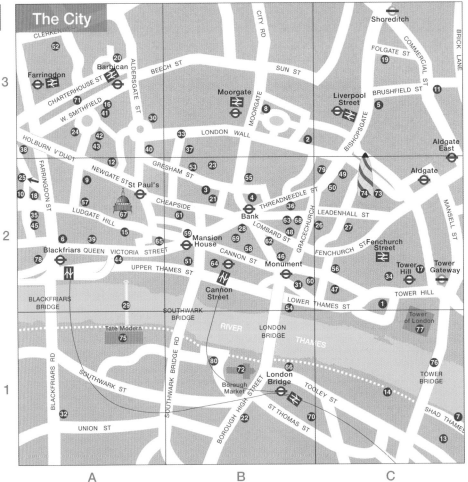

The City

Shoreditch

CLERKENW...

52

Farringdon

Barbican

20

BEECH ST

CITY RD

SUN ST

Moorgate

8

FOLGATE ST

COMMERCIAL ST

BRICK LANE

19

Liverpool Street

5

11

ALDERSGATE ST

CHARTERHOUSE ST

71

W. SMITHFIELD

16

41

24

30

42

43

38

HOLBURN V'DUCT

12

9

NEWGATE ST

LONDON WALL

33

37

23

53

55

BRUSHFIELD ST

BISHOPSGATE

Aldgate East

Aldgate

2

MANSELL ST

25

10

18

FARRINGDON ST

St Paul's

GRESHAM ST

3

21

CHEAPSIDE

4

THREADNEEDLE ST

36

79

49

50

74 73

LEADENHALL ST

26

27

35

45

57

67

LUDGATE HILL

61

Bank

6

39

15

65

59

Mansion House

28

69

LOMBARD ST

63 68

48

62

GRACECHURCH ST

Fenchurch Street

Tower Hill

17

Tower Gateway

Blackfriars

78

QUEEN VICTORIA STREET

44

51

58

CANNON ST

46

Monument

56

FENCHURCH ST

34

UPPER THAMES ST

64

31 60

47

1

TOWER HILL

Cannon Street

LOWER THAMES ST

54

BLACKFRIARS BRIDGE

29

SOUTHWARK BRIDGE

RIVER

LONDON BRIDGE

THAMES

Tower of London

77

Tate Modern

75

80

72

66

London Bridge

76

TOWER BRIDGE

BLACKFRIARS RD

SOUTHWARK ST

SOUTHWARK BRIDGE RD

Borough Market

BOROUGH HIGH STREET

TOOLEY ST

14

32

UNION ST

22

ST THOMAS ST

70

SHAD THAMES

13

A   B   C

1

2

3

1) All Hallows by the Tower C:2 *(p.29)*
2) All Hallows Church B:3 *(p.118)*
3) Banco Commerciale Italiana B:2 *(p.143)*
4) Bank of England B:2 *(p.121, 189)*
5) Bishopsgate Institute C:3 *(p.163)*
6) Black Friar Public House A:2 *(p.337)*
7) Blueprint Café, Design Museum C:1 *(p.344)*
8) Britannic House B:3 *(p.185)*
9) Central Criminal Court, Old Bailey A:2 *(p.178)*
10) Cheshire Cheese Public House A:2 *(p.269)*
11) Christ Church, Spitalfields C:3 *(p.95)*
12) Christ Church, Newgate A:2 *(p.64)*
13) The Circle, Queen Elizabeth St C:1 *(p.216)*
14) City Hall C:1 *(p.236)*
15) City of London Information Centre A:2 *(p.245)*
16) Cloth Fair A:3 *(p.259)*
17) Crescent, City of London C:2 *(p.119)*
18) Daily Express building A:2 *(p.268)*
19) Dennis Severs' House C:3 *(p.131)*
20) Florin Court A:3 *(p.259)*
21) Frederick Place B:2 *(p.115)*
22) George Inn B:1 *(p.335)*
23) The Guildhall B:2 *(p.16, 40)*
24) Haberdashers' Hall A:3 *(p.262)*
25) Dr Johnson's House A:2 *(p.127)*
26) Leadenhall Market C:2 *(p.359)*
27) Lloyd's of London C:2 *(p.214)*
28) Mansion House B:2 *(p.118)*
29) Millennium Bridge A:2 *(p.369)*
30) Museum of London A:3 *(p.17)*
31) The Monument B:2 *(p.367)*
32) Palestra A:1 *(p.250)*
33) Pizza Express, Alban Gate B:3 *(p.345)*
34) Port of London Authority C:2 *(p.184)*
35) Reuters Building A:2 *(p.267)*
36) Royal Exchange B:2 *(p.358)*
37) St Alban B:3 *(p.65)*
38) St Andrew, Holborn A:3 *(p.66)*
39) St Andrew by the Wardrobe A:2 *(p.66)*
40) St Anne & St Agnes A:3 *(p.67)*

41) St Bartholomew the Great A:3 *(p.34)*
42) St Bartholomew the Less A:3 *(p.261)*
43) St Bartholomew's Hospital A:3 *(p.261)*
44) St Benet, Paul's Wharf A:2 *(p.68)*
45) St Bride, Fleet St A:2 *(p.68)*
46) St Clement Eastcheap B:2 *(p.70)*
47) St Dunstan in the East C:2 *(p.70)*
48) St Edmund the King & Martyr B:2 *(p.71)*
49) St Ethelburga's C:2 *(p.50)*
50) St Helen's Bishopsgate C:2 *(p.38)*
51) St James Garlickhithe B:2 *(p.71)*
52) St John's Priory A:3 *(p.36)*
53) St Lawrence Jewry B:2 *(p.72)*
54) St Magnus the Martyr B:2 *(p.72)*
55) St Margaret, Lothbury B:2 *(p.73)*
56) St Margaret Pattens C:2 *(p.74)*
57) St Martin within Ludgate A:2 *(p.75)*
58) St Mary Abchurch B:2 *(p.75)*
59) St Mary Aldermary B:2 *(p.76)*
60) St Mary at Hill B:2 *(p.77)*
61) St Mary-le-Bow B:2 *(p.77)*
62) St Mary Woolnoth B:2 *(p.96)*
63) St Michael Cornhill B:2 *(p.78)*
64) St Michael Paternoster Royal B:2 *(p.79)*
65) St Nicholas Cole Abbey A:2 *(p.80)*
66) St Olaf House B:1 *(p.195)*
67) St Paul's Cathedral A:2 *(p.61)*
68) St Peter upon Cornhill B:2 *(p.81)*
69) St Stephen Walbrook B:2 *(p.83)*
70) The Shard B:1 *(p.251)*
71) Smithfield Meat Market A:3 *(p.139, 264)*
72) Southwark Cathedral B:1 *(p.32)*
73) Spanish & Portuguese Synagogue C:2 *(p.51)*
74) Swiss Re Headquarters C:2 *(p.238)*
75) Tate Modern A:1 *(p.230)*
76) Tower Bridge C:1 *(p.367)*
77) Tower of London C:1 *(p.31)*
78) Unilever House A:2 *(p.192)*
79) Vertigo, Tower 42 C:2 *(p.344)*
80) Winchester House B:1 *(p.304)*

Roman Wall and 19th-century statue of Trajan, Tower Hill

01

IN THE BEGINNING

IN THE BEGINNING

"And dream of London, small and white, and clean,
The clear Thames bordered by its gardens green"
William Morris

There is little evidence of pre-Roman habitation in the London area, just a few small settlements along the river Thames west of Whitehall. One explanation for this is that the river acted as natural barrier and border between tribes of Britons – the Atrebates, Regni and Cantiaci, who lived south of the Thames, and the powerful Catuvellauni tribe, who lived to the north.

For at least six centuries before the Roman occupation of Britain, the country had enjoyed substantial links with a trade network that stretched from the western Mediterranean, Spain, southern Gaul to northern Germany and the Baltic Islands. The Thames acted as a super highway transporting raw materials and goods from Britain's abundant natural resources, copper from Wales, tin from Cornwall.

Archaeologists tell us that conditions in the area settled by the Romans were idyllic with the land almost entirely covered with a mix of open oak and hazel woodland. Small clean and clear flowing rivers, such as the Fleet and the Walbrook, poured into the Thames, then wider than it is today with small boggy islands at various points. The impetus for bridging the Thames, at a point not far from where London

Bridge is today, may have been a military one, but it also made for an attractive and convenient place to settle and trade.

Almost within living memory of the Roman conquest of 43 CE the southern half of Britain was a hive of activity: road building, setting up trading posts and establishing towns. Londinium, as Roman London was to become known, with its establishment as a major port, was central to this activity as at high tide the area could be reached by merchant ships that sailed up the Thames laden with goods from all parts of the Empire.

Founded in about 50 CE on the north bank of the Thames, early Londinium must have resembled a frontier town of the Wild West filled with pioneering merchants and dealers. Settlement began in the area that is today the City of London. Flimsy, wooden dwellings, warehouses and a small fort were hurriedly constructed and the town rapidly expanded, becoming the largest town in Britain in just ten years.

However this fledgling town was destroyed in 60 CE by the Iceni tribe, from the area known today as East Anglia, led by their queen

Boudicca. She also razed Colchester and St Albans to the ground in her revolt against Roman rule. But by 70 CE Londinium was once again a boomtown with a programme of public works in place and within 30 years prestigious buildings such as the Amphitheatre, the Governor's Palace and Public Baths, now built from durable stone and tile, were gracing its streets. Domestic dwellings and shops were still made from wood, closely packed together and generally situated on the busier, noisier streets.

The central, and perhaps most characteristic feature of any Roman town was the Forum, of which Londinium could boast the largest example in the northern Roman provinces, about 600 feet square in total. Situated approximately at modern Cornhill, such a complex consisted of a large central open space surrounded by buildings which housed the town hall and legal centre. The open space was used by the populace as a venue for conducting religious and official business, as well as serving as a market place.

This was a period of great prosperity for the town and for builders and planners this meant that new problems required new solutions. Continuous supplies of food and goods needed to be brought in from outside and it is about this time that the wooden landing stage that had passed as the town's port facility was superseded by a well-built quay, with warehouses of commercial proportions.

Such was its importance Londinium received a visit from Emperor Hadrian in 122 CE and by 200 CE a defensive wall surrounded the city. This wall, almost two miles in length, anywhere between 9 and 15 feet thick, was made from Kentish ragstone. The whole of Londinium was enclosed within about 330 acres in total. Gateways controlled access and allowed the passage of the major Roman roads

During the 3rd century CE the population of Londinium began to shrink considerably, due in large to an economic downturn. Nevertheless the citizens of the town were notably wealthier than ever before, with homes made from stone, or at least only half-timbered. Interiors were brightened with mosaics and wall paintings and possibly one or two rooms had the luxury of a hypocaust system of central heating.

The end of the 4th century saw the decline of the Roman Empire as a whole and by the mid 5th century Londinium was abandoned and its once grand public buildings and busy streets were left to fall into decay.

There is virtually nothing left to see of Roman London. Although archaeology can confirm the existence and position of buildings, what size they were and what materials they were made of, there is not much in the way of written evidence to tell us what the buildings actually looked like. To bridge this gap we have to consider what Roman architecture was like generally and apply this to London's remains in order to get some sort of picture of Londinium's principal buildings.

Many of the outward forms of Roman architecture are clearly taken from the Greek. In colonising Greece during the 2nd century BCE the blossoming Roman Empire was able to exploit the skill of Greek builders who had perfected a standard post and lintel type of construction. Greek buildings were composed entirely of horizontal blocks supported by columns and walls – this was a style of architecture characterised by straight lines and a complete absence of arches or curves.

However such construction had its constraints. The span between columns was limited, as was the weight bearing capacity, and therefore buildings could be no more than two storeys high. This was not enough for the Romans who wanted the architecture of their empire to make a strong statement of authority and this was very important to an acquisitive empire. The solution to the need for taller, more lavish buildings was found through the ingenious combination of the column and the rounded arch – a system that allows for a much higher load-bearing capacity.

The rounded arch is a distinctive feature of Roman architecture, as are the orders, or columns. The Romans had five different styles of columns, (see opposite page) three of which were copies of Greek orders – Doric, plain with no fancy carving; Ionic, with fluted or scrolled capitals (that is the uppermost part of the column); and Corinthian with a capital decorated with carved acanthus leaves. All three Greek orders had fluted shafts. To this the Romans added the Tuscan order, like the Greek Doric but even plainer in appearance as the shaft was not fluted, and lastly Composite, similar to the Corinthian, but with more elaborate carving on the capital.

The influence of Greco-Roman building cannot be overestimated, with many of their forms becoming part of the common language of western architecture. Indeed the very word 'architecture' is derived from the Latin and one of the most widely read and respected works on the subject is Vitruvius's De architectura libri decem (Ten Books of Architecture). Written sometime between 31 BCE and 14 CE, Vitruvius' treatise highlighted the affinity between architecture and engineering and his work went on to influence a succession of architects over the ages, including Inigo Jones whose work in the 17th century is discussed in the following chapter.

Plunder, neglect and the destruction over the centuries has resulted in few Roman remains to be seen in London today. However, archaeologists continue to turn up interesting finds, examples of which can be seen in-situ in the undercroft of All Hallows by the Tower on Byford Street (see p.29). In addition, three Central London museums have extensive Roman displays, helping us to imagine what Londinium would have been like:

Tuscan

Doric

Ionic

Modern Ionic

Composite

Corinthian

In The Beginning

Above: Capitals of the Five Classical Orders and of the Modern Ionic Order

Guildhall

Guildhall Yard, EC2P 2EJ • Tel 020 7332 3700 • www.guildhall-art-gallery.org.uk • Nearest transport: Bank LU • See website for opening times and admission charges

During the 1988 preparation work for an extension to the Guildhall in the heart of the City, short stretches of Roman wall were discovered. Much excitement ensued when it was realised that what had been found was the site and remains of the amphitheatre – which would have been used for gladiatorial combat, animal fighting, public executions and religious ceremonies.

A line set into the paving in the square in front of the Guildhall denotes the location of the amphitheatre, whilst archaeological finds relating to the site are in the basement of the Guildhall Art Gallery – a short walk from the Museum of London. *Area Map p.8, B:2*

British Museum

Great Russell Street, WC1B 3DG • Tel 0207 323 8299 • www.thebritishmuseum. ac.uk • Nearest transport Holborn LU and Russell Square LU • Admission free except for major exhibitions • See website for opening times

The Weston Gallery of Roman Britain houses an extensive display of artefacts from the Roman occupation, although not necessarily from Londinium. The museum also houses a fascinating collection of Greek and Roman architectural remains, offering an excellent insight into how the various orders were used and the role of elements such as capitals, cornices and friezes. *Area Map p.2-3, B:2*

Museum of London

London Wall, EC2Y 5HN • Tel 020 7001 9844 • www.museumoflondon.org.uk • Nearest transport Barbican LU & Rail and St Paul's LU • Admission free • See website for opening times

A wonderful resource in the heart of the City of London. Archaeological finds and atmospheric room reconstructions show how Roman Londoners would have lived and worked. There is also a section of old Roman city wall which can be glimpsed from the museum. *Area Map p.8, A:3*

Rose window with stained glass designed by Sir James Thornhill in 1722, north transept, Westminster Abbey

02

LONDON BEFORE WREN

LONDON BEFORE WREN

*"Go where we may, rest where we will,
Eternal London haunts us still" Thomas More*

The monk and historian The Venerable Bede (672-735) tells us that even after the end of Roman rule London was a 'mart of many nations'. For many years archaeologists and historians were baffled as to where the latest settlers in London, the Saxons and the Angles – Germanic tribes from Northern Europe who settled in Britain from the late 4th and 5th centuries onwards – actually lived. The first St Paul's, a wooden structure, was in place on the site of the present Cathedral by the early 7th century, but there is no evidence of other early settlement within the abandoned Roman city. It would appear that, initially at least, the Saxons avoided the site of Londinium and settled along the Thames valley at places such as Croydon, Mitcham, Rainham, Hanwell, and Twickenham.

However, during the building of the new extension to the Royal Opera House in Covent Garden in the 1980s, remains were found of the elusive Saxon town of 'Lundenwic'. They had settled a mile or so to the west of the ruined Roman city, underlying what is today the West End and the Aldwych, the name which may refer to the 'old town'. It was not until the later Saxon period, from the expulsion of invading Danes by King Alfred in 886 until the Norman invasion of 1066, that the area within the old Roman walls was used again.

There is nothing left standing of the Saxon period, save a few traces at All Hallows by the Tower (see p.29), due mainly to their preference for building timber structures, which had no permanence above ground, or for re-using Roman brick from the City area, thereby usually confusing matters. Because it is regarded as a time of cultural unenlightenment, the period of about 400 years between the departure of the Romans and the arrival of the Normans is often referred to as the 'Dark Age'. This is a little unfair given the beautifully crafted articles produced in this period, examples of which can be seen in the British Museum.

However, one very important Saxon architectural legacy to posterity is the concept of the 'Hall' dwelling – one large room, open to the rafters, constructed of whole or split logs, with a fire for cooking and warmth at the centre. The size of the construction depended upon how many people had to be catered for. This simple structure was the basis of later 'Halls' for meetings and dining such as at Westminster, the City (Guildhall see p.40) and was central to community living in institutions such as the Inns of Law (see Section Two 'Walking London's Architecture' p.257) and the colleges of Oxford and Cambridge.

The Norman invaders were prolific castle and church builders, the finest examples of which in London are to be found at the White Tower and St John's Chapel (see Tower of London p.31). The Tower was one of three castles built in the area, the others being Baynard's Castle and Montfitchet Castle, the remains of both perished in the Great Fire of 1666.

There are two notable characteristics of Norman architecture. The first is the use of enduring materials such as stone, or the re-use of available Roman bricks. The second is the rounded arch, borrowed from Roman builders and the reason why Norman architecture is often called 'Romanesque'. The rounded arch was found to be strong in the extreme and experimentation with the pointed arch did not come until much later. The ground plan of a Norman church is always in the shape of a Latin cross, with the altar almost without exception at the east end of the building – in the direction of Jerusalem – with the main entrance at the west end.

Many Norman French words have been absorbed into our everyday language such as lodge, grange, vale and forest, and place names from this period still resound in London – Barbican, Savoy, Old Bailey, Charterhouse.

The term 'Gothic' is a Renaissance term of abuse – describing a style humanists found barbaric and anti-classical, but which embraced several changes in architectural thought and application between the 12th and 16th centuries.

The Gothic style is generally held to have begun with the rebuilding of St Denis in France in the 1140s, under the auspices of Abbot Suger (1081-1151) who clearly understood the impact architecture could make. He wanted a large building with plenty of room for the perambulation of pilgrims on feast days and, as he firmly believed in the transcendental power of light and colour, he demanded large stained glass windows.

On entering a Gothic church the impression is of great height. This is created by the actual height of the building and by the optical illusion created by the columns, arches and ribs all pointing upwards. An exterior feature of Gothic church building is the flying buttress, the function of which is to counterbalance the outward thrust exerted on the seemingly impossibly tall, thin walls. The best example of Gothic architecture in London is the nave of Westminster Abbey (see p.25).

Medieval London had a rich and sophisticated government and, by virtue of its wealth and size, was more independent than other cities. Some individuals became so rich they were able to lend vast sums to the crown if the king was in need of extra cash. One such wealthy individual was Richard Whittington, businessman, entrepreneur and philanthropist, who died 1423. He financed the first public toilets in the City, and was three times Lord Mayor of London. Whittington had financial dealings with three monarchs, Richard II, Henry IV and Henry V and was the same person loosely portrayed in the apocryphal story of young 'Dick Whittington and his Cat', retold every year in pantomime.

Despite the proliferation of rich and powerful individuals, London was a place of extremes of wealth and poverty. The livery companies, some dating from the early 12th century, not only looked after the interests of their members but also built enduring premises. The great churches and monasteries of this period are impressive, so too are the inns of courts and the houses of noblemen, but the back streets, dark and overhung, would have contained rough dwellings. Whilst the main thoroughfares would have been kept relatively clean, other lesser streets were smelly places, littered with animal dung and industrial waste, such as animal parts discarded by leatherworkers.

The average life expectancy for Londoners during this period was just over 30 years with an infant mortality rate of 30% and Bubonic plague regularly afflicting rich and poor alike. Attempts were made to 'zone' activity in order to contain dirt and pollution, such as having specific areas for butchers on the edge of the City. Others took the view that health terrors were caused by immorality – a moral city was a healthy one – so prostitutes, beggars and lepers were subject to regular summary expulsions. However, rich citizens were able to invest in their spiritual wellbeing by financing monasteries, setting up alms houses or providing wards for unmarried mothers, as a way of avoiding divine retribution.

The start of the 15th century saw London, along with the rest of Europe, emerging from a century of trauma – the 'Hundred Years War' and the Black Death had devastated the population and the accompanying economic recession affected many. Industry, farming and business recovered gradually, and by the end of the century a new confidence and a revival in international trade was being felt; in part due to improvements in navigation and the acquisition of new empires.

By the early 16th Century, Henry VIII was changing the face of London with the construction of palaces in Whitehall, St James and Greenwich and projects such as the royal dockyards at Deptford and Woolwich, bringing relief to the overcrowded City docks. The once dominant monasteries were now no longer the most impressive buildings in London. After the Dissolution of the Monasteries, which took place between 1535 and 1540, the confiscated land and buildings were sold to friends and supporters of the King, but not many of them could afford lavish new buildings, so adaptation was the order of the day.

It was Cardinal Wolsey who acknowledged the Renaissance fashions emanating from Italy, by commissioning an Italian sculptor to produce roundels of the Roman Emperors for his fabulous new Hampton Court, which was architecturally every inch a late medieval castle.

The Reformation had driven a wedge between England and Catholic Italy and so trade and political ties were established with the Protestant Low Countries, and England's ideas of the Renaissance were initially imported via Antwerp rather than Rome or Florence. The reigns of Mary and of Elizabeth saw little in the way of Royal building. Elizabeth chose to encourage her courtiers, the new men who rose up in wealth and influence under the Tudor monarchy, to build for her. The Queen preferred to be entertained in such 'prodigy houses' rather than at court, and spent much of her reign going from one house to another, along with her colossal entourage. Such a house would be built with a range of state apartments – a great chamber, withdrawing chamber and bedroom fit for a monarch – all financed by the host.

It was under Elizabeth's successor James, who came to the throne in 1603, that Renaissance architecture was embraced and the first building to be started in this new style was the Queen's House at Greenwich by Inigo Jones (see p.44).

What was so new about the Renaissance style? The architect now had to be mindful of the ideals of proportion and symmetry, using Classical inspiration and mathematical precision to create unified, balanced structures. Inigo Jones (1573-1652) was the first architect in England to implement these ideals. Despite his humble background, Jones had travelled extensively in Italy, studying the Roman remains a full century before it became de rigeur for every fashionable young man of means to do so. He became Surveyor of the King's works in 1615 and in the following year received the commission from Queen Anne, wife of James, to design a new pavilion at Greenwich.

Jones' first work for the Royal household was as a masque designer, working in collaboration with the dramatist Ben Jonson, when they turned traditional court entertainment into a theatrical and intellectual display of excellence. Masques combined music, drama, dance and art and Jonson and Jones were the European masters of the genre – until they quarrelled and the partnership was ended in 1632. However, by this time, Jones was well established as an architect, responsible for England's first truly Renaissance buildings – the Banqueting House, the Queen's House, the first Protestant Church and the first London Square at Covent Garden (see p.48).

However, with the execution of Charles in 1649 and inauguration of the Commonwealth under Cromwell all such work was stopped and Jones's services were no longer required. Inigo Jones died in 1652, eight years before the Restoration that would witness the rise of the architectural genius – Christopher Wren.

Westminster Abbey

Westminster Abbey

Dean's Yard, SW1 • Tel 020 7222 5897 • www.westminster-abbey.org • Nearest transport St James's Park or Westminster LU • See website for opening times and admission charges

Westminster Abbey, or more correctly The Collegiate Church of St Peter, Westminster, is a living, breathing place of Anglican worship with regular daily and Sunday services throughout the year as well as a host of special services.

Since William the Conqueror's coronation here on Christmas Day 1066, most English monarchs have been crowned at the Abbey. The building has become the focus for national sorrow, such as the funeral of Princess Diana in 1997, and celebration – services of thanksgiving and royal weddings, most recently that of Prince William and Catherine Middleton, the Duke and Duchess of Cambridge. Millions of television viewers from all around the world watched the marriage ceremony and saw the Abbey in all its splendour with an avenue of 25ft trees, field maples and hornbeams, decorating the nave and emphasising its lofty Gothic dimensions.

The royal couple made their vows standing on the newly restored Cosmati pavement in front of the High Altar. Unlike Roman or medieval mosaics, Cosmati work consists of geometrical patterns built up from pieces of stone, purple porphyry, green serpentine, yellow limestone, as well as opaque coloured glass, cut into a variety of shapes: triangles, squares, circles, rectangles etc. The pavement covers an area of 24 feet 10 inches (7m 58cm) square and had been covered by carpet for the past 150 years until the restoration work was completed in 2010.

A Benedictine monastery had been established on the site by the Saxons from as early as the 7th or 8th Century. Subsequently sacked by the invading Danes, and restored by King Edgar (944-75) the abbey fell into disrepair.

It was the Saxon King Edward the Confessor who decided to build a magnificent church on the site, regardless of cost. Between 1045-50 he built what was in reality a classic Norman church – years before the Norman invasion of 1066. Edward had spent 25 years in exile in Normandy and had not only admired its architecture but understood the impact a church building could have as a force within the kingdom. Edward's church was to be larger than any in Normandy. He also had his residence built alongside, thus establishing the site of the Palace of Westminster. Very soon the medieval town grew around this 'west minster'.

Little is left of Edward's Norman church as subsequent monarchs have left their mark on the Abbey. There is a depiction of the building stitched into the Bayeux Tapestry – how accurate is open to debate.

After the Confessor's founding of the Abbey, the monarch who has made the greatest architectural contribution to the place is Henry III. During his long reign in the 13th Century, Henry, with far more ambitious good taste than cash, undertook many major building projects. At Westminster he added the Lady Chapel to the east side of the existing Abbey (1220 to 1245) and as soon as this was completed he had the Norman church demolished to make way for a magnificent new construction. The full extent of this new building was never fully realised and its plan has been lost to us, nevertheless Henry's legacy is, in the words of Nikolaus Pevsner, 'the most French of all English Gothic churches'.

The building and repair of the Abbey was paid for by the Crown until 1698 when an annual payment for upkeep was granted by Parliament. The names of the masons and architects associated with the Abbey include Henry Yevele, Sir Christopher Wren, Nicholas Hawksmoor, John James, James Wyatt, Edward Blore and Sir George Gilbert Scott.

In mid-2009 the Dean of Westminster announced plans for an estimated 23 million pound package of improvements to the fabric of the building. These include a visitor and conference facility and, most controversially, a stone corona – a crown-shaped roof – over the lantern that lights the most sacred part of the church, in front of the High Altar. Completion is planned in time to celebrate the Queen's diamond jubilee.

The available space in this little book only allows the briefest outline of some of the highlights of this magnificent building:

The Exterior. Well worth taking the time to have a closer look – especially if time does not allow a visit to the inside of the Abbey. Of particular note is the North Transept, this is the 'short arm' of the Latin cross that faces Parliament Square. Indeed for many years this served as the state entrance from the Palace of Westminster – three porches under pointed gables are reminiscent of work at Chartres, with beautifully carved figures; a splendid rose window and two-tiered flying buttresses.

Visitors to the Abbey today are admitted via the West Front, an architectural mix of the 12th, 14th, 15th and 16th centuries. The most iconic part of this building, the twin towers, are a strange but pleasing mix of Gothic and Classical detail. They date from the early 18th century (designed 1734, built 1735-45) and were the last project of Nicholas Hawksmoor and completed after his death. It is odd to think that this is the most widely known of all his works, though few people identify him with Westminster Abbey.

Great Cloister. A reminder that this building was once a monastery for this is where the monks of the Abbey would live and study. The visitor has to imagine glass in the windows, rushes on the floor, chairs, tables and log fires keeping the whole area warm. Surprisingly large; each cloister is approximately 100 feet in

Chapter House,
Westminster Abbey

length, but there is very little of the 11th-century building remaining since much of it was destroyed in a fire in 1298. Most of the building dates from the 13th to the 15th centuries.

Pyx Chamber. The word 'pyx' means box – in this case a box for money. It derives its name from the fact that this was at one time the site of the crown treasury. This, and the undercroft, are the only remains of the original Norman church. This chamber, sometimes referred to as the Chapel of the Pyx, and the museum, were formed from the undercroft of the monks' dormitory.

The Nave. Only 35 feet wide but the tallest in England at 102 feet (31 metres); Salisbury Cathedral, the next in height, is 84ft (25.5 metres). It was begun in 1246, making it the first example of High French Gothic architecture to be built in England. The tall, thin walls only stand upright with the aid of the massive external flying buttresses, which are a work of art in themselves.

Chapter House. Begun in 1246, this octagonal vaulted room of eight bays, supported on a single pier, has a spectacular tent-like appearance. The huge windows with heraldic crests and the beautifully tiled floor date from 1259. From about 1400 to 1547 this room was used for Parliamentary meetings.

Chapel of Henry VII (also known as the Lady Chapel). Built between circa 1503-15, when it replaced the Lady Chapel of 1220-45.

The superb pendant fan vaulting makes this arguably the most spectacular surviving ceiling of its time.

Feretory – Chapel of St Edward the Confessor. This Chapel, containing the shrine of St. Edward the Confessor, lies east of the Sanctuary at the heart of the Abbey. It is closed off from the west by a stone screen, probably dating from the 15th century, carved with scenes from the Confessor's life. Many past Kings and Queens are buried here, and the chapel has been a place of pilgrimage – particularly for the sick who would come to the shrine on their knees seeking a cure.

This Chapel is richly decorated and of particular note is the Cosmati work on the base of the Confessor's shrine – red and green porphyry and glass mosaics set into Purbeck stone.

There are many works of art and monuments to see within the Abbey – over 450 if the grave–slabs are included. Poets' Corner, located in the South Transept, is almost a 'Who's Who' of English literature, and always popular with visitors. Geoffrey Chaucer, author of the Canterbury Tales, was the first poet to be buried here in 1400. He held the post of Clerk of the King's Works at the nearby Palace of Westminster for a short time, and would have been very familiar with the Abbey.
Area Map p.6, B:1

All Hallows by the Tower

Byward Street, EC3R 5BJ • Tel 020 7481 2928 • www.ahbtt.org.uk • Nearest transport Tower Hill LU • See website for opening times

This interesting church located very close to the Tower of London in the City was built as a daughter church of Barking Abbey, Essex and first mentioned in documents dating from 1086.

All Hallows can claim to be the only City church with standing fabric from the Anglo Saxon period; a section of the south-west wall and part of the north-west corner of the nave. Two sections of Roman tessellated pavement are also to be seen, one still in situ between the Saxon foundations of the tower, the other recently re-laid as part of the crypt flooring.

Most of the pre-17th century fabric of the church was destroyed in a fire in 1650, the church was rebuilt between 1658-59 making it the only London church to have work carried out during the Commonwealth. The church again suffered extensive damage from enemy bombing during the Second World War and drastic reconstruction was undertaken by Lord Mottistone of Seely and Paget architects. The same firm were commissioned to add the spire to the brick tower during the 1950s.

Do not miss the exquisite font cover dated 1682 and attributed to Grinling Gibbons – a feast of carved leaves, cherubs, fir cones and flowers.

Many historical figures are associated with this church – William Penn, founder of Pennsylvania was baptised here and John Quincy Adams, 6th President of the USA, married here in 1797. *Area Map p.8, C:2*

The White Tower, Tower of London

Tower of London

Tower Hill, EC3 • Tel 0870 756 606 (information line) • www.hrp.org.uk • Nearest transport Tower Hill LU & Tower Gateway DLR • See website for opening times & admission charges

The Tower of London, built by William the Conqueror in the south-east angle of the existing Roman wall, sometime after 1077, has been a royal palace, fortress, prison, place of execution, jewel house, mint, arsenal and royal zoo. Successive monarchs have added various buildings thereby bequeathing a complex mix of architecture from various periods, such as the Cradle Tower (1348-1355), New Armouries (1663) and the Waterloo Barracks (1845). However, as at Westminster Abbey, Henry III made a significant mark.

The oldest and most familiar building within the walled 12 acre site is the central keep, the White Tower. It was a bold statement by the conquering Normans, and initially served as a stronghold as well as a palace. The Tower walls, in parts 12 feet thick, were originally made from Kentish ragstone with Caen stone dressings, specially shipped over from Normandy. The Caen stone has now been replaced with Portland stone. Originally the walls were whitewashed, hence the name. The White Tower is a roughly square building with turrets on each of the four corners. The whole roofline was crenellated until the mid 16th century when ogee caps were added. Each of the three original floors (the fourth was added later) is divided into three distinct departments.

One of the architectural highlights of the Tower is St Johns Chapel on the second floor. This is perhaps one of the finest early Norman structures remaining anywhere. It is massive and solid with a tunnel-vaulted nave – a feature almost unique in England. With its two-level arcade, powerful round piers below and dramatic arches it certainly is one of the most impressive spaces in London. Pleasingly unadorned, to the modern eye at least, the Chapel lost its screens and stalls during the Reformation. *Area Map p.8, C:1*

Southwark Cathedral

Montague Close, SE1 9DT • Tel 020 7367 6700 • www.southwarkcathedral.org.uk • Nearest transport London Bridge LU & Rail • See website for opening times

Amidst the railway tracks, roads, blocks of flats and offices and in the shadow of the approach to London Bridge stands Southwark Cathedral. Built on the site of a much earlier church this former Augustinian Priory of St Mary Overie (meaning St Mary 'over the river') has its Norman and medieval plan still pretty much intact. This is despite serious fires in 1212 and 1390 which destroyed most of the fabric of the building. Subsequent rebuilding and renovation have nonetheless left the choir and retro-choir undisturbed and for this reason the Cathedral can lay claim to being the 'oldest Gothic building in London'.

A successful new building project was opened in 2001 providing the Cathedral with new ancillary accommodation, including a theological library, shop and refectory. The old and new parts of the building marry perfectly, which is due to the careful use of materials; limestone and Norfolk flint under a Westmoreland slate roof. This extension, the work of architects Richard Griffiths and Ptolemy Dean, was nominated in the 2002 prestigious RIBA Stirling Prize for architectural excellence.
Area Map p.8, B:1

Westminster Hall

Houses of Parliament, Palace of Westminster, SW1 • www.parliament.uk/visiting • Nearest transport Westminster LU • Entrance by ticket – please apply to your local MP, paid guided tours are also available during the Summer Opening, see website for more details

The Hall was originally a Norman addition incorporated into the old Palace of Westminster built by Edward the Confessor as the principal residence of the monarch and remaining so until the reign of Henry VIII. Thereafter it was used mainly as a meeting place for Parliament, a use it has retained through to the present day. The Hall, described by many as the greatest royal hall in Europe, is, along with the Jewel Tower, the only surviving parts of the old Palace. Built by William II (also known as William Rufus) in 1099, some of the original masonry still survives but the Hall was heavily renovated during the reign of Richard II when the magnificent hammerbeam ceiling was added. *Area Map p.6 B:1*

Left: Jewel Tower, old Palace of Westminster, where rib vaulting and ceiling bosses, usually found in church buildings, are used in a secular setting

Jewel Tower

Abingdon St • SW1 3JY • Tel 020 7222 2219 • www.english-heritage.org.uk • Nearest transport Westminster LU • See website for opening times and admission charges

The Jewel Tower was built in the south-west corner of the old Palace of Westminster grounds in 1365/66 to house the personal treasure of King Edward III. The Tower had been moated as an effective additional form of security, the remains of which can still be seen.

The building is L-shaped, has three floors each consisting of just one large room, with a fireplace and a smaller inner-room. The polygonal turret contains the stone staircase. The ground floor rooms are a little grander than the upper floors, with an interesting vaulted ceiling and three bosses depicting comical faces. It is believed that this building was constructed by the great mason Henry Yevele, who was responsible for work on the nave at Westminster Abbey next door. The only jarring note of the Tower is the size and shape of the windows. These were enlarged and dressed with Portland stone in the early 18th century when the building was used as a record repository for the Parliament Office.

The Tower now houses a small museum containing items relating to the old Palace of Westminster. *Area Map p.6, B:1*

St Bartholomew the Great

West Smithfield, EC1A 7JQ • Tel 020 7606 5171 • www.greatbarts.org • Nearest transport Farringdon or Barbican LU & Rail • See website for opening times & admission charges

This church was founded in 1123 as an Augustinian priory by Rahere (a compassionate and enterprising monk). He established the kernel of the world famous St Bartholomew's Hospital and in 1133 received royal permission to hold an annual fair, which raised a considerable sum of money for his work – see Bartholomew Walk p.257.

Very little of the 12th-century church remains, however what survives is one of the most beautiful buildings in London. Originally a modest building of a choir, ambulatory and Lady Chapel, enlargement took place during the next 100 years with the addition of transepts and crossing, as well as a lengthening of the nave which gives the whole building the feel of a classic Norman church. The splendid gateway of 1595 marks where the original nave finished.

The part of the priory serving as a hospital survived the Reformation but the monastery itself was closed, the church sold off to the parish and part of the nave demolished. The crypt was used as a wine and coal store; the Lady Chapel became private dwellings and a print works (Benjamin Franklin worked here during 1725); horses were stabled in the cloisters; a blacksmith operated in the north transept and a carpenter set up a workshop in the sacristy. The building was also used as a non-conformist meeting place and a school at various times throughout its history. It is a small miracle there was any fabric left to work with but the eminent architect Aston Webb spent from 1884-96 restoring the building to what we see today.

The church contains many notable features including an oriel window, installed in 1517, overlooking the choir (probably to act as a watch tower to keep an eye on the gifts left at Rahere's tomb). The crossing has splendid, solid Romanesque pillars and the earliest pointed arches in London dating from 1145-60. The medieval font dates from around 1405, and served in the baptism of painter William Hogarth in 1697. The interior was used in the filming of 'Four Weddings and a Funeral' (1994) and 'Shakespeare in Love' (1998).

Area Map p.8, A:3

Right: The Norman choir of St Bartholomew the Great

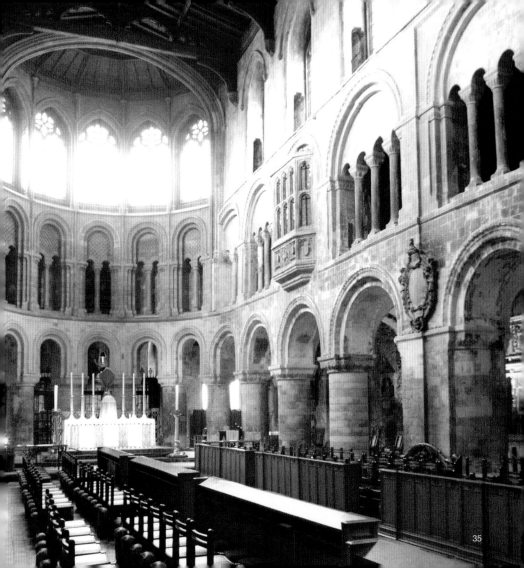

The Priory Gate, St John's Priory, built in 1504 from Kentish ragstone

St John's Priory

St John's Gate, St John's Lane, Clerkenwell, EC1M 4DA • Tel 020 7324 4070 • www.museumstjohn.org.uk • Nearest transport Farringdon LU & Rail • See website for opening times

Established in about 1140, the Knights Hospitallers' Priory of St John covered about six acres in Clerkenwell and was the English headquarters of the Order of St John. The Order was founded to give succour to pilgrims and Crusaders, and in 1877 became the St John's Ambulance Brigade.

After the dissolution of the monasteries during the reign of Henry VIII, the Priory buildings were put to various uses, the residence of Queen Elizabeth I's Master of Revels; a pub; a coffee shop, reputedly run by the father of the painter William Hogarth; and as the offices of 'The Gentlemen's Magazine'. The St John's Ambulance Brigade have their head office on the premises, thus bringing the story full circle.

What is left of architectural interest is a fine 12th-century crypt over which a Georgian parish church was built; the original church having been circular, similar to Temple Church. Also of note is the large and impressive St John's Gate, built in 1504, its grand size denoting the importance of the Priory. The museum contains many items of interest such as illustrated manuscripts and items relating to the history of the Order. *Area Map p.8, A:3*

St Pancras Old Church

Pancras Road, NW1 • Tel 020 7387 4193 •
www.posp.co.uk • Nearest transport King's
Cross LU & Rail • See website for details

Amid the ongoing redevelopment in the King's Cross area, sits the St Pancras Old Church. Given its present surroundings, it is difficult to believe that this little church was, at one time, encircled by fields, and once served a country parish that stretched from what is now the Russell Square area all the way to Kenwood in Hampstead.

The church is named after Pancratius, an orphaned boy living in the household of the Emperor of Rome who, on refusing to relinquish his Christian beliefs, was martyred in 304 CE; a basilica was later built in his honour on the Aurelian Way. During the time of the Roman occupation of London the River Fleet was navigable to just beyond where the church is sited today. Legend tells us that an encampment here raised the first place of worship in the name of St Pancras, the anglicised version of his name. What form this building took can only be guessed at as no trace of it remains. However a carved altar stone dating from the 6th or 7th century and an entry in the Doomsday Book of 1086 confirm the church's earlier existence. This makes it one of the oldest sites of continuous Christian worship in London.

The fairly substantial Norman church had been reworked during the 12th century and

Above: The Soane Mausoleum in the Churchyard is one of only two Grade I listed monuments in London. The design was a direct influence on Giles Gilbert Scott's design for the red telephone box

dramatically remodelled during the 19th century, with mixed success. It is a pity that during this latter work the medieval tower was removed in order to extend the church west and add a south facing entrance porch and tower. The church was last renovated in 1979-80. There are many fine monuments in the churchyard including that of the eminent architect Sir John Soane and his family (illustrated here).

St Helen's Bishopsgate

Great St Helen's, EC3A 6AT • Tel 020
7283 2231 • www.st-helens.org.uk •
Nearest transport Liverpool Street LU &
Rail • See website for opening times

An interesting church that escaped damage in
the Great Fire of 1666 and World War II, only
to sustain serious damage by IRA bombing in
1992 and 1993. The architect Quinlan Terry
restored and reworked the interior between
1993-95 to provide a more flexible space for
worship. This little church, now almost hidden
amid a thicket of tall, shiny office blocks,
started life circa 1200-1215 as a Benedictine
nunnery. However there was already a parish
church on the site, possibly 11th or early 12th
century, and the nun's new church was built
alongside the existing building. This has given
the church its odd appearance of having two
'main' entrances almost side by side, one for
the nuns, and one for the parish. The naves
are now one, but it is possible to trace their
original configuration.

The church has a number of noteworthy
features, not least of which is the Shakespeare
window which dates from 1884 (he is believed
to have lived nearby); a richly decorated pulpit
dating from circa 1633 and a superb collection
of pre-1666 monuments. *Area Map p.8, C:2*

*Right: The west end of St Helen's Bishopsgate with its
compact timber bell-turret against the soaring Swiss
Re building, see p.239*

Eltham Palace

Court Yard, Eltham, SE9 5QE • Tel 0208 294 2548 • www.elthampalace.org.uk • Nearest transport Eltham Rail • See website for opening times & admission charges

Eltham Palace was built on a site that has been occupied by substantial houses since Saxon times. In 1275 it was owned by the Bishop of Durham who presented it to the first Prince of Wales, who became King Edward II. It was a favourite royal palace until Henry VIII's reign, when Greenwich was favoured. Eltham was sold off during the Commonwealth and was subject to an inglorious history until 1931 when the exceedingly wealthy Stephen Courtauld purchased the lease and embarked on a six-year restoration programme of the old Hall. He also built an entirely new adjoining house. Within a mere eight years the lease was sold to the Army Education Corps and in 1995 the property was acquired by English Heritage.

The Great Hall dates from 1475, measures 100 feet by 36 feet, and still has its superb original hammerbeam ceiling; the only survival of the Palace's medieval splendour. The house built during the 1930s is Art Deco in style which, whilst not pleasing the purists, does provide a terrific contrast to the Hall. Of particular note is the entrance hall where the glass dome illuminates some extremely elegant period furniture and a circular carpet beneath. Both buildings are set in romantic, moated gardens.

Guildhall

Gresham Street, London, EC2 • Tel 020 7606 3030 • www.guildhall.cityoflondon.gov.uk
• Nearest transport Bank LU • The Guildhall is open to the public when not in use, see
website for details

There had been a guildhall (from the Anglo Saxon 'gild' meaning payment – a place where citizens paid their taxes) on this site for many years, although this particular building was begun in 1411. Enemy bombing in 1940 destroyed the complex of Medieval buildings, of which the Guildhall was the only survivor. Post-war restoration was carried out by Sir Giles Gilbert Scott who also added new office accommodation on the north wall. Further work during the 1960's added more offices as well as a new L-shaped library. The building of the new art gallery during the 1990s was delayed by the exciting discovery of remains of a Roman amphitheatre (see previous chapter). The art gallery, designed by Richard Gilbert Scott, was opened in 1999.

The Guildhall is the City's largest secular building and is still an important focus of official ceremonies and celebrations. Much of its 15th-century perpendicular architecture is still in evidence – with its characteristic lightness of stonework and splendid windows with notably accomplished tracery.

Another interesting feature of the Guildhall is the 1788/89 porch by George Dance the Younger. Made mainly from Portland stone, it is arguably the earliest example of Indian influence in English architecture; a form which went on to be labelled 'Hindoo-Gothic'. At this time there was much debate amongst architects and intellectuals as to the origins and nature of 'the Gothic', and here Dance is experimenting with these forms. Another theory is that the inclusion of such eastern motifs and echoes may well have been a nod of recognition towards the City's vital trading links with the Orient. *Area Map p.8, B:2*

St Margaret's Church

Westminster, Parliament Square, SW1 • Tel 020 7222 5152 • www.westminster-abbey.org • Nearest transport St James's Park or Westminster LU • Admission free • See website for opening times and details of services

If this church stood anywhere else in London it would probably receive far more attention, however, being in the shadow of the magnificent Westminster Abbey many visitors overlook this lovely building. Built 1482-1523, but with a much earlier, perhaps late 11th-century foundation, it is the only surviving pre-Reformation church in Westminster. Built in a Perpendicular style, the final flowering of the Gothic style, the interior was heavily restored during the 18th and 19th centuries, the last time by George Gilbert Scott in 1877. The church exterior is somewhat dominated by a tower built in 1734-5.

St Margaret's has been the official parish church of Parliament since April 1614 and is where Samuel Pepys, John Milton and Winston Churchill were married.

This church has an interesting selection of stained glass windows ranging from the very early 16th century to a fabulous example of John Piper's work – an abstract titled 'Spring in London' and dated 1968. *Area Map p.6, B:1*

St James's Palace

Cleveland Row, Marlborough Gate, SW1 • www.royal.gov.uk • Nearest transport Green Park LU • No public entry apart from service attendance. Services are held at 8.30 am and 11.15 am in the Chapel Royal or The Queen's Chapel on Sundays throughout the year, except for August and September. In the Chapel Royal, they are held from the first Sunday in October to Good Friday, inclusive. In The Queen's Chapel services take place from Easter Sunday to the last Sunday in July, inclusive

Although not open to the public (apart from the chapel) there is plenty of St James's Palace to see from the street. The complex of buildings includes Clarence House, latterly the home of the late Queen Mother and now Prince Charles's London residence.

The Palace was built by Henry VIII between 1531-40, at the same time Whitehall was under construction and would appear to have been intended to house the monarch's heir rather than the king himself. When Whitehall burned to the ground in 1698 St James's became the focus of the Royal court in London. This association however was relatively short-lived as George III thought St James's unsuitable and eventually moved to Buckingham House (later Palace).

When a fire in 1809 destroyed much of St James's Palace, restoration work was carried out by John Nash almost immediately.

The wall and gatehouse which face onto Cleveland Row are the oldest parts of the Palace to survive, with the Tudor brickwork (red brick with blue brick diapering) dating from 1531-40 with later alterations. The gatehouse is typical of early Tudor design with its octagonal turrets. The ogee topped cupola and clock face were added 1832.

The Chapel Royal is also part of the original range of buildings but was heavily renovated by Robert Smirke in 1836/37. The beautiful decorative ceiling dates from 1540 and is still very much intact. It was in this remarkable chapel that King Charles I took communion on the morning of his execution and in which Queen Victoria and Prince Albert were married in November 1840.

Close by is St James's Park, which at one time was a swamp but which Henry VIII had drained in 1533 and stocked with deer for the royal hunt.
Area Map p.6, A:2

Staple Inn

Holborn, EC1 • Nearest transport Chancery Lane LU • No public access – apart from shops on ground floor

This is a rare survivor of Elizabethan architecture in Central London and despite extensive restoration it is still a very impressive building. The front of this half-timbered building is in two halves – the slightly shorter half is probably just the older of the two, dating from 1586. Both parts have two overhanging storeys and the shops on the ground floor, which are still just one room apiece, as they were originally planned. The Staple Inn gives us a tantalising glimpse of what London looked like prior to the Great Fire of 1666.

Area Map p.2-3, C:1

Charlton House

Charlton Road, SE7 8RE • Tel 0208 856 3951 • www.greenwich.gov.uk • Nearest transport Charlton Rail • See website for access details

The last remaining example in London of a truly Jacobean house. It was built for Sir Adam Newton, tutor to the eldest son of James I, who died as a teenager before he could become King Henry IX. Instead his younger brother became the ill-fated King Charles I. Constructed in the E-plan favoured at the time, as this allowed more light into the core of a building, Charlton House is a massive three-storey mansion with four symmetrical bay windows. It was built between 1607 and 1617 of red brick with stone dressing and each of the four towers that grace the corners is topped with an ogee roof. The interior contains a hall of double height, much fine panelling (mostly, alas, not original), interesting stone and marble fireplaces and a superb carved staircase. The House sits in very pleasant gardens and parkland.

It is interesting to compare the bulkiness of this house with the work of Inigo Jones as his Queen's House (see following page) began a mere four or so years later. Inigo Jones may well have been familiar with Charlton as he, like Sir Adam Newton, was in the employ of the Royal Household.

The Queen's House, Greenwich

National Maritime Museum, Greenwich, E10 9NF • Tel 020 8858 4422 • www.nmm.ac.uk • Nearest transport Cutty Sark DLR, Greenwich & Maze Hill Rail • Admission free • See website for opening times

This riverside location was once the site of the Palace of Placentia, the birthplace of Henry VIII and his daughters Mary and Elizabeth. It was a favourite royal residence with an armoury and a tiltyard complete with romantic medieval towers and was conveniently close to the Royal Naval yards at Deptford and Woolwich.

In 1616 work began on the Queen's House, commissioned for the wife of James I, Anne of Denmark who unfortunately died three years later when work stopped on the House. The half-completed construction was covered in thatch and only finished in 1635 for Henrietta Maria, Charles I's queen.

The Queen's House was the first wholly classical building in England and is considered to be one of the most important buildings in British architectural history; there simply had been nothing like it before. Inigo Jones built what was effectively a small (just 110 by 120 feet) two-storey square Italian villa. Built in brick, with rusticated stone facings up to the first floor level on its north and south sides and plastered elsewhere, a pure white house contrasting with the heavy-looking piebald Tudor and Jacobean buildings of the time. The central loggia on the second floor overlooking Greenwich Park is pure Palladio, with a balustrade and Ionic columns with intricately carved capitals.

The interior contains many gems such as the royal apartments and the Great Hall, a 40-foot cube which Jones designed in accordance with Palladio's rules of proportion. The beautiful 'Tulip' staircase, so-called because of the flower motifs on the finely crafted wrought-iron balustrade, was the first cantilevered spiral staircase in Britain. One of the most significant works of architecture in London, the whole building was sympathetically restored from 1984-90.

Tulip Staircase, The Queen's House

The Banqueting House

Whitehall, SW1 • Tel 020 7839 8918 • www.hrp.org.uk • Nearest transport Westminster LU and Embankment LU • See website for opening times and admission charges

On its completion the Banqueting House drew the comment from a contemporary observer that the building was 'too handsome for the rest of the palace'. Built 1619-22 as part of the Whitehall Palace complex, really a collection of buildings of varying quality and style, Inigo Jones's Banqueting House was not only a more than satisfactory provision of a new reception hall and masquing house but also a momentous triumph in the history of English architecture.

Begun after Jones's Queen's House at Greenwich, but completed many years earlier, the Banqueting House also incorporated elements of Palladio's Vicenzan architecture.

The Banqueting House is approximately 110 feet in length and 55 feet in height, being therefore a double cube, its seven bays are divided by Ionic pillars with Corinthian pilasters above. Externally the two main elevations match. The three middle bays have attached columns whereas the outer bays have pilasters doubled at the outer edge of the building for emphasis. To add further interest to the façade different coloured masonry was used; Oxfordshire stone at the lower level with Northamptonshire stone above and Portland stone for all the main architectural detailing and the parapet, which runs the length of the building, both front and back. However, only Portland stone was used during subsequent renovation, principally by Sir William Chambers during the late 18th century and by Sir John Soane in the early 19th.

Seeing inside this building is very rewarding. The brick groin-vaulted undercroft, which originally sported a grotto and fountain, was the venue for Charles I's notorious drinking parties. The vast ceiling of the main room is particularly memorable. Divided into cornices and enriched with gilded carvings, it is more in keeping with classical Italian style than the rather fussy English fashion of the time. The whole building and its decoration, all coolly Classical, contrast with the ceiling panels, painted by Rubens, from which tumble colour and vigour. In place by 1635, the nine paintings proclaim the blessings of the reign of James I and glorify the Stuart dynasty. The paintings were commissioned by Charles I and one wonders whether he may have glanced upwards to take a last look at them as he was led through this room on his way to be executed outside in the cold on 30 January 1649. *Area Map p.6, B:2*

Left: Banqueting House (pictured) survived the fire of 4 January 1698 which destroyed the rest of Whitehall Palace, the monarch's principal residence since 1530

The Piazza & St Paul's Church, Covent Garden

Covent Garden Piazza, Covent Garden, WC2 • Transport Covent Garden LU

St Paul's, Bedford St, WC2E 9ED • Tel 020 7836 5221 • www.actorschurch.org • Nearest transport Covent Garden LU

It is hard to imagine when walking through the now bustling Piazza that this land was once used for growing provisions for Westminster Abbey. When Henry VIII closed the monasteries the whole area was given to Sir John Russell, the first Earl of Bedford and it was the 4th Earl who decided to develop the land. Between 1629-37 what emerged was London's first residential square, designed by the most fashionable architect of the day, Inigo Jones.

Influenced by recent Parisian and Italian building, Jones produced a plan of individual houses behind a common, continuous façade in a Classical design. The development attracted wealthy residents who enjoyed the novelty of living in the grand terraced housing. Jones's church of St Paul sat to the south of the square. However, within two decades the 5th Earl wanted a larger return on the investment and had a fruit and vegetable market built at the centre of the square. The smarter residents promptly decamped to newer squares in town and less desirable occupants moved in. Jones's houses had all been demolished by 1890. What remains is the Georgian central market place, considered the best preserved in England, built for the 6th Earl in 1828 and restored and renovated after 1974 when the market moved to larger premises in south London. The three terraces of market buildings now house small shops and restaurants. To get a flavour of what Jones's houses were like we can look at Bedford Chambers in the locality. Built 1877-79 by the eminent architect Henry Clutton and in a slightly larger scale, they do nonetheless resemble Jones's design especially in terms of proportion.

The Church of St Paul was built at the same time as the Piazza and was the first parish church to be built since before the reign of Queen Elizabeth. Jones's challenge was to build a church appropriate for the Protestant Church of England. His plans gave concern to his patron that the building would be likened to a barn to which Jones replied 'Then you shall have the handsomest barn in England'. The main body of the church feels wide for there are no side chapels or alter screen and the fittings are simple, with a notable carved wreath by Grinling Gibbons who is buried in the churchyard. Externally, the most striking feature of the church is the portico with two square piers, one at each corner of the porch-front with two Tuscan columns between.

St Paul's is known as the 'actors church', because it is located so close to Drury Lane and it is here that many notable thespians have their funerals and memorials. *Area Map p.6, B:3*

Fulham Palace

Fulham Palace and Museum, Bishops Avenue, SW6 6EA • Tel 020 7736 3233 • www.fulhampalace.org • Nearest transport Putney Bridge LU • See website for opening times and admission charges

The eminent architectural historian Nicholas Pevsner called this 'one of the best medieval domestic sites in London'. Set in 13 acres of beautiful grounds by the Thames, this was the country residence of the Bishop of London from 704 until 1973, having been acquired by the Saxon Bishop Waldhere. Archaeological evidence shows that the site has been occupied since the Neolithic period.

Fulham Palace is an interesting mix of building styles – the earliest surviving part being the great hall which dates from about 1480 with 16th-century additions. The hall underwent changes in decoration as well as function, from chapel to drawing room, as each incumbent Bishop endeavoured to make his mark on the Palace. The rest of the building is mostly Tudor and of particular note is the exquisite brickwork which makes an interesting contrast with the machine made bricks of the Victorian era.

Since 1973 the Palace has been leased to the Borough of Fulham and is now a museum. Among the exhibits is a fascinating model of the building – colour coded to help visitors identify the various architectural styles.

Above: West Courtyard, Fulham Palace

St Ethelburga's, Bishopsgate

St Ethelburga's Centre for Reconciliation and Peace, 78 Bishopsgate, EC2N 4AG • Tel 020 7496 1610 • www.stethelburgas.org • Nearest transport Liverpool Street LU & Rail • See website for opening times

It is hard to imagine that during the Medieval period this was the largest building in the area – now it is one of the smallest. Miraculously untouched by the Great Fire of London in 1666 and enemy bombing during the Blitz, this beautiful little church was extensively damaged by an IRA bomb in 1993. Building insurance does not, as a rule, cover for acts of terrorism and so much debate ensued regarding the possibility of fund raising before it was decided to rebuild as a Centre for Reconciliation and Peace.

Following restoration by the architectural firm of Purcell Miller Tritton, who specialise in church and cathedral work, in November 2002 St Ethelburga's was reconsecrated and started a new phase of its life.

The saint, after whom this church is named, was a 7th-century English Benedictine abbess, but the earliest evidence of a place of worship on this site is from about 1200. The present church fabric dates from the late 14th century with much of the shattered remains of this building being re-used – including much of the main tower and the 1671 weather vane both of which were spared in the blast. The main entrance on to Bishopsgate was restored to look as it did originally, the collapsed roof has been replaced by a new steel structure and the Portland stone mullioned windows are new. Of particular note is the east window depicting St Ethelburga gathering up the fragments from the previous shattered window which was made by Helen Whittaker. The new altar and lectern, is also worthy of attention and is made from the remains of the previous old organ loft.

In the tiny garden at the east end of the church sits a tent, opened in May 2006, as a place for the meeting of all faiths. The tent was designed by Professor Keith Critchlow, a world expert in sacred geometry, using the universal languages of geometry, algebra, astronomy and harmony. Made using traditional Bedouin techniques, it is a 16-sided structure covered in woven goat's hair and is a place of extraordinary peace and tranquillity.
Area Map p.8, C:2

Right: St Ethelburga's, Bishopsgate. Now dwarfed by its neighbours, St Ethelburga's was once the largest building in Bishopsgate

Spanish and Portuguese Synagogue, Bevis Marks, City

4 Heneage Lane, off Bevis Marks, London EC3A 5DQ • Tel 020 7626 1274 • www. bevismarks.org.uk • Nearest transport Aldgate LU • See website for opening times and tour details

Dating from 1699-1701, this is the oldest surviving synagogue in England and it is still a thriving place of Jewish worship. It was built by Joseph Avis, a Quaker carpenter, in a style reminiscent of the simpler Wren churches that were being built elsewhere in the City, mixed with elements from the Great Synagogue of Amsterdam built in 1675. There are many highlights, including 12 Corinthian columns, one for each of the tribes of Israel, supporting the gallery and the seven superb brass chandeliers that hang low – representing the days of the week.

The building is often open for visitors. Regular tours are available, and highly recommended. *Area Map p.8, C:2*

Temple Church

Temple Lane, EC4 • Tel 020 7353 3470 • www.templechurch.com • Nearest transport Blackfriars LU/Rail, Chancery Lane LU • See website for opening times & admission charges

This church was built for the Knights Templar, an organisation formed at the end of the 11th century for the protection of Christian pilgrims journeying to and from the Holy Land. The churches they built throughout Europe were based on the circular design of the Church of the Holy Sepulchre in Jerusalem. Temple Church is one of the last surviving examples of such a church in England. The building was consecrated in 1185 in the presence of King Henry II and was dedicated to St Mary. Associated with many historic events, such as the mediation between King John

and the Barons in 1215, the Knights Templar nonetheless fell out of favour at the beginning of the 14th century. On confiscation of this church by the Crown it was leased to lawyers of the Middle and Inner Temples.

The circular nave of the Temple Church is a very fine example of the Transitional phase of architecture between the Norman and Gothic, indeed probably one of the first buildings to incorporate Gothic themes in England. The main piers in the nave are of Purbeck marble, its first use as a building material in London.

Many famous architects – Wren, George Gilbert Scott, Robert and Sidney Smirke, Decimus Burton among them – have supervised restoration of the church at one time or another and their involvement is a testament to its architectural significance.

With superb acoustics this is a popular venue for concerts and is very much a thriving, working church as well as an immensely interesting building to visit. Visitors should not miss the life-size Purbeck marble effigies of knights dating from the 13th century.

For other buildings in the area of 'The Temple' see Fleet Street & Beyond Walk, p.266.

Temple Church, a building in transition, with revolutionary pointed Gothic arches beneath a blind arcade of intersecting round arches of the old Norman style

Crosby Hall

Crosby Hall, at junction of Cheyne Walk and Danvers Street, SW3 5AZ • Nearest transport South Kensington, Gloucester Road and Sloane Square LU

Although this is one of the oldest buildings in Chelsea it originally stood in Bishopsgate in the City, where it was the Great Hall of the 15th-century Crosby Place. Built between 1466 and 1475 by an unnamed mason for Sir John Crosby, a wealthy City merchant, this former city mansion was familiar to Shakespeare who makes mention of it in 'Richard III' as the scene of Gloucester's plotting. Indeed the building was occupied by Richard whilst he was Duke of Gloucester. The Hall was moved stone by stone from Bishopsgate to Chelsea in 1910 in order to rescue it from proposed demolition and a plaque on the side of a modern banking house marks its original position. It was then incorporated into the buildings of the British Federation of University Women and used as a dining hall, but is now a private residence and not open to the public. The Hall was owned by Sir Thomas More for a period after 1523, and it is perhaps fitting that it now sits in what was once More's orchard.

There is no public access to this building, but it can be readily viewed from the street.

All Saints (Chelsea Old Church)

Cheyne Row, SW3 5LT • Tel 020 7795 1019 • www.chelseaoldchurch.org.uk • Nearest transport South Kensington, Gloucester Road and Sloane Square LU• See website for opening times & services

The chancel of this church dates from the 13th century, two chapels from the early 14th century, the More chapel on the south side was built in 1528 for Sir Thomas following the death of his first wife and the nave and tower were built in about 1670. Some beautifully carved capitals and a little 17th-century Flemish stained glass survived the terrible bomb damage that the church sustained during the Second World War. The many interesting monuments and the calm atmosphere make this church interior a very special space.

Lambeth Palace

Lambeth Palace Road, SE1 7JU • Nearest transport Lambeth North LU • Lambeth Palace is not open to the public but tours can be arranged by writing to the Booking Department at the above address. Lambeth Palace is part of the London Open House scheme (see p.377 for more information)

The palace and official London residence of the Archbishop of Canterbury, the most senior cleric of the Church of England, has occupied this site since 1207. This is the last remaining bishopric palace of any size along either bank of the Thames; the others all disappeared with the Reformation.

The simple but beautifully constructed undercroft of the Palace chapel dates from before 1240. The west doorway with its noted trefoiled opening are all that remain of the original building, the rest of which was damaged by Second World War enemy bombing and now restored. The water tower, also called Lollards' Tower, dates from 1435 and was used as a prison in the 17th century. The Gatehouse dates from about 1495 and is an excellent chance to see the red bricks used extensively in high quality Tudor building. The Great Hall of 1663, is also built of brick but with stone dressings and is a magnificent example of Gothic architecture with buttresses, pointed windows and a high-pitched roof with a splendid hammerbeam ceiling. Since the 19th century the Hall has been used as a library. The principal offices and residence are the work of the architect Edward Blore (1787-1879) and all, according to the novelist Walter Scott, 'in the best Gothic taste'. *Area Map p.6, C:1*

St Paul's Cathedral, see p.61

03

WREN & THE
RE-BUILDING OF THE CITY

WREN & THE RE-BUILDING OF THE CITY

"Resurgam – I shall rise again"

At certain points in its history London has been a city of ruins and with its tindery mix of thatch and timber was accustomed to conflagration, whether by act of vandalism or by accident. The spark that ignited Thomas Farriner's bakery on 2nd of September 1666 in Pudding Lane started what history recalls as 'The Great Fire of London'. The fire raged for four days and nights and destroyed five-sixths of the City; 460 streets containing approximately 13,200 houses were lost, four of the seven City gates, 85 churches and 44 halls of livery companies were razed to the ground. The human misery caused by such catastrophe is incalculable but there were those who saw the sweeping away of the seething, stinking, plague-ridden streets with their mish-mash of buildings as an opportunity for urban renewal.

Even before the ashes of the fire had cooled plans for a more modern city were submitted to the Crown by, amongst others, Robert Hooke, John Evelyn and Christopher Wren. It is Wren's name that became synonymous with the re-building of the City, even though the vision he put forward was ignored.

Christopher Wren had spent the previous year, 1665, in Paris. Whether to avoid the plague that was ravaging London or to see for himself the extensive building work that was taking place

under the glitteringly extravagant Louis XIV, this was the one and only time Wren ventured abroad. Paris enjoyed imposing buildings, squares, theatres and aristocratic hotels (mansions) as well as the Chateau de Versailles and its gardens, all constructed in conformity with the ideals of the Italian Renaissance. Architects of the calibre of Leonardo da Vinci and Cellini had been employed at the French court since the beginning of the century, and during the summer of 1665 the great Italian architect Bernini was also in Paris having been summoned by Louis XIV to work on the Louvre. Bernini and Wren met only briefly but the encounter must have made an impact on the young man, who was on the threshold of greatness himself.

Architecture in the 17th century was not as yet a profession and Christopher Wren, without building skills and experience, was merely a gentleman-amateur. Educated at Westminster and Oxford, he was Professor of Astronomy and a scientist of outstanding reputation by the age of 29. His first venture into architecture arose when his aged uncle, who happened to be the Bishop of Ely, asked him to design the new chapel he was sponsoring at Pembroke College, Cambridge. The resulting construction was considered to be a successful, if unimaginative, example of a neo-classical building. His next buildings of note were both in Oxford, the Sheldonian Theatre and a new quad at Trinity College.

On his return from Paris in late 1665, Wren was appointed to restore St Paul's Cathedral, which shall henceforth be referred to as Old St Paul's to differentiate it from the post Great Fire building. Old St Paul's was one of the largest medieval cathedrals in England, 585ft long and 489ft high to the top of its spire. The main body of the cathedral was started in the 11th century and its spire renewed in 1315 after a fire. The spire was struck by lightening and rebuilt circa 1444 only to be struck again in 1561, when a decision was made not to re-build it. Without its hapless spire the building looked like a huge, squat ship, dwarfing all around it. We owe our knowledge of what Old St Paul's, and indeed the City as a whole, looked like from the drawings and engravings of Wenceslaus Hollar who worked in London in the 1650's.

Magnificent as it must have been, the old cathedral suffered neglect after the Reformation and much abuse during the Civil War when Cromwell's men, and their horses, were housed in the nave and various other parts of the building were let to traders. Stained glass windows, carved woodwork, effigies, statues and an Inigo Jones porch were wantonly destroyed and the dilapidated roof finally caved in. Wren's restoration plans were rendered unnecessary when the cathedral burnt to the ground along with most of the City. The vision Wren and his contemporaries had

for the City was for it to be re-built in a similar fashion to Paris or Rome with a regular street plan. However, the survival of London as an important commercial capital depended upon its immediate reconstruction and there was simply neither the time or the will to resolve the complicated land titles that each plot had accrued over the centuries. Therefore rebuilding could only be carried out on the lines of the existing streets. In October 1666 the King appointed Wren as one of three Crown Commissioners, to join with three nominees of the City to consider the methods of rebuilding and these were eventually encapsulated in a series of Acts of Parliament to safeguard against such a catastrophe ever happening again. These were:

i) The structural standardisation of new-build houses in three specific types, all made from brick, with specified floor-height and wall thickness; this point in fact set a trend for house building throughout the whole country. The Commissioners had no say over the actual design of what was to be built, even though the King demanded a 'much more beautiful city' to replace the old one.

ii) The provision of a Thames-side quay and conversion of part of the River Fleet into a canal.

iii) The authorisation for collection of a tax on coal imports into London to pay for a limited number of public works. This amount was subsequently found to be wholly inadequate and had to be trebled within a couple of years.

It took nearly three months to complete the demolition of the charred remains of the City and clear the rubble that lay everywhere. Labourers and skilled workers were brought in from all over the country to fulfil anticipated demand. Disputes between landowners and tenants had to be resolved and money had to be found to cover the cost of rebuilding. At this time there was no such thing as fire insurance (although this eventually came about as a result of the Great Fire) and little or no compensation; so only those City Companies, institutions, colleges and private individuals with enough capital invested elsewhere had the means to begin rebuilding immediately. Indeed many wealthy private individuals chose not to rebuild their London houses within the City but moved west instead.

Important buildings, such as the Royal Exchange, the Custom House, the College of Arms and many of the City Livery Companies' halls were under reconstruction within three or four years of the Great Fire, having been forced to carry on their business elsewhere in the meantime.

Perhaps as compensation for not being able to implement his overall plan for the City, Christopher Wren was charged with the task of personally overseeing the rebuilding of the City churches and St Paul's Cathedral. The whole project was to be financed from the aforementioned Coal Tax, which could only barely cover the actual construction and fabric of the churches. The interior fittings and decoration were to be the responsibility of the parish, although in most cases advice

was sought from Wren. Of the pre-Great Fire churches 85 out of 107 had been destroyed and it was decided to rebuild only 51 of them. However many of the churchyards and burial grounds still exist and can be visited.

Wren was assisted by Robert Hooke and Edward Woodroffe. Exactly how much input Wren had in each individual church is debatable, but he was in overall control. Many of the designs had to fit into awkward spaces and most of the churches are easy to pass by at ground level but they do display an astonishing variety of invention. This is particularly so with regard to the spires Wren added to each church, which lent the City an elegance and an element of fantasy not seen before, and gave the country a blueprint for Protestant church building.

It was not until 1675 that Wren was able to start work on St Paul's Cathedral. His first design was rejected by the clergy who were hostile to its Classical lines. What they wanted was more or less a straight replacement of the Gothic Old St Paul's with its high nave and lower side aisles but what Wren envisaged was a high dome which would act as a focal point for the City as a whole. Wren got his way by encouraging the clergy to agree to one design and then fundamentally altering it as the Cathedral was being built.

St Paul's Cathedral

Ludgate Hill, EC4 • Tel 020 7236 4128 • www.stpauls.co.uk • Nearest transport St Paul's LU • See website for opening times, admission charges and access details (Cathedral occasionally closes at short notice for special services)

The foundation stone for Wren's master-piece, laid 21 June 1675, bears the inscription 'RESURGAM', Latin for 'I shall rise again', and was a relic from the Old St Paul's destroyed by the Great Fire of 1666. The new Cathedral, the fourth on the site, was completed in 1708, with the interior furnished by 1710. Christopher Wren personally oversaw the project from beginning to end, a unique feat, for nowhere else in the world has one Cathedral had just one architect and although his plans had to be approved by the Cathedral dean and chapter, what we see today is the pure product of Wren's genius. Whereas his City churches are essays in northern Protestant order, the design of St Paul's has its roots in the grand architecture of the Renaissance and the Baroque. The Cathedral bears comparison with, and indeed in some parts arguably surpasses, Michaelangelo's St Peter's in Rome.

In order to provide a visually adequate substructure on which to place the dome Wren doubled the apparent height of the building by raising false screen walls on top of the aisle walls all round the cathedral. This also enabled him to conceal the flying buttresses that support the vault of the choir as well as giving the whole building a Classical feel. The porticoes that extend from the transepts and

the much-photographed western towers were both influenced by buildings that were under recent construction in Rome, such as Rainaldi's Church of Gesu e Maria and Bernini's Santa Maria della Vittoria – so much inspiration from a city unvisited by Wren.

The familiar outline of St Paul's is due mostly to its great dome. It is almost hemispherical, and sits more sedately, more majestically than the elongated Roman type. However, this dome, that has dominated the London skyline for so long and is regarded by many to be the most beautiful in the world, is actually one of three structures. Such a large dome would have been fine viewed from the outside, but the observer inside the cathedral looking upwards would have had the feeling of staring into a vast cavernous hole and so, as with St Peter's in Rome, another smaller, saucer shaped dome was placed inside to solve the problem. Wren went further by placing a golden ball and cross, 23 feet high and weighing 7 tonnes, on top of the outer dome and in order to support its weight he introduced a third dome, or perhaps cone is a better description, made of brick and placed between the two others.

As wonderful as it is to view from the outside, a visit to the interior of St Paul's is a must. The crypt contains Wren's tomb; he was one of the first to be buried here when he died at the age of 91. National figures including Lord Nelson and the Duke of Wellington are also buried here. There are numerous monuments and notable statues such as the one by Flaxman

of Sir Joshua Reynolds. The crypt also holds the plans and models made by Wren of the Cathedral itself.

But no visit to St Paul's would be complete without a visit to the famous dome. A mere 259 steps takes one to the Whispering Gallery, so named because by a quirk in its construction a whisper against one wall can be heard on the opposite side. A further climb will take one to the Stone Gallery that encircles the outside of the dome and of course provides a fantastic view over London. However just 530 steps from ground level will take you to the highest point, the Golden Gallery. It is said Wren, in his mid-seventies, was hauled up here in a basket once a week to inspect the work in progress.

This iconic building celebrated its 300th birthday in 2010 and has recently undergone a £40 million-restoration with an intensive programme of external cleaning and improved access for visitors with disabilities.
Area Map p.8, A:2

Left: The Dome, St Paul's Cathedral. It was Wren's intention that the interior of the dome should be decorated with mosaics, which would have been unique in England at that time. However eminent painter Sir James Thornhill was commissioned to provide monochrome depictions of the life of St Paul instead. Eventually mosaics designed by Alfred Stevens in 1864 were used in the spandrels

WREN'S CITY CHURCHES

Before the Great Fire of 1666 the City of London had 107 parish churches, all highly individual, built in different periods and in various styles. The Great Fire destroyed 85 of the 107 and a decision was made that only 51 would be rebuilt. In addition, St Andrew's Holborn, which whilst untouched by the fire and not strictly within the City was included as its crumbling fabric made it a special case. Wren was put in charge of the whole project, with Robert Hooke as one of his assistants, with the rather restrictive brief that the churches had to be rebuilt within their existing, frequently irregular and cramped plots. However notwithstanding these limitations, Wren and Hooke designed and built an amazing variety of airy, well lit buildings. Without an English Protestant church tradition, they looked to Dutch Protestant churches for inspiration.

Of these 51 churches only 24 complete buildings and six towers remain. These are listed below in alphabetical order rather than by merit or date.

Most of these churches are open to the public Monday to Friday, unless stated. Many have regular services of worship and lunchtime concerts – please telephone the individual church for details. If you are only able to see one, St Stephen Walbrook is highly recommended.

Christ Church, Newgate St

Newgate Street, EC1 • Nearest transport St Paul's LU • The tower can be viewed at any time

The first church on this site dated from the mid 13th century and was built by Franciscan friars (also known as Greyfriars). It was rebuilt in the early 14th century and was the second largest medieval church in the City, the largest being Old St Paul's. After the Dissolution of the Monasteries in 1536, Christ Church was used as a store for wine rumoured to have been plundered from French ships, the chancel became a parish church and the King's printer set up shop in the nave.

When Wren rebuilt the church after the Great Fire he made use of the medieval foundations and lower walls and the church therefore remained comparatively large. Enemy bombing during the Second World War destroyed the fabric of the main body of the church but the tower, regarded by some as the most beautiful in London, was mercifully spared. The spire, which has been likened to a square version of the one belonging to St Mary-le-Bow, was the subject of preservation work during the 1960s and a small garden has been formed where the church used to be.
Area Map p.8, A:2

St Alban

Wood Street, EC2 • Nearest transport St Paul's LU • The exterior of the tower can be viewed any time

As with so much of the City, the small area surrounding this tower has witnessed a great deal of history. It is believed that the first building on the site was the chapel of King Offa, dating back to the 8th century. An 11th-century Saxon church certainly stood here and was enlarged over the centuries until it perished in 1666. Rather than design a completely new church, Wren appears to have been content to construct between 1682-8 a fairly faithful replica of what was lost to the Great Fire. The church was destroyed by enemy bombing in 1940, leaving Wren's beautiful Perpendicular Gothic tower standing forlorn and alone.

The tower was renovated during the 1960s and in 1984-85 it was converted into a private house and is now used as offices. Nothing remains of the churchyard used during the 18th and 19th centuries by the Barber-Surgeon's Company for burying the remains of executed criminals whose bodies had been used for dissection. *Area Map p.8, B:3*

Left: St Alban, Wood Street, a sacred site since the 8th century now surrounded by traffic and the 21st-century City

St Andrew, Holborn

Holborn Circus, EC4 3AB • Tel 020 7353 3544 • www.standrewholborn.org.uk• Nearest transport Chancery Lane LU or Farringdon LU & Rail • See website for opening times, services & events

There has been a church on this site since at least 959 CE which, although untouched by the Great Fire, had been pitifully neglected and Wren was charged with its rebuilding. The work started in 1684 and it took just two years to complete what was the largest of Wren's churches. Wren kept the 15th-century tower and refaced it in Portland stone. The interior is similar to St James's Piccadilly (completed 1682), also by Wren, with its barrel-vaulting, groin-vaults on Corinthian columns over the aisles and a two-storey Venetian window in the chancel. Enemy bombing during 1941 destroyed much of the building, the outer walls and tower surviving, but a faithfully reconstructed church was completed in 1961.

Although the original furnishings have been lost, there is much of interest. The organ is modern but sits within a case donated by the composer Handel in 1750, and the pulpit and font are from the Foundling Hospital.

On the outside wall of the west end of the church are 17th century statues of a young boy and girl from a nearby former parish school. St Andrew's now houses the Royal College of Organists.
Area Map p.8, A:3

St Andrew by the Wardrobe

St Andrew's Hill & Queen Victoria Street, EC4V 5DE • Tel 020 7329 3632 • Nearest transport Blackfriars LU & Rail • See website for opening times, services & events

So named because of its proximity to the building where royal ceremonial robes and arms were stored from the mid 14th century. A church has occupied this spot since about 1170 and this unadorned red brick rectangular church with its plain tower was one of Wren's last City churches (1685-94).

Over time 'improvements' to Queen Victoria Street robbed St Andrew's of its churchyard and have somewhat elevated the building so it is now very easy to pass by without noticing it. The original furnishings were destroyed by enemy bombing in 1940, and were replaced by a collection from other Wren churches, such as the font and font cover made for St Matthew Friday Street, which was demolished during the 19th century. There is also a splendid stained glass window depicting the conversion of St Paul made for Bulstrode Park in Buckinghamshire in the early 18th century.
Area Map p.8, A:2

St Anne and St Agnes

St Anne & St Agnes, Gresham Street,
EC2V 7BX • Tel 020 7606 4986 • www.
stanneslutheranchurch.org • Nearest
transport St Paul's LU, Barbican LU & Rail
• See website for opening times, services
& events

Wren designed this small church to a cross-
in-square plan, although it is believed Robert
Hooke was heavily involved in its actual
construction. A modest weatherboard
pyramid with a square lantern tops the roof.
The church sustained fire damage during
World War II and the subsequent renovation
did not include the original elaborate interior
decoration, which suited the church's new
role as a place of Lutheran worship. Services
are now held in Amharic, English and Swahili.
Area Map p.8, A:3

*Right: St Anne and St Agnes. Here, as with other
City churches, Wren creates a sense of light and
space in a relatively small building*

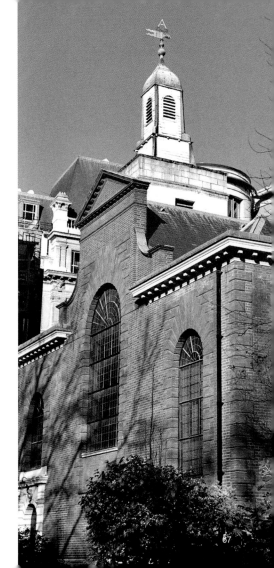

67

St Benet

St Benet

Paul's Wharf, Queen Victoria Street, EC4V 4ER • Tel 020 7489 8754 • Nearest transport Blackfriars LU & Rail • Please telephone for opening times

This delightful little church of red and blue brick chequerwork is thought to be the design of Robert Hooke rather than Wren, though it is attributed to the latter. The exterior is heavily influenced by Dutch church building and inside there is some interesting 17th-century furniture, such as a carved communion table. There has been a church on this site since at least the early 12th century and it is believed that the architect Inigo Jones was buried in the chancel on his death in 1652, but his memorial was destroyed in 1666. Much of the churchyard was lost in a road-widening scheme of 1870 and further 'improvements' left the church virtually marooned on its own small island. The nearby College of Arms uses St Benet for worship and since 1879 it has been the London Church of the Welsh Episcopalians, conducting a number of its services in Welsh.

Area Map p.8, A:2

St Bride

Fleet Street, EC4Y 8AU • Tel 020 7427 0133 • www.stbrides.com • Nearest transport St Paul's LU, City Thameslink Rail • See website for opening times, services & events

Named for St Bridgit, the daughter of a 5th-century Irish prince of Kildare, it is believed that a building of some sort has occupied this site since the Roman occupation of Britain. Many famous people are associated with this church. Wynkyn de Worde, apprentice to William Caxton who brought the first press to England in 1471, set up his printing works alongside the medieval church and thus inaugurated Fleet Street, 'the street of ink', as the centre for the printed word in England. Worde was buried in the churchyard in 1535.

Wren started work on replacing the ruined medieval church in 1671, finishing seven years later. The magnificent spire was added in 1701-03. This is the tallest of all Wren's spires at 226 feet and is said to have inspired a local baker, William Rich, to create the first tiered wedding cake. The spire is telescoped in five stages, becoming slimmer as it reaches its peak, and is similar to an unexecuted design Wren made for the steeple of the old St Paul's

Cathedral. The spire is notable not only for its height and beauty but also because it defiantly withstood enemy bombing during World War II, which was severe enough to melt the bells within. However the extensive damage to the fabric of the church allowed the eminent archaeologist Professor Grimes to discover Roman and medieval remains that had lain hidden for hundreds of years. These are now on display in the Crypt along with a comprehensive and entertaining history of the church and the surrounding area.

Restoration work took place between 1955-57 and Wren's barrel-vaulted ceiling, oval clerestory windows, and five-bay nave, with paired Tuscan columns were faithfully rebuilt. It was decided not to replicate the galleries that once ran along both sides of the nave. Of particular note is the trompe l'oeil painted by Glyn Jones that creates the illusion of a half-domed apse. *Area Map p.8, A:2*

Left: St Bride, Fleet Street. Wren's tallest spire completed in 1703 it measured 236ft (72m,) shortened by 10 feet (3m) in 1764 and an inspiration for wedding cakes ever since

St Clement Eastcheap

Clement's Lane, EC4N 7AE • Tel 020 7283 2711 • Nearest transport Monument LU; Please telephone for opening times

Wren built this, his plainest church, between 1683-87 to replace the 11th-century church. The exterior is stuccoed brick with stone quoins and dressings, and, with neither steeple nor cupola is considered 'too plain' for some. However there are some interesting furnishings – particularly the large pulpit and tester and a carved wooden font cover depicting a caged dove. *Area Map p.8, B:2*

St Dunstan in the East

St Dunstan's Hill, off Lower Thames Street, EC3 • Nearest transport Monument LU • The tower and remaining walls can be viewed at any time

One of two churches in London named for a Saxon Archbishop of Canterbury. The original 13th-century church was noted for its wealth and for the prosperity of its parishioners; indeed repairs undertaken after the Great Fire were paid for by a private benefactor. Wren added the steeple in 1695-1701 in a Gothic style, no doubt to match the patched-up body of the church. Enemy bombing during World War II rendered the building a shell once again, and this is how it remains today, although a garden was planted in the ruins in the early 1970s. *Area Map p.8, C:2*

St Edmund the King & Martyr

Lombard Street, EC3V 9AN • Tel 020
7626 9701 • Nearest transport Bank LU •
Please telephone for opening times

There has been a place of worship on this site
for almost a 1,000 years and it was named
after the 9th-century King of East Anglia, killed
by Viking invaders. The eponymous king also
gave his name to the town of Bury St Edmunds
in Suffolk.

There is very strong evidence that Wren's
assistant Robert Hooke was responsible for
much of the work on the body of this church.
Another of Wren's assistants, Nicholas
Hawksmoor, is thought to have designed the
spire, originally adorned with 12 decorative
flaming urns and topped with a weathervane.
The urns were inexplicably removed during late
19th-century renovation by William Butterfield,
whose taste was for the Gothic rather than
anything that even hinted at the Baroque.

The building now houses The London Centre
for Spirituality. *Area Map p.8, B:2*

St James Garlickhithe

Garlick Hill, EC4V 2AL • Tel 020 7236
1719 • www.stjamesgarlickhythe.org.uk •
Nearest transport Mansion House LU • See
website for opening times, services & events

This is perhaps one of the unluckiest buildings
in London. The original Norman church was
destroyed in the Great Fire, Wren's church was
subject to inappropriate restoration during the
19th century, it was bombed during World War
II and then in 1991 a tall crane, working on a
nearby building, fell on it! Happily it survived
and what the visitor sees today is very much
what Wren completed in 1674. With its interior
of white walls, ceiling and columns, with just a
few touches of gold, and its many windows of
clear glass, this luminous building is known as
'Wren's Lantern'. *Area Map p.8, B:2*

St Lawrence Jewry

Gresham Street, EC2V 5AA • Tel 020
7600 9478 • www.stlawrencejewry.org.uk
• Nearest transport Bank LU • See website for opening times, services & events

Named for a 3rd-century Roman who refused
to denounce Christianity, this church has
been the Corporation of London's official
place of worship since the Guildhall chapel
was demolished in the early 19th century.
Unusually for a City church it stands quite
detached at the head of King Street, one
of only two new roads built in the City
immediately after the Great Fire (the other
being Queen Street) and laid to ease the route
between the Thames and the Guildhall.

The interior of St Lawrence is an essay in
white Corinthian pilastered walls, gold leaf and
magnificent chandeliers hanging from the richly
coffered ceiling. When built in 1670-87 it was
one of the most expensive of Wren's churches.
Gutted by enemy bombing on 29th December
1940, the church was fully restored in 1957.
Area Map p.8, B:2

St Magnus the Martyr

Lower Thames Street, EC3R 6DN • Tel
020 7626 4481 • www.stmagnusmartyr.
org.uk • Nearest transport Monument LU
• See website for opening times & services

Built 1671 76 with its 185 feet steeple added
in 1703, this church was named for St Magnus
the Viking Earl of Orkney who lived 1080-1116.
The church stood at the approach to the Old
London Bridge. So busy was the route that
in 1762 the approach was widened, reducing
the church by two bays at its west end, and so
isolating the solid square tower.

The visitor will not fail to notice that, in
comparison with other Wren churches, the
interior is fairly sumptuous. The furnishings
for City churches were the responsibility of the
parish and St Magnus is fortunate in having
many of its original fittings which, unusually, are
very much in continental Baroque style. Some
additions were made during the 1920's when
the church was embellished further for Anglo-
Catholic worship.

Some fine paintings are contained within the
church – Moses and Aaron on the reredos,
and a Virgin and Child in the style of Van Dyck.
There is also an interesting model of the Old
London Bridge. On the west exterior wall is a
clock dating from 1709, which was a famous
London land-mark for some 200 years until
obscured 20th-century buildings.
Area Map p.8, B:2

St Margaret Lothbury

Lothbury, EC2R 7HH • Tel 020 7726 4878 • www.stml.org.uk • Nearest transport Bank LU • See website for opening times, services & events

The original church on this site dated from the 12th century with 15th-century additions. Wren's church was built between 1683-92, with the plain square tower completed in 1700. The tower and its distinctive fine lead spire are thought to be the work of Robert Hooke.

Entrance to the building is via the stone-clad south side, through the tower, much in the style of London medieval churches. Wren may well have kept the old foundations and building pattern here. Much of the exquisite furnishing comes from now demolished London churches such as the superb carved font which was originally at St Olave Jewry. *Area Map p.8, B:2*

Right: St Margaret Lothbury, one of Wren's many and varied spires

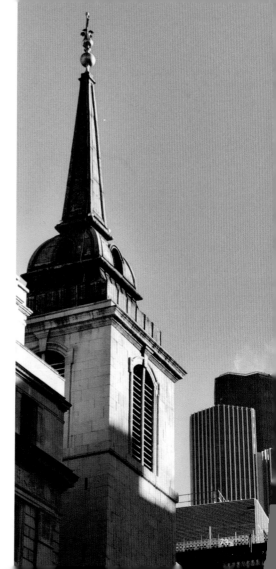

St Margaret Pattens

Eastcheap, EC3M 1HS • Tel 020 7623 6630 • www.stmargaretpattens.org • Nearest transport Monument LU • See website for opening times, services & events

The unusual name of this church has two possible explanations, either it is named for a wealthy parishioner canon of St Paul's, Ranalf Patin or the name refers to the pattens, wooden shoe covers, which may well have been made in the vicinity.

The original 12th-century church on this site apparently collapsed and was rebuilt in the 16th century. Wren's church was built between 1684-89 with the lead-covered spire, added 1698-1702, thought to be by Nicholas Hawksmoor. The exterior of the church is built mainly of Portland stone and the interior consists of a plain rectangular nave.

Many of the interior furnishings survive including now rare examples of twin canopied churchwardens' pews, an hourglass in an iron stand used for timing sermons and a punishment bench with a carved Devil's head.
Area Map p.8, C:2

Left: St Margaret Pattens. The lead-covered spire, at nearly 200 feet (61m), is the only one of the rebuilt City churches to be designed in a medieval style

St Martin within Ludgate

40 Ludgate Hill, EC4M 7DE • Tel 020 7248 6054 • www.stmartin-within-ludgate.org.uk • Nearest transport City Thameslink Rail, St Paul's LU • See website for opening times, services & events

Situated close to the west end of St Paul's Cathedral on a site near the old Lud Gate, Wren's church of 1677-86 incorporates part of the Roman city wall. The church is built on a centralised plan, a cross inside a square – the cross being defined by columns supporting the barrel vaulting. From the tower rises a lead spire, which is thought to be influenced by Dutch design.

The church of St Martin was fortunate to suffer little from 'improvements', renovations and World War II bomb damage and is therefore a relatively good example of Wren's design. However, Robert Hooke's diary tells of at least 31 visits to the site at both the design and construction stages, which might suggest St Martin is more his work than Wren's. *Area Map p.8, A:2*

St Mary Abchurch

Abchurch Lane, off King William Street, EC4N 7BA • Tel 020 7626 0306 • Nearest transport Bank LU & Cannon Street LU/ Rail • Please telephone for opening times, services & events

This church was built by Wren between 1681-86 on the site of a medieval church. Constructed from dark red brick with stone quoins and a tower on its north-west corner, which carries a slender lead-covered spire. The rather plain exterior is of Dutch influence and gives no hint of the sweetest of Wren's interiors.

The small interior has no aisles and is made to look spacious by the placement of a shallow dome on eight arches. This dome was splendidly painted in 1708 by William Snow and colourfully depicts a heavenly choir with sun rays and clouds. Also of major interest is the very large carved reredos known to be by Grinling Gibbons, the only such example of his work on this ambitious scale in the City.

Enemy bombing during World War II caused extensive damage to the church. The dome had to be restored and the precious reredos had been blown into over 2,000 pieces. Miraculously the restoration has brought St Mary back to something like its former glory, the restoration taking over seven years to complete. *Area Map p.8, B:2*

St Mary Aldermary

Watling Street, EC4M 9BW • Tel 020 7248
4906 • Nearest transport Mansion House
LU • Please telephone for opening times

'Aldermary' denotes that this church of St
Mary is the oldest in the City. At first sight one
can hardly believe that this is a Wren church
given that it is one of the finest examples of
17th-century Gothic revival in the country.
The main body of the church was built with
money from a private benefactor under
the supervision of Wren and this may go
some way to explain the deviation in design
from other contemporary City churches.
Stone refacing during the late 19th century
accentuates this difference. A visit inside the
church reveals a unique example of a Wren
fan-vaulted ceiling with some late 19th-century
carved Gothic furnishings and panelling.
Area Map p.8, B:2

*Right: St Mary Aldermary. A fine example
of Wren's Gothic Revival work*

St Mary at Hill

St Mary at Hill, EC3R 8EE • Tel 020 7626 4184 • www.stmary-at-hill.org • Nearest transport Monument LU • See website for opening times, services & events

Wren was able to reuse three walls and most of the tower of the medieval church on this site first mentioned in the 12th century. But 19th-century renovations, during which 3,000 bodies were exhumed from the churchyard and re-interred at Norwood Cemetery, and a serious fire in 1988 requiring extensive repairs has left the church as a mixture of periods. Nevertheless this is a lovely little church, being a simple brick building with stone trimmings tucked away down a small side-street. The interior is a rectangular space which has been subtly divided by the four free-standing fluted columns of the central square, on which the vaults rest, with emphasis given to Wren's central plan by the shallow dome in the middle.

For many years this church has been associated with the fish trade, which was carried out at nearby Billingsgate and the surrounding streets. The fishmongers guild still hold their Harvest Festival service at St Mary's. *Area Map p.8, B:2*

St Mary-le-Bow

Cheapside, EC2V 6AU • Tel 020 7248 5139 • www.stmarylebow.co.uk • Nearest transport Bank LU or St Paul's LU • See website for opening times, services & events

If a child is born within the sound of Bow Bells, so the legend tells us, he or she can declare themselves a Cockney. Cynics may point out the bells are hard to hear above the roar of the passing traffic. However, the 11th-century medieval church previously on this site had to contend with the cacophony of a medieval market outside in Cheapside.

On commencement of work on the site after the Great Fire, Wren not only found he could reuse the medieval crypt but was also delighted to find part of a gravelled roadway on which to build the church tower. The steeple cost almost as much as the rest of the building and is, at 224 feet, second only to St Bride in height and was the first to be built on a post Great Fire church (1678-80). The Basilica of Maxentius in Rome apparently inspired the square nave with its three wide arches on piers.

Enemy bombing in 1941 caused extensive damage to the steeple and bells, but the tower remained upright. The interior, however, had to be radically repaired and all the furnishings were renewed between 1956-64.

There is a great café in the Crypt – see 'Eat and Drink Architecture' p.333. *Area Map p.8, B:2*

St Michael Cornhill

St. Michael's Alley, Cornhill, EC3V 9DS • Tel 020 7248 382 • www.st-michaels.org.uk • Nearest transport Bank LU • See website for opening times, services & events

As with St Mary at Hill, St Michael's contains a mix of periods. It would appear that the body of the church was rebuilt after the Great Fire at the behest of the parish rather than Wren and his Commissioners. Perhaps it was felt that repair rather than rebuild was the order of the day. The original medieval tower was demolished and rebuilt between 1715-22 by Wren's office in a Gothic style to a design by Nicholas Hawksmoor. George Gilbert Scott carried out renovations between 1857-60 in the High Victorian Style removing most of the original furnishings but adding a superb Gothic porch on the north side. *Area Map p.8, B:2*

St Michael Paternoster Royal

College Hill, Upper Thames Street, EC4R 2RL • Tel 020 7248 5202 • Nearest transport Cannon St LU & Rail, Mansion House LU • Please telephone for opening times

There has been a church on this site since at least 1100. The building that perished in the Great Fire had been built in 1409 by the famous Lord Mayor of London, Richard (Dick) Whittington, who lived close by. Wren built its replacement between 1685-94 as a plain rectangular church with a tower, which has arched windows and a pierced parapet. To this was added a steeple (1713-17) considered to be one of the most beautiful in the City.

This was one of the last churches to be repaired (1966-68) following severe damage sustained by bombing in World War II. Fortunately much of the furnishings from the 17th century survived, such as the carved reredos. There is also a charming stained glass window depicting Dick Whittington (see opposite).

The term 'paternoster' refers to the rosary makers who worked in the locality and the 'royal' in the church's name is thought to be a corruption of 'La Reole', after the area of France with which a nearby wine-importer had business dealings. *Area Map p.8, B:2*

Left: St Michael Paternoster Royal. Stained glass window depicting Dick Whittington by John Hayward, installed 1968

St Nicholas Cole Abbey

Queen Victoria Street, EC4V 4BJ • Nearest transport Blackfriars LU & Rail • Currently not open to the public

Not very far away from St Paul's Cathedral and the Millennium Bridge, this church has a splendid spire surmounted by a gilded ship. 'Cole Abbey' is thought to be a corruption of the term 'cold harbour', a temporary shelter for travellers.

Wren rebuilt this church slightly larger than its Medieval foundation in order to accommodate parishioners from the nearby St Nicholas Olave, which was not rebuilt after the Great Fire.

This rectangular building of Portland Stone has large, arched windows, some of which contain some interesting modern (1960's) stained glass by Keith New. The north-west steeple has an inverted trumpet-shaped spire crowned by a weathervane in the shape of a ship which once sat atop the now demolished nearby St Michael's Queenhithe.

The interior has a flat, uncovered ceiling and plain walls except for gilt Corinthian pilasters and panelling. Despite extensive bomb damage in 1941, much of the late 17th-century furnishings have been beautifully preserved – notably the font cover and pulpit.

Changing street patterns and extensive building in the City has resulted in the church finding itself amid busy roads and this has given it a somewhat isolated air. From 1982 until 2003 the church was used by the Free Church of Scotland and the future of the building has looked rather uncertain.

Recently, however, a 125 year lease on the building has been acquired by Culham, an endowed educational charity formed out of the closure in 1980 of a Church of England teacher training college. Their plans are to provide a unique National Centre for Religious Education.

In order to accommodate the necessary facilities for the National Centre and its ancillary support, the architects Maxwell Hutchinson and Matthew Swinhoe of the Hutchinson Studio have designed a two-storey 'box' which will sit in the nave divorced from the existing panelled walls by an ambulatory. This and other facilities necessary for the buildings new role, such as a restaurant/café, will be sympathetically designed to respect the historic fabric of the church. *Area Map p.8, A:2*

St Peter upon Cornhill

Cornhill, EC3V 9DS • Tel 020 7283 2231 • Nearest transport Bank LU • Telephone for details and opening times

Wren, assisted by Robert Hooke, built this church between 1677-84. The crowded site, a site of worship since at least Saxon times, gives us a glimpse of what London was like before 19th and 20th-century road widening schemes left some churches marooned. Access to the church is through the door between the Ionic columns of the porch that protrude onto Cornhill from between the Victorian shops on either side.

An attractive feature of this small church is the brick tower and leaded dome with an obelisk-like spire of copper, topped with a weathervane in the shape of the key of St Peter. The attractive, small churchyard affords a very good view of the spire.

One of this church's boasts is that Felix Mendelssohn played the newly installed organ here in 1840. He obviously enjoyed the experience as he returned for an encore two years later!

Regular services are no longer held here and the church is now under the wing of St Helen's Bishopsgate, where details of access to St Peter's may be obtained. *Area Map p.8, B:2*

Left: St Peter upon Cornhill

St Stephen Walbrook

39 Walbrook, EC4N 8BN • Tel 020 7283 4444 • www.ststephenwalbrook.net • Nearest transport Bank LU • See website for opening times, services & events

Located behind the Mansion House in close proximity to its neighbours it would be easy to dismiss this church with its dull exterior at street level, despite its magnificent spire. However, this is one of the most remarkable church interiors in London, if not the whole country. It is known for certain that Wren was closely involved in the design and construction of St Stephen and was paid a 20 guinea bonus because the finished project so delighted the parishioners. Wren may have used the building of this church as an experimental model for St Paul's Cathedral, and he certainly employed the same group of craftsmen.

This is one of the largest of the City churches of this period and what greets the visitor is a light and airy interior. Sixteen carefully spaced Corinthian columns, all of equal height, give the nave an exquisite sense of division. The beautiful coffered and moulded dome sits on eight arches supported by eight of the columns. Very little alteration took place during the 18th and 19th centuries but extensive renovation work needed to be carried out during the 1980s when the building was in imminent danger of collapse. This work, costing approximately £1.3 million, was done with great care and sensitivity, but there was controversy concerning the reordering around a new altar, an eight foot circle of Travertine marble by Henry Moore.

Another contemporary touch was the light-coloured wooden curved benches which replaced the old box pews.

The eminent 16th-century composer John Dunstable and the architect and playwright John Vanburgh (1664-1726) are buried here. It is from this church that the then rector, Chad Varah, founded The Samaritans. *Area Map p.8, B:2*

Left: St Stephen Walbrook exterior

Chiswick House; see p. 107

04

FROM RESTORATION
TO GEORGIAN

FROM RESTORATION TO GEORGIAN

"Oh bear me to paths of fair Pell Mell! Safe are thy pavements, grateful is thy smell." John Gay

When the monarchy was restored to Britain in 1660, Charles II and his entourage brought back from their enforced exile continental ideas and tastes that were to change the face of much of London. One of the first projects the King undertook on his return was the remodelling of St James's Park and opening it to the public. The Park's main feature was a straight canal, tree lined in the French style. Pall Mall was laid out alongside the Park, this too has a continental flavour as its name refers to pell mell (pallo a maglio in Italian) a game played with a mallet and ball and popular with the Court.

The wealthy in society built their houses in the newly fashionable West End of London – St James's, Soho, Westminster, Piccadilly and Mayfair. Following Inigo Jones's example in Covent Garden of 1629, the London square became a desirable place to live as well as a golden opportunity for speculative building. Terraces of tall houses resembled one large mansion enabling those with aspirations to be vague as to how much of it they actually lived in. Squares laid out in this period were St James's (1661), Leicester (1670), Golden (1677) and Bloomsbury, which is thought to have been the first, planned in early 1661 by the Earl of Southampton.

Three sides of Bloomsbury Square contained terraced houses, whilst the fourth side was taken up with the Earl's own large abode, Southampton House. Here, as with other schemes, the aristocratic model of development went on alongside smaller-scale speculative building. Most of the Square has been subsequently rebuilt, but numbers 9-14 retain some fabric and certainly the proportions of the original houses.

Some of the building schemes executed in the 1660s, particularly those in Soho, were shoddily constructed and needed replacement when their 60-year lease expired. Subsequent redevelopment, during 1730-40s, was dominated by the fashion for the Palladian Revival style. The renewed interest in the work of Inigo Jones was perhaps a reaction to the Baroque architecture perfected by Wren and Vanbrugh (see Greenwich Walk page 274). The architect Colen Campbell mooted a national architectural style over the 'affected and licentious' Baroque, which was considered to carry too many associations of foreign tyranny and absolutism. He suggested a return to the 'Antique Simplicity' found in the Queen's House, Greenwich and the Banqueting House, Whitehall.

However, the return to the works of Jones and Palladio required a reinterpretation. Instead of being a vehicle for Stuart pretensions, Palladianism was viewed as a way of adapting the buildings of Roman antiquity to suit the governing classes. As the Roman patrician travelled from his country estate to the Senate, so the English gentleman travelled from his country estate to Parliament. The work of Burlington and Kent especially embraced Palladio's architectural philosophy (see p.89).

By 1760 Neoclassicism, had become fashionable, by-passing Palladianism to return to the pure forms of Greek and Roman architecture, as practised by Robert Wood, James Stuart and Robert Adam (see p.108).

London was by far the largest city in Europe by 1700, with a population of 600,000, but most of its citizens did not enjoy the privilege of good living conditions. The writings of Smollett and the paintings of Hogarth show a world of squalor and want. Many of those flooding into London were refugees, particularly Huguenots from France after the persecution of 1685, who settled in the East End, working mainly in the textile trade. The Government became alarmed at this influx of non-conformists with unknown political allegiances and so the 1711 Building of Fifty New Churches Act was passed to reassert the primacy of the Established Church. This work was to be paid for from a tax on the purchase of coal with a brief to build the churches in stone with towers or steeples;

no doubt influenced by Wren's City churches. Only 12 of the churches were built, the most notable being – St John's Smith Square (Archer, see p.336), St Mary-le-Strand (Gibbs, see p.102) and St Mary Woolnoth, (Hawksmoor, see p.96).

The 18th-century growth in state and commerce generally led to buildings for specific official purposes, for example the Admiralty (see Whitehall Walk p.325) and Sir William Chambers' creation, of one of the first purpose-built office complex's in Europe at Somerset House (see p.316). Also built were barracks, hospitals, theatres, opera houses, coffee houses, banks and bridges and London became the first 'consumer society' in the world as shops sprang up all over the capital. It had been usual to convert ordinary houses but purpose-built shops with large windows were now becoming commonplace; number 34 Haymarket has probably the oldest shop front in London and numbers 165-167 Bond Street date from the 1770s.

Gentlemen's clubs were an 18th-century invention, and were often named after their original owner. Two such can still be found in St James's Street, Westminster and are, more or less, in their original form. Boodles was built in 1775-76 in the Adam style and Brooke's, dating from 1776-78 is by the architect Henry Holland.

Another 18th-century phenomenon was the emergence of the architect as an arbiter of taste and design. An architect could so designate himself by virtue of his academic training in the subject. His whole approach to design and construction was based on theoretical knowledge rather than observation and practical experience, the tools by which a master mason or master carpenter learned his trade. That is not to say a medieval mason would have been ignorant of geometry, for how else would he have been able to build the Gothic churches with their impossibly tall walls. Cooperation between master masons and other master craftsmen would have been paramount to the production of fine buildings.

The rise of the architect began in the 17th century when the tastes of many of London's patrons, principally the Royal Household and in particular the Stuart dynasty, coincided with those of Inigo Jones. Jones was well-travelled and well-versed in the work and writings of Andrea Palladio, the master of Italian Renaissance architecture. Palladio interpreted all that was elegant about Roman building and applied this vision to 16th-century villa and palazzo building with notable success. Jones used Palladio's theories in his own work at the Queen's House, Banqueting House etc. He was able to do so, in part, because Palladio had set his ideas on paper in his architectural treatise *I quatro libri dell'architettura*, (The Four Books of Architecture), published in 1570. Architecture was henceforth the marriage of the practical to the theoretical.

Inigo Jones paved the way for others, such as Wren, Vanbrugh and Nash who, like him, were holders of posts within the Royal Works. However, although positions within the Works were prestigious and, to a large extent, lucrative, the knowledge gained therein was not felt to have been passed on thoroughly enough. It therefore became usual from the early part of the 18th century for practising architects to take on articled clerks who learned their profession 'on the job', at the drawing board, attending lectures and, if funds were sufficient, travelling in Europe, principally to Northern Italy, Rome and Greece.

The Royal Academy of Arts, founded in 1768, incorporated architecture into its remit and appointed a Professor of Architecture. In 1791 a group of leading London architects set up 'The Architects' Club' with a mission to define the profession and qualifications of an architect. A few years later, in 1809, The London Architectural Society formed to provide lectures and a library. In 1810 the first tentative steps were taken to institute a Royal Academy of Architecture, but its first official meeting was not held until 1835.

To follow are listed, as far as possible, in date order, the 18th century's leading architects and some of their work still to be seen in London. Many were 'amateur' architects in that they did not rely on their architecture practice to earn a living, and were wealthy gentlemen in their own right. Most had travelled abroad, some extensively so having been on the 'Grand Tour', and this is where many found the inspiration to try their hands at architecture.

Previous page left: Chiswick House, see p.104
Previous page right: Apsley House, see p.114
Opposite: Somerset House, see p.316

SIR CHRISTOPHER WREN
(1632-1723)

See the previous chapter for St Paul's Cathedral and the City churches. Other buildings by Wren are:

St James's, Piccadilly

197 Piccadilly, W1J 9LL • Tel 020 7734 4511 • www.st-james-piccadilly.org • Nearest transport Piccadilly Circus LU • See website for opening times, services & events

The area surrounding the church was granted to Henry Jermyn, Earl of St Albans in 1662 for residential development. In 1672 Wren was commissioned to design and build the new parish church, which was eventually consecrated by the Bishop of London on 13 July 1684. Built of red brick with Portland stone dressings St James's is a supremely elegant building. Its interior is wide and spacious with galleries on three sides supported by square pillars and handsome Corinthian columns carry the barrel vault of the nave.

The font and reredos are by Grinling Gibbons and are stunning examples of his work and make a visit to this charming church even more worthwhile. Sculpted in white marble the font depicts scenes from Genesis, whilst the reredos of carved limewood is of garlands of flowers and a pelican with her young. St James's is a lively place with a busy café and a popular crafts market held in the courtyard from Wednesday to Saturday with an antiques market on Tuesdays. *Area Map p.6, A:2*

Royal Hospital Chelsea

Royal Hospital Road, SW3 • Tel 020 7881 5209 • www.chelsea-pensioners.co.uk • Nearest transport Sloane Square LU • See website for opening hours, details of guided tours and chapel service times

Built at the behest and expense of Charles II as a home for war-wounded and elderly soldiers, the Royal Hospital was inspired by the magnificent Hôtel des Invalides in Paris. Although nothing like as grand as the Paris model it is considered by its residents to be a 'homely' space in which to live. Built between 1682 and 1691, 476 old soldiers had moved in by 1689.

Built of two coloured brick with some Portland stone dressings, the Hospital was Wren's largest domestic commission, built in a

Dutch style but with Classical porticoes and trimmings. The buildings are arranged around three open courtyards, the longest of which fronts the road and houses both the Hall and Chapel. From the central octagonal, domed vestibule turn left into The Great Hall, which contains some superb paintings, including two by the 18th-century portraitist Allan Ramsay, as well as tattered banners from historic military campaigns. This wood panelled room, which is still used for dining, has a very plain, flat ceiling and large round-headed windows. The tunnel-vaulted Chapel has an apse with the Resurrection painted by Sebastiano Ricci.

The central courtyard, the Figure Court, is enclosed by buildings on its northern, eastern and western sides, but the southern side is open with a view to the grounds and the river. The statue of Charles II dressed as a Roman Emperor, from which the Court takes its name, is the work of Grinling Gibbons.

Visitors are welcome here and permitted to visit the Hall, Chapel and courtyards. The Long Wards are not open to the public as they are still very much in use by ex-soldiers, known as Chelsea Pensioners, whose scarlet uniforms cut quite a dash in this part of town.

Kensington Palace

Kensington Palace

Kensington Palace State Apartments, Kensington Gardens, W8 4PX • Tel 0844 482 7777 • www.hrp.org.uk • Nearest transport High Street Kensington LU, Queensway LU or Notting Hill Gate LU • See website for opening times and admission charges

In his capacity as Royal Surveyor Wren built various additions to the London residence of the monarch, Whitehall Palace, all of which have since been demolished. In 1688 James II was deposed and William and Mary were crowned. However the new King found Whitehall damp and instructed Wren to transform the newly purchased Nottingham House, in the more benign area of Kensington, into a Palace where they would reside.

This building became Kensington Palace, although it was not known as such until the 18th century. To save cost, Wren initially made use of the modest scale of the original house and the material used was chiefly brick. The main entrance is under the clock tower into Clock Court with the King's Staircase on the far right of the Court, which once took visitors up to the Royal Suite. The Court now serves as the private quarters for residents and visitors now enter through the back of the Palace.

The tastes of the Dutch King of England are clearly reflected in this building, in that it has more than a passing resemblance to his own country retreat in Holland, Het Loo, near the town of Apeldoorn, but on a much smaller scale. Remodelling and enlargement was subsequently undertaken by William Kent and Nicholas Hawksmoor.

George II was the last reigning monarch to live here, although Wren's Clock Court remains a residence of the royal family, most notably Diana Princess of Wales who lived here from her marriage until her death.

For more information about the Kensington Palace Orangery see 'Eat and Drink Architecture' p.333.

Other buildings by Christopher Wren:

- St Clement Danes, see 'Strand Walk' p.314
- The Royal Observatory etc, see 'Greenwich Walk' p.276
- The Monument, see 'Architecture with a View' p.367

NICHOLAS HAWKSMOOR
(1661-1736)

Born in Nottingham Nicholas Hawksmoor was, by the age of 18, employed in London as Sir Christopher Wren's 'domestic clerk'. He assisted Wren in making drawings for St Paul's Cathedral and many of the City churches. He also assisted Vanbrugh on his two most fabulous buildings, Castle Howard in Yorkshire and Blenheim Palace in Oxfordshire. In 1711 Hawksmoor was appointed as one of two surveyors to oversee the Fifty New Churches Act, and at last was recognised as a major architectural force in his own right. Part of the genius of Hawksmoor was his mastery of architectural forms from Classic through Gothic and Renaissance to Italian Baroque, but in a style that remained utterly personal, and almost impossible to categorise.

See 'Walking London's Architecture' for details of Hawksmoor's work in Greenwich (p.274).

Christ Church, Spitalfields

Commercial Street, E1 • Tel 020 7247 7202 • www.christchurchspitalfields.org • Nearest transport Aldgate East LU or Liverpool Street LU & Rail • See website for opening times, services & events

Another glorious example of Hawksmoor's genius and considered by many to be his best church, yet it has suffered a chequered history and was nearly demolished during the 1960s. The building was started in 1714, and consecrated in 1729 but became neglected over the ensuing years and had to be closed in 1957 as it was felt to be a dangerous structure. Conservationists fought and won a hard battle and money was raised for the restoration of Christ Church by selling-off St John's, Smith Square as a concert hall (see 'Eat and Drink Architecture' p.336).

This church is now used extensively during the Spitalfields Festival and for other concerts during the year. It is a truly fantastic architectural tour de force. Just to look at the giant columns and plaster decorated ceiling is worth the journey alone. *Area Map p.8, C:3*

Left: Christ Church Spitalfields. Hawksmoor's bold and muscular example of Baroque architecture

St George's Bloomsbury

Bloomsbury Way, WC1A 2HR • Tel 020 7242 1979 • www.stgeorgesbloomsbury. org.uk • Nearest transport Holborn LU or Tottenham Court Road LU • See website for opening times, services & events

This is the last of the 12 churches built under the Fifty New Churches Act. At this time Bloomsbury was served by St Giles Church, but this arrangement was seen to be unsatisfactory by the new, relatively wealthy residents of the area who objected to having to enter the unsavoury neighbourhood.

Consecrated in 1731, St George's was the sixth and last of Hawksmoor's London churches, and is considered by many to be one of the finest buildings in the capital. The interior deserves close inspection; the galleried nave is a almost a cube, thus complying with the Classical style; the rich mahogany altar and marquetry reredos are a unique feature for a London church.

The exterior is dominated by the large Corinthian portico. It is believed that the inspiration behind the portico was the Roman Temple of Bacchus at Baalbek in the Lebanon. Looking up at the steeple we see a statue of King George I atop the stepped pyramid whose design was based upon Pliny's description of the Mausoleum at Halicarnassus in what is now Turkey. Particular attention was given to the steeple during the recent restoration. *Area Map p.2-3, B:1*

St Anne, Limehouse

Three Colt Street, Limehouse, E14 7HP • Tel 020 7987 1502 • www.stanneslimehouse.org • Nearest transport Westferry DLR • Please telephone for opening times and services

Started in 1714 as one of the first of the 'Fifty Churches' of the 1711 Act, it was not completed until 1724 and then remained unused for six years due to the lack of funds with which to pay the clergy. The huge portico at the west entrance and the tower are characteristically complex. The tower is said to be Hawksmoor's version of a 15th-century lantern tower and is complete with a clock (said to be the second highest placed clock in the country after the Big Ben clock face on the Houses of Parliament). The tower and clock were a landmark for generations of sailors, on their way to or returning from every corner of the world; alas the ships pass no more.

The interior is impressive with four huge, full height columns dividing the nave. A superb stained glass window at the east end by Charles Clutterbuck depicting the Crucifixion of Christ was installed during a very faithful reconstruction of the interior by Phillip Hardwick, following a serious fire in 1850. St Anne's received further renovation and cleaning between 1983-93 by Julian Harrap.

St Mary Woolnoth

Lombard Street, EC3 • Tel 020 7626 9701 • Nearest transport Bank LU • Please telephone for opening times and services

Aptly described as situated 'on the prow' of Lombard Street and Bank, this church's curious name dates back to a Saxon noble called Woolnoth, or possibly Wulfnoth, who founded a temple on the site. Hawksmoor's church is the only one built in the City under the 'Fifty Churches' Act of 1711. Given a very cramped site, he created a unique exterior, especially when one considers his other churches were built on spacious 'greenfield' sites. The interior feels larger than expected and its design is based on the Egyptian Hall, as described by the Roman writer Vitruvius.

The church has been threatened with demolition many times, especially during the 19th century when City sites were at premium and 18th-century church architecture was of low priority. St Mary Woolnoth is unique in having an underground station below it, during the construction of which The City and Southern London Railway cleared the church vaults, transferring the bodies buried there to a cemetery in Ilford, and sunk lift shafts directly beneath the church. *Area Map p.8, B:2*

West Towers, Westminster Abbey

Dean's Yard, SW1 • Tel 020 7222 5897
• www.westminster-abbey.org • Nearest
transport St James's Park LU or Westminster LU

This project was Hawksmoor's last and he
died before it was completed. These towers
show his extraordinary ability for imitation and
innovation and are one of only two examples of
his Gothic work in London, the other being the
tower of St Michael, Cornhill (see p.78). So well
do the towers sit with the rest of the west end
of the Abbey, it is hard to persuade the casual
onlooker that the towers only date from the
18th century. *Area Map p.6, B:1*

*Right: West Towers, Westminster Abbey. One of
Hawksmoor's last projects, completed nine years after
his death. Inspiration for the design may well have
come from the 14th-century west towers of Beverley
Minster on which he worked earlier in his career*

SIR JOHN VANBRUGH
(1664–1726)

Of Vanbrugh one contemporary said 'Van's genius, without thought or lecture, is hugely turn'd to architecture'. However, Vanbrugh's life was an extraordinary one even if we do not take into consideration his architectural achievements: he was also in his time a wine merchant, soldier, prisoner (in the Bastille of Paris) as well as a successful playwright.

It is not known when Vanbrugh decided to try his hand at architecture but by 1669 he was designing Castle Howard in North Yorkshire for the Earl of Carlisle. By 1702 he was Wren's principal colleague on the Board of His Majesty's Works and the following year was appointed to the Board of Directors of Greenwich Hospital. He was later given the opportunity to create his most memorable building; Blenheim Palace in Oxfordshire, a gift to the Duke of Marlborough as a mark of royal gratitude for his military achievements against the French. A master of the Baroque, Vanbrugh's work was flamboyant, theatrical and exuberant. His massive, muscular style worked best when applied to the large-scale projects he undertook but towards the end of his life Vanbrugh did champion architects of the Palladian movement, such as Burlington.

Vanbrugh Castle

Westcombe Park Road, SE3 • Nearest transport Maze Hill Rail • No public Access

In 1718 Vanbrugh bought 12 acres of land at Maze Hill in order to build homes for himself and his family, while he was working on projects at Greenwich nearby. His own, the only building remaining, is now divided into private apartments and so is not open to the public.

Finished in 1726, this turreted, palatial building, resembling a Scottish castle or fortress, still stuns and amuses the unsuspecting! It is thought to be Britain's first sham castle – a sort of Gothic pile without a trace of Gothic detailing!

Royal Arsenal, Woolwich

Woolwich SE18 6ST • Nearest Transport Woolwich Arsenal Rail & DLR • 'Firepower' museum • Tel 020 8855 7755 • www.firepower.org.uk

During the building of Blenheim Palace the Duchess of Marlborough had a spectacular falling-out with Vanbrugh, which led to his resigning the commission in 1716. His friendship with the Duke continued and this led to the architect being given the commission for designing buildings for the Board of Ordnance. The most important buildings in this group, and still extant in London, can be found at the Royal Arsenal at Woolwich which is just along the River Thames from Greenwich.

It is probable, but by no means beyond doubt, that Vanbrugh was responsible for the building of the Brass Gun Foundry of 1717; The Model Room of 1719 and the Gun Bore Factory of the early 1720s. All the buildings are simply constructed in brick and together make a very interesting group.

The 76-acre site at Woolwich has a long history. In 1512 Henry VIII established a Royal Dockyard here and by 1671 it became the largest complex for the manufacture and storage of armaments and military equipment in Britain. King George III gave the Arsenal a Royal Charter in 1805 in honour of its importance in the Napoleonic Wars. During the First World War some 80,000 were employed here in armament manufacture. Despite this glorious past the site was closed by the Ministry of Defence in the late 1960s.

The London Development Agency took control of the land in 2000, when it was decided to create a new mixed use urban quarter. The first phase has provided over 1,000 homes in a mix of 22 converted Grade I and II listed buildings and new build blocks. These include the Greenwich Heritage Centre, Firepower (a museum showcasing the history of the Royal Regiment of Artillery), shops, cafés and other commercial and light industrial use. Outdoor spaces have been transformed with landscaping and public art.

The building of a further 3,000 homes, as well as a health centre, hotel, offices, cafés, shops and a new cinema, are currently underway and will make this a new London neighbourhood with transport links that include the Riverside Thames Bus and the planned London Crossrail route.

See also:
• King William Block, Greenwich Hospital, 'Greenwich Walk', (p.280).

THOMAS ARCHER
(1668-1743)

Born to a wealthy Warwickshire family and educated at Oxford, he travelled in Europe for four years. During his time in Italy he studied the work of Bernini and the influence is evident in Archer's designs, which are almost pure continental Baroque.

St Pauls's Deptford

Diamond Way, Deptford, SE8 3DS • Tel 020 8692 0989 • Nearest transport Deptford Bridge DLR • Please telephone for opening times and services

Pevsner described St Paul's as 'One of the most moving 18th-century churches in London: large, sombre and virile'. Built 1713-30 as part of the 1711 'Fifty Churches Act', it is certainly one of the foremost Baroque churches in London, if not the country. The visitor is greeted at the west end by a large semi-circular portico, surmounted by a tall English steeple. The interior has notable features such as a curving Venetian window at the apse on the east end, great solid Corinthian columns and the original pulpit with graceful iron stairs.

Russell House, Covent Garden

43 King Street, Covent Garden, WC2 • Nearest Transport Covent Garden LU • no public access other than ground floor shop when open

If you stand with your back to the porch at the front of the Church of St Paul, Covent Garden by Inigo Jones and glance to your left you will see Russell House. A lovely stuccoed house built 1716-7 by Archer as a home for Admiral Russell, 1st Earl of Oxford, it has four giant Composite pilasters on street-level rusticated piers, and tall, slim windows with gentle elliptical heads. Restored to its former glory in 1977, the building had for many years been used as a fruit store for Covent Garden Market. The ground floor of this handsome building is now a fashion shop. *Area Map p.6, B:3*

See also:
- St John, Smith Square, 'Eat and Drink Architecture', p.336

Left: St Pauls Deptford

JAMES GIBBS
(1682-1754)

Born into a modest Scottish Catholic family, Gibbs was unable to fund a 'Grand Tour' and as a young man stayed with relatives in Holland before enrolling at the Scots College in Rome with a view to taking Holy Orders. Fortunately for us, the young Gibbs decided that his real calling was architecture and he became a pupil of the great Carlo Fontana. Consequently Gibbs had a thorough, professional training in Italian architecture, unlike his contemporaries who were merely observers. On his return to England in 1709, the only obstacle to a glittering career was his religion. Ironically, one of his first major commissions was to design the church of St Mary-le-Strand as one of the 'Fifty New Churches' under the Act intended to promote Protestant worship! Not adverse to self-publicity, he published two editions of his drawings and in 1732 published his Rules for Drawing the Several Parts of Architecture.

St Mary-le-Strand

Strand, WC2 • Nearest transport Temple LU, Charing Cross LU & Rail • Tel 020 7836 3126 • www.stmarylestrand.org • See website for opening times & services

Marooned in the middle of a busy London thoroughfare and a short walk from the delights of the Covent Garden area, this small church is worth dodging the traffic to visit. The advantage of it being stranded on an island is that it can be viewed from all sides. Dating from 1714-17, this building, probably more than all his others, reflects Gibbs' training under Fontana, even though Gibbs had to make modifications to please his masters. The original design for the tower was too 'Roman' for Whigish taste and so something a little more Palladian was produced instead. The semi-circular entrance porch is exquisite as is the interior with its richly coloured stained glass windows, particularly the work in the apse by Sidney Toy (1947). *Area Map p.6, C:3*

Octagon of Orleans House

Riverside, Twickenham, TW1 3DJ • Tel 020 8831 6000 • www.richmond.gov.uk/arts • Nearest Transport St Margaret's Rail or Richmond LU then bus 33, 490, H22, R68, R70, 290 alight at The Crown Pub / Lebanon Park • See website for opening times

Built in the early 1720's as an almost freestanding garden room and place for entertainment, the building is of brick with stone window dressings. The fairly plain exterior is in stark contrast to the richly decorated baroque interior. This is the work of renowned Swiss stuccatori Giovanni Bagutti and Guiseppe Artari, who also decorated St Peter, Vere Street and St Martin-in-the-Fields for Gibbs.

Set in a peaceful woodland area near the River Thames, the Octagon is part of the Orleans House Gallery and is maintained by The London Borough of Richmond.

St Peter, Vere Street

Vere Street, W1G 0DQ • Nearest Transport Bond Street LU

Of brown and orange brick with stone quoins and Tuscan portico and pediment, this church sits on its own little island just off busy Oxford Street and was built for the Earl of Oxford 1721-24. With very pretty plasterwork by Bagutti and Artari, this church has been cited by some as the 'testing ground' for Gibbs much larger work – St Martin-in-the-Fields.

The building is now the offices of the London Institute of Contemporary Christianity.
Area Map p.4, C:1

See also:
• St Martin-in-the-Fields,
  see 'Whitehall Walk' p.323
• St Bartholomew's Hospital, see
  'Bartholomew Walk' p.261

LORD BURLINGTON (RICHARD BOYLE, 3RD EARL OF BURLINGTON) (1694-1753)

Having inherited extensive properties in the country and London at the age of ten, wealth enabled Burlington to travel as well as patronise the talented. He championed the music of the young Handel, the paintings of Kent and supported the Italian sculptor Guelfi. He employed the talent of Colen Campbell in his quest to restore the principles of Palladian architecture to the position enjoyed at the time of Inigo Jones before the cultural wilderness that was the Commonwealth intervened. Campbell and Burlington collaborated on the remodelling of the latter's family home in Piccadilly, which was subject to further, more extensive, alterations during the 19th century.

However by the early 1720's Burlington was acting as his own architect, assisted by Henry Flitcroft, who was later to design the church of St Giles-in-the-Field. Their earliest work is the Dormitory at Westminster School (gutted during World War II and much altered since with no public access).

Chiswick House

Burlington Lane, W4 • Tel 020 8995 0508 • Nearest transport Chiswick Rail • www.chgt.org.uk • See website for opening times and admission charges

Described by Sir Kenneth Clark in his book *Civilisation* as a 'masterpiece of domestic architecture', Chiswick House was inspired by Palladio's famous Villa Rotonda – but it is no slavish copy. Built between 1727 and 1729 the house was designed by Burlington to be the setting for his extensive art collection. This was housed on the first floor along with a bedchamber and dressing room for Lady Burlington. The lower floor housed Burlington's library and his private apartments. The domestic offices, kitchen etc, remained in the adjacent Jacobean house.

The plan of Chiswick House is a square with an interior of octagonal halls and a slightly flattened dome, also octagonal, with four small windows. The elegant exterior double staircase leads to the portico which, even with six solid Corinthian columns, appears to float. Burlington ingeniously used obelisks to contain the chimneys so necessary for the English climate and on either side of the portico are statues of Inigo Jones and Palladio by the leading 18th-century sculptor Rysbrack.

The sumptuous interior is at odds with the monochrome exterior, but is very much in the spirit of the work of Inigo Jones. Indeed most

of the chimneypieces in Chiswick House are based on designs in Burlington's Collection by Jones and many of the rooms have painted ceilings by William Kent.

The original Jacobean house was demolished in the 1780's in order to add wings to Burlington's villa, but these were taken down shortly afterwards. Chiswick House stayed mostly within the ownership of Burlington's family but by the early 1950's it needed extensive repairs. This work was undertaken by the Ministry of Works at the behest of Middlesex Council and since 1984 Chiswick

House has been cared for by English Heritage. Connoisseurs of architecture will have fun spotting Burlington's influences in the house and references to the works of classical interpreters Palladio and Scamozzi. For the rest of us it is just a joy to behold – a sparkling gem of a building set within an exquisite public park.

Also of note is the gateway and new café. The gateway was originally designed by Inigo Jones for a house in Chelsea and erected at Chiswick in 1738. The café was named RIBA London Building of the Year 2011, see 'Eat and Drink Architecture' p.353 for more details.

WILLIAM KENT (1685-1748)

Although from a humble Yorkshire family, as a talented painter Kent enjoyed the patronage of wealthy gentlemen who financed his visits to Italy over a period of ten years. In the winter of 1715 whilst in Rome he met the Earl of Burlington who became a patron, collaborator and friend. On his return to England in 1719 Kent received commissions from the great and wealthy, being called upon to restore Ruben's ceiling at the Banqueting House and in 1739 he became Portrait Painter to the King – a post he never assumed.

Kent became interested in architecture during his stay in Italy and had studied the works not only of Palladio but also buildings in Rome by Guilio, Romano and Raphael. The influence of these latter two artists/architects can be seen in Kent's preference for rusticated wall-surfaces over the smooth exteriors associated with Palladian architecture.

Among Kent's most prestigious works outside the capital are the garden buildings at Stowe in Buckinghamshire and Holkham Hall in Norfolk, on which he collaborated with Lord Burlington. One of Kent's major London projects, the Courts of Justice, originally stood approximately where the public entrance to the House of Commons is today, but was irreparably damaged by fire in 1834.

44, Berkeley Square, Mayfair

44 Berkeley Square, W1J 5AR • www.theclermontclub.com

One of the finest town houses in London, this house was built 1742/44 for Lady Isabella Finch. She was sometime Lady in Waiting to Queen Caroline, who, being a single woman, required a house for entertaining as much as for domestic convenience. The house is of brick construction with stone quoins and detailing at the ground floor, particularly around the front door. The interior has an exquisite staircase, which, starting with a single flight fans out to both sides taking guests up to the important first floor, piano nobile, and the great salon with its three tall pediment windows overlooking the square.

The house is now owned by the Clermont Club, a private members club with no public access. However, the club's website has some superb photographs of the interior.

See also:
- Treasury Building and Horse Guards Parade, see Whitehall Walk' p.320
- Chiswick House (Interior), see p.104

SIR WILLIAM CHAMBERS
(1723-96)

During the period of the 1770s and 1780s English architecture was dominated by two very talented men. The first, William Chambers initially made his name by producing work in the Chinese style and later as the leading exponent of Palladianism, the second was Robert Adam who gave his name to a style of his own.

Born in Gothenburg to Scottish parents, William Chambers showed a great interest in architecture but was obliged to work for the family mercantile business. In this capacity he travelled extensively to Africa, India, Ceylon and, most importantly, China, where he studied and drew the buildings he saw. It was not until the age of 27 that Chambers began his architectural studies in earnest in Paris, under the tutelage of Blondel at l'Ecole des Arts, and he went on to study for a further five-years in Rome.

Within two years of his return to England in 1755 he published his first book, *Designs for Chinese Buildings* and was appointed 'Tutor of Architecture' to the future King George III. Princess Augusta, employed Chambers to lay out the grounds at Kew and furnish it with buildings of an Oriental flavour. His royal patronage continued when he was appointed Treasurer of the newly founded Royal Academy in 1768 and the King's Surveyor-General in 1782.

The King's Observatory, Richmond

Old Deer Park, Kew Road, Richmond, TW9 2AZ • Nearest Transport Richmond LU & Rail

Set in the centre of the historic Richmond Deer Park, which majestically sweeps down to the Thames, the King's Observatory was designed by William Chambers for George III. Made of Portland stone, the building contains two octagonal rooms surmounted with what appears a fashionable cupola, but is in fact a moveable dome, inside which were the main telescopes. The building was completed in time for the King, a keen astronomer, to observe the transit of Venus across the face of the Sun on 3rd June 1769.

See also:
• Somerset House, see 'Strand Walk' p.316

ROBERT ADAM (1728-92)

Born the second son of William Adam, a successful Scottish architect and entrepreneur, Robert Adam enjoyed a background of relative privilege. He moved in intellectual circles, had access to his father's excellent library and was sufficiently wealthy to be able to travel extensively in Europe. However, Adam was not a gentleman of leisure and, like his father, was thoroughly versed in the craft of building. One important result of this was his concern with every detail of his architectural projects – very different from the dilettante, gentleman architects of this period.

On his return from his travels in early 1758 Adam decided to settle in London and was soon joined by his two younger brothers, James, also an architect and William junior, a banker. In 1761 Robert Adam was given one of two new posts of Architect of the King's Works (the post until then had been 'Surveyor of the King's Works'). The other post went to Sir William Chambers who was Adam's rival rather than his colleague. Indeed Chambers was successful in blocking Adam's membership to the Royal Academy on the grounds that his work was 'too eclectic'. However, Adam proved his scholarship by producing three volumes entitled *Works in Architecture of Robert and James Adam*. Perhaps more importantly, Robert Adam had a whole style of architecture named after him and even for those with little interest in the field, the term 'Adam Style' will bring to mind buildings and interiors in the Classical manner.

Over the next 30 years Robert Adam went on to expand the repertoire of English domestic architecture from strict Palladianism to include a much wider range of classical sources. He became one of the most sought after and busiest architects of his day and his wealthy clients adored the new decorative style all of which was designed by Adam, including the door fittings. Although public commissions eluded him, at the time of his unexpected death in 1792 at the age of 63, Robert Adam had over 30 commissions from all parts of the country in hand. At his funeral in Westminster Abbey his coffin was borne to its last resting place by a Duke, two Earls, a Viscount and a Baron.

There are very few unaltered, from the foundations to the chimney tops, Adam buildings. Indeed there is little of his work to see in central London – much was swept away by road-widening schemes, 'improvements', enemy bombing etc. Despite the sad loss of much of his work, Adam was a master of renovation and interior design, as three of his most important houses Syon, Osterley and Kenwood, all described below, illustrate.

The vast collection of plans and drawings by Robert and James Adam was obtained by Sir John Soane in 1833, and can be viewed at his museum, see p.122.

Syon House

Syon Park, Brentford, TW8 8JF • Tel 020 8560 0882 • www.syonpark.co.uk • Nearest transport Gunnersbury LU & Rail then bus 237 or 267 • See website for more details

Originally the site of a 15th-century abbey and of a noble house since 1547, Syon House has belonged to the Percy family, Earls and Dukes of Northumberland, since 1594 and was extensively reconstructed by the tenth Earl in the 17th century. The title died out with his son and was not recreated until 1750 when Sir Hugh Smithson became Earl of Northumberland. It was for him that Robert Adam refashioned the old house by creating a first floor, or piano nobile level, and a complete set of parade rooms, through which the guests and hosts would promenade at the frequent, fashionable parties. These new rooms were created within the old structure. The exterior is very simple, castellated and stuccoed.

Entrance to the house is through the Hall to the Ante-room (see below right), the Great Dining Room and the State Drawing Room to the Gallery. This principal route takes the visitor through a sequence of splendid chambers, each different from the last yet all related by similar uses of classical motifs. Adam's use of colour adds to the drama with the prevailing ivory and black of the Hall giving way in the next room, the Ante-room, to an essay in sumptuous gold. Adam draws on a wide range of sources, mixing ancient Greek and Roman motifs in an idiosyncratic manner and then arranging them in a unified scheme.

Lansdowne House

9 Fitzmaurice Place, Berkeley Square, W1J 5JD • www.lansdowneclub.com • Private members club, no public access

Now a private members club, Adam designed this house for Lord Bute between 1762 and 1768 as a town mansion standing in its own, large garden. This is an early example of Adam's town houses. Road improvements in the area during the 1930s meant major alterations to the property were necessary and part of the Adam interior had to be sacrificed when Adam's original stone façade was pushed back 40 feet to make way for the road. The discarded Adam Drawing Room, complete with exquisite decorations executed by Cipriani and Zucchi, was shipped off to America and now resides in the Philadelphia Museum of Art and can be viewed on www.philamuseum.org.

Home House

20 Portman Square, W1H 6LW • www. homehouse.co.uk • Private members club, no public access

The commission for this house was originally given to the architect James Wyatt, but after a falling out with the Countess of Home a year into the project he was sacked and Robert Adam was engaged to complete the job in 1775. The interior, especially, is everything one imagines an Adam house to be – very light, elegant and glamorous. The exquisite staircase, reminiscent of Kent's at 44 Berkeley Square, has a single flight to the first floor and then swings out on both sides, lit by a circular skylight. Miraculously, much of Adam's original interior decoration, some started by Wyatt, survives.

Home House remained a private residence until, in 1926, Samuel Courtauld housed his growing art collection here, becoming the basis of the Courtauld Institute of Art; the collection moving to larger premises at Somerset House in 1989 (see p.316). The house was then listed on the 'Buildings at Risk Register' until it received extensive and highly successful renovation by Fielden and Mawson, conservation architects, between 1996 and 1999.

The house is now a private members club. The club has a superb website which really gives an excellent impression of the interior of the house. *Area Map p.4, B:1*

Osterley Park

Jersey Road, Isleworth, Houndslow, TW7 4RB • Tel 020 8232 5050• www.osterleypark. org.uk • www.nationaltrust.org.uk • Nearest transport Osterley LU then 25min walk• See website for opening times and admission charges

Osterley Park was originally built as the country seat for Thomas Gresham in 1575. The house was bought in 1761 by wealthy banker Robert Childs, who, like many of his contemporaries, employed Robert Adam to transform his home. As with Syon, the old-fashioned exterior of the house, with its red brick wings around a courtyard and towers at each corner topped with ogee caps, belies its interior. Adam added a magnificent screen of Ionic columns to form a double portico at the centre of the front elevation, with the house being entered by a flight of stairs. Inside, the decorative scheme of the Etruscan Dressing Room is particularly sumptuous, Adam drawing on ancient Herculaneum and the classicizing work of his contemporary Josiah Wedgwood for inspiration.

Owned by the National Trust since 1949, the house is considered to be the most perfectly preserved of all Adam's work. The grounds have a magnificent lake complete with anglers, water fowl and a flashing kingfisher. The stable block has interesting Elizabethan brickwork and an early 18th-century cupola and clock. All this is a mere 45 minute tube ride from the centre of London.

Kenwood

The Iveagh Bequest, Kenwood, Hampstead Lane, NW3 7JR • Tel 020 8348 1286 • www.english-heritage.org.uk • Nearest transport Golders Green LU then bus 210, Gospel Oak & Hampstead Heath Rail • Admission free • See website for opening times

Kenwood stands on the crest of the ridge between Hampstead and Highgate and looks towards central London. On the site of a much older house, Kenwood was rebuilt in about 1700 and between 1764-79 was remodelled by Robert Adam for its owner William Murray, 1st Earl of Mansfield. To the existing brick house Adam added the porch, library and ante chamber, embellished and decorated the remainder of the interior and encased the whole exterior in white stucco. The wings of the house are a post-Adam addition.

On the north façade of the house Adam added the huge portico, with four fluted Ionic columns and Grecian scrolled capitals supporting the massive pediment. As you pass through the portico look up to see the rather striking decoration beneath the pediment.

The Library, sometimes referred to as 'The Great Room', is regarded as one of the finest 18th-century British interiors. The room is an unusual shape, a double cube with semi-circular apses and a coved ceiling inspired by ancient Roman baths.

Kenwood houses a renowned art collection, which includes works by Jan Vermeer, Frans Hals and Rembrandt as well as portraits by Gainsborough, Reynolds and Romney.

This elegant house sits in extensive grounds, landscaped by Repton in 1793, which beautifully incorporate some fine 20th-century sculpture by, among others, Reg Butler, Barbara Hepworth and Henry Moore.

Above: Kenwood House south front
Opposite: Antechamber to the Dining Room

Apsley House

149 Piccadilly, W1 • Tel 020 7499 5676
• www.english-heritage.co.uk • Nearest
transport Hyde Park Corner LU • See
website for opening times and admission
charges

Built 1771-78 by Robert Adam for Lord Apsley,
but extensively remodelled by James Wyatt
and his family from 1807 onwards. Further
renovations have largely ignored its Adam
origins, although a few of the rooms still
conform to his ideals – if you look really hard.

Originally the house address was 'No1
London' because it was the first building
past the tollgate into the capital for travellers
eastward. Apsley House was once the home
of Arthur Wellesley, 1st Duke of Wellington,
soldier and politician, and today houses the
Wellington Museum and a glittering array of
artworks acquired courtesy of the Iron Duke's
military successes, among them paintings by
Velasquez and Correggio.

The Adelphi

Royal Society of Arts, 8 John Adam Street,
WC2 • Tel 020 7930 5115 • www.thersa.
org • Nearest transport Charing Cross LU
& Rail • Usually open to the public first
Sunday of the month from 10am-1pm, but
please telephone to confirm

This building's name is derived from the Greek
'adelphoi' meaning 'brothers' – in honour of
Robert, John and William Adam. Between
1768 and 1774 terraces of houses were built
in this area using a series of arches and
subterranean streets to counteract the slope
from the Strand to the river. The scheme was
a financial disaster and only by resorting to a
public lottery for the unsold houses, did the
family avoid ruin.

Regrettably, most of the scheme was
demolished in 1936. Only a few of the original
houses remain – Nos 6-10 and 18 Adam
Street, 4-6 John Adam Street, 1-3 and 9
Robert Street. The buildings are now offices
without public access

No. 8 John Adam Street, now home to the
Royal Society of Arts, was one of the last
buildings to be completed in 1774. Built
from stone with a temple front of fluted Ionic
columns, it is perhaps the best Adam façade
in London. The RSA has a great website were
you can see most of the rooms using their virtual
tour. *Area Map p.6, B:3*

Frederick Place

Off Old Jewry, City of London EC2 •
No public access

A surprising find at the heart of the City,
these houses were built during the same
period as the Adelphi project and were also
constructed as a speculative venture. It has
been many years since these buildings served
as private residences, most are now offices,
and consequently they have been subject to
alteration. However, it is fun to look for original
Adam traces. See – Numbers 6, 7 and 8
Frederick Place and Number 35 Old Jewry.
Area Map p.8, B:2

Fitzroy Square

Off Tottenham Court Road, W1 • For
information about the Georgian Society
telephone 087 1750 2936 or consult their
website www.georgiangroup.org.uk

Some of Robert Adam's last London work
can be seen in Fitzroy Square. In early
1790 Charles Fitzroy, Lord Southampton,
commissioned the highly fashionable Adam
to design a handsome square of houses on
his land here. However, at the time of Adam's
sudden death in 1792 only the south and east
sides had been completed. These buildings are
typically Adam – light, elegant, stuccoed with
rustication at the ground floor.

'Victorianisation', 'improvement' and bomb-
damage during World War II has left this
square in rather a sorry state but the efforts of
caring residents and organisations such as the
Georgian Group ensure a better future for this
wonderful group of buildings.

Indeed, the Georgian Group, a national charity
for the preservation for our Georgian heritage,
occupies one of the best-preserved buildings
at number 6. The Group often hosts exhibitions
and lectures that are open to the public.
Area Map p.2-3, A:2

See also:
• The Admiralty Screen, 'Whitehall Walk' p.325

JOHN NASH (1725-1835)

Nash was the leading architect of the English Regency period pursuing a neo-classical vision with the patronage of the Prince Regent. He began his working life as a designer of country houses with the landscape gardener Repton, and by the early 19th century had become a prosperous member of the Whig party and in an ideal position to put his architectural ideas into practice in the capital. The forging of a form of classical architecture with stucco walls, huge porticos and various orders of columns and entablatures defined the Regency style.

Among Nash's key works are the Regents Park terraces, All Souls Church (1822-24) as well as the layout of Regent Street and Trafalgar Square. For more information about Nash refer to the John Nash Walk, see p.284'.

Right: Cumberland Terrace, Regent's Park. The grandest of the Nash terraces built around the park. Best described as 'Romantic Picturesque', his work is often criticised for its impure style, see p.287-288

GEORGE DANCE THE YOUNGER (1741-1825)
& GEORGE DANCE THE ELDER (1695-1768)

George Dance Senior and Younger are often considered collectively simply because they often worked together in the City. However the father's reputation has been somewhat eclipsed by his son's prodigious talent. The building George Dance Senior is noted for is the Mansion House built at the heart of the City and described below.

Dance the Younger spent his early years learning the craft of architecture in his father's studio, but only after he had spent many years of travel in Europe and study in Rome accompanied by his brother Nathaniel, an accomplished painter.

His first work was to design the church of All Hallows, London Wall in the City, detailed below. Dance was only 26 when he was given this extraordinary commission in 1765, but this may have been due to his father's position as Clerk of the City Works, an influential and potentially lucrative post that would be passed to the son in due course.

It was in this capacity that both Dance Senior and Younger executed some of their most notable projects, such as the now demolished Newgate Prison, built 1770/8 – and, despite its grim purpose, said to have

been the most impressive Classical building in the whole of London. It was pulled-down in 1900 to accommodate present Central Criminal Courts.

George Dance the Younger turned his hand to an array of interesting design projects throughout his career including town planning patterns such as at Finsbury Square (1777); the road pattern of Southwark, radiating from St George's Circus (1785); the highly original façade to the Guildhall (page 40); he was also responsible for adding the Sculpture Gallery (now the Ballroom) to Adams Lansdowne House (1792); and the design of the building for the Royal College of Surgeons in Lincolns Inn, now much altered (1806/10), and alterations to the Mansion House, as described below. He is noted for his stormy relationship with his brilliant pupil, the irascible John Soane, who purchased Pitzhanger Manor in Ealing, designed by Dance in 1770, and promptly re-built it.

Mansion House

Mansion House Place, City of London, EC4N 8BH • Tel 020 7626 2500 • www.cityoflondon.gov.uk • Nearest Transport: Bank or Mansion House LU • No public access except tours by a City Guide every Tuesday at 2pm • See website for details

This prestigious commission was won by Dance the elder in 1734 with a brief to provide lodging for the Mayor, who until then lodged at one of the City Halls during his term in office. Dance was forced to squeeze a lot of building into a small, awkward space. Faced with Portland stone, the building is rusticated at basement level.

The grander front of the building is no longer used as the main entrance due to it's close proximity to the busy road. In 1846 stables at the (west) rear of the building in Walbrook, were demolished and a Doric porch was erected as the new main entrance to the building. As with the exterior, the interior has a nod toward Palladian architecture, but again many find the rather excitable ornamentation difficult to digest.

The Mansion House is still in use today for its original purpose and is the venue for lunches, dinners, banquets and meetings with guests of the Lord Mayor. There are two very large ceremonial rooms in the building, the Ballroom and the Egyptian Hall. The latter has a magnificent tunnel vault roof added by George Dance the Younger in 1795/6, which rests on the giant Corinthian columns of his father's design.

All Hallows Church

All Hallows on the Wall, 83 London Wall, EC2M 5ND • Tel 020 7588 2638 • www.allhallowsonthewall.org • Nearest transport Moorgate LU and Liverpool Street LU & Rail • Open to the public most Fridays 11am-3pm (please telephone to check)

All Hallows was built to replace a medieval church that stood on Roman foundations on the same site, hugging the City wall.

The plain exterior is of yellow and pink brick with Portland stone dressings. Also of Portland stone is the short Italianate tower placed at the west end, with a pedimented door, clock and a domed cupola. The aisleless interior has engaged Ionic columns supporting an enriched plaster vault. The simple space was a great inspiration to one of Dance's pupils – John Soane.

The church has been adapted to provide meeting and exhibition space for charitable organisations and other users but the main sanctuary area is in its original state.
Area Map p.8, B:3

Right: All Hallows Church, London Wall. George Dance the Younger designed this church on his return from study in Italy, his first commission when he was a mere 24 years of age

Crescent, City of London

Crescent, off The Minories, EC3 • Nearest transport Tower Hill LU • No public access

A fine row of eleven handsome four-storey houses which date from 1765 to 1770. When originally built the crescent stood in a field between, what were then, London's two largest hospitals for the mentally insane – St Luke's and Bedlam. It was here Dance the younger introduced London to the concept of residential crescents and circus's, so fashionable and popular in Bath.

Today offices, rather than private residences, occupy the site. The Crescent is certainly worth a visit, although difficult to find amid the towering buildings that now surround it.
Area Map p.8, C:2

See also:
• St Bartholomew the Less, 'Bartholomew Walk' p.261

Sir John Soane
(1753-1837)

'The ruling passion of my life (is) to be distinguished as an architect', so said Sir John Soane, the son of a Reading bricklayer who went on to enjoy great success in his chosen career. Soane did indeed become a distinguished architect, was awarded many prestigious surveyorships (Whitehall, Bank of England) and undertook the role of Professor of Architecture at the Royal Academy for many years.

Soane was a pupil of George Dance junior and it has been suggested that together they introduced what the latter liked to call 'the poetry of architecture' into the rather austere classical tradition, by which he meant the role that natural light could play in a building. Soane's buildings are characterised by an innovative approach to lighting and fenestration with devices such as top lighting and coloured glass used to particular effect.

Right: Sir John Soane's Museum, see p.122

Bank of England

Bank of England Museum, Bartholomew Lane, EC2R 8AH • Tel 020 7601 5545 • www.bankofengland.co.uk/museum • Nearest transport Bank LU • Admission free • See website for museum opening times

Soane was appointed to the Surveyorship in 1788 at the commencement of this major building project. The Bank, quite naturally, needed to be wrapped in a secure, windowless wall and thus most of the interior needed to be top-lit which is where Soane's genius lay. Alas, much of his work has since been rebuilt in the name of progress. Thankfully for Soane's admirers a replica of the very finest of his work at the Bank, the domed Stock Office built in 1792, can be seen at the Bank of England Museum. *Area Map p.8, B:2*

Dulwich Picture Gallery

College Road, SE21 7AD • Tel 020 8693 5254 • www.dulwichpicturegallery.org.uk • Nearest transport West Dulwich Rail • See website for opening times and admission charges

Designed and built between 1811-14 this was Britain's first public art gallery and a natural vehicle for Soane's clever use of top lighting. Using brick with stone dressings, Soane managed to produce a wonderful building with a very limited budget. Thanks to a major restoration programme the galleries once again look magnificent and an exciting new bronze and glass 'Visitor Wing' by Rick Mather houses an excellent café.

The gallery contains some outstanding works of art by Poussin, Rembrandt, Murillo, Gainsborough and Watteau, amongst others.

Sir John Soane's Museum. Soane left this house, really a gigantic cabinet of curiosities, for 'students and amateurs' to enjoy

Sir John Soane's Museum

13 Lincoln's Inn Fields, WC2A 3BP • Tel 020 7405 2107 • www.soane.org • Nearest transport Holborn LU • Admission free • See website for opening times

Soane moved to this house in 1812 and in 1833 obtained an Act of Parliament that enabled him to leave it to the nation intact, as a museum for the study of 'Architecture and Allied Arts'. It is packed with the items he collected throughout his long life – architectural drawings, models, casts, pieces of sculpture, stunning items from antiquity, a collection of paintings by Hogarth – including all eight stages of The Rakes Progress, as well as some very good sculpture by, amongst others, Flaxman and Banks.

The Museum is actually three houses knocked into one and the exterior is more eclectic than its Georgian Mannerist Neo-classical neighbours. Soane added a three storey stone loggia to the façade, topped with statuary. The interior contains a series of architectural delights: the oval staircase which sweeps gracefully up to the yellow drawing room, the clever use of mirrors to create light and space in the main ground floor room, the neo-Gothic 'Monks Parlour' and the basement rooms whose arrangement is reminiscent of a Roman catacomb which has been crammed with interesting objects. Make an appointment in advance and you will be able to peruse some of the 30,000 architectural drawings Soane collected, including some by Wren and Robert Adam. *Area Map p.2-3, C:1*

Holy Trinity Church, Marylebone

Holy Trinity Church now known as 'One Marylebone Road', NW1 4AQ • Tel 020 7380 1663 • www.onemaryleboneroad. com • Nearest transport Great Portland Street LU • No public access

Built 1824/28 as a Commissioners Church, a term used for a number of churches built during the first half of the 19th century in response to the population shift from rural to urban areas. The term is derived from the Church Building Commission which was established in 1824 to organise the building of these Anglican churches.

Unusually the altar was placed at the north end, rather than the more conventional east. The main entrance is at the south, through Soanes unpedimented portico of four huge Ionic columns. The rather busy two stage tower, complete with clock and weather vane, sits atop the building. Deconsecrated in 1955, it served as offices for various publishing houses until 2007 when it was sympathetically restored to become a smart social venue. If you are not fortunate enough to receive an invite, do look at their website where you can see some excellent photographs of the interior. *Area Map p.4, B:2*

SIR ROBERT SMIRKE
(1781-1867)

At the age of 16 Smirke began working in the office of Sir John Soane, but left within months to work with George Dance junior. Smirke enjoyed an immensely successful career, being awarded some very plum commissions. A dedicated Greek Revivalist, it has been suggested that his work consisted of the same couple of Grecian formulae used over and over and that his reputation for reliability and as a good business manager outweighed his architectural flair.

Right: The Main frontage, The British Museum, by Sir Robert Smirke and considered to be his finest achievement

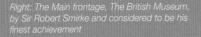

British Museum

Great Russell Street, WC1B 3DG • Tel 020 7636 1555 • www.thebritishmuseum.ac.uk • Nearest transport Holborn LU or Russell Square LU • Admission free except for major exhibitions • See website for opening times

Arriving at the corner of Great Russell Street, particularly from Gower Street, its hard to imagine that such a narrow street could possibly accommodate a museum, let alone this monumental neo-classical building. It was built by Smirke 1823-47 as a massive extension to Montague House, the original, rather modest museum building, and was designed to a courtyard plan. Wings and floors were added piecemeal, when funds allowed. The first phase was built on the east side specifically to house George III's library acquired by the Museum in 1823. The King's Library, as the wing is known, has recently been renovated and re-opened to the public as the Enlightenment Gallery, but minus the books (which are housed in the new British Library – see p.226).

The façade, one of the most memorable and imposing in London, was the last part of Smirke's project to be built in 1847, when Montague House itself was demolished to make way for the great Ionic colonnade and portico.

The architect's brother, Sidney Smirke, designed and built the domed Reading Room, finished in 1857, which filled Robert's courtyard. For a description of the 21st-century alterations to this see p.232. *Area Map p.2-3, B:1*

Other buildings by Sir Robert Smirke:

- Canada House, see 'Whitehall Walk' p.323
- King's College, see 'Strand Walk' p.316
- St James's Palace, see p.42

OTHER 18TH CENTURY
BUILDINGS OF INTEREST:

Dr Johnson's House

17 Gough Square, EC4A 3DE • Tel 020 7353 3745 • www.drjohnsonshouse.org • Nearest transport Chancery Lane LU and Blackfriars LU & Rail • See website for opening times and admission charges

The lexicographer, writer and conversationalist Samuel Johnson (1709-84) lived in this atmospheric house whilst he wrote his Dictionary of the English Language. The house, built in 1700, contains furniture and fittings dating from Dr Johnson's time here. This house is a real gem, an oasis of calm surrounded by a sea of offices.
Area Map p.8, A:2

Left: Dr Johnson's House interior. The property, probably built for a merchant, was restored by architect Alfred Burr in 1911-12 prior to it opening to the public

Keats House

Keats Grove, NW3 2RR • Tel 020 7435 2062 • www.keatshouse.cityoflondon.gov.uk • Nearest transport Belsize Park and Hampstead LU and Hampstead Heath Rail • See website for opening times and admission charges

This was the home of the eminent poet John Keats (1795-1821) who was 23 years old when he moved into the eastern half of this house (it used to be a pair of semi's). At this date Hampstead was not really part of London but a fairly secluded village surrounded by fields. Keats wrote some of his finest poetry here, including 'Ode to a Nightingale' whilst sitting under a plum tree in the garden. Sadly he died at the tender age of 25 whilst on a trip to Italy, having written some of the most memorable poetry in the English language.

Built in 1815, interior of Keats House has been sensitively restored thanks to a Heritage Lottery Grant of almost half a million pounds. The refurbishment sought to reflect the original decoration of the property, creating a living space that Keats would have recognised and providing an authentic example of Regency style.

Geffrye Museum

Kingsland Road, E2 8EA • Tel 020 7739 9893 • www.geffrye-museum.org.uk • Nearest transport Liverpool Street LU & Rail or Old Street LU & Rail • Admission free • See website for opening times

This excellent museum takes the form of a series of rooms each one displaying the interior of a period home, from Elizabethan times up to the present. The museum is housed in a row of beautifully built 18th-century almshouses and also features a lovely garden with period garden 'rooms'.

Right: Geffrye Museum. Almshouses have been a traditional charitable endowment since the Middle Ages, this building was endowed by Sir Robert Geffrye for the Ironmongers Company and built 1715. Of stock brick and red brick dressings, the long U-shape building has a central bay with a clock set in its pediment and a charming bell-cupola above

John Wesley's House

7 City Rd, EC1Y 1AU • Tel 020 7253 2262 • www.wesleyschapel.org.uk • Nearest transport Old Street & Moorgate LU/Rail • Admission free • See website for details

Whilst thought to have been designed by George Dance the Younger, as part of a large complex, this attribution is uncertain. Only one house and the adjoining chapel were built in 1778/79 and this is where John Wesley (1703-91), evangelist and founder of Methodism, spent his last eleven winters – he spent his summers touring the country and preaching. The four-storey stuccoed building with Coade stone dressings is a good example of a Georgian town house. Since 1898 the house has been a museum and the interior has been, as far as possible, restored to look as it did when Wesley was in residence.

Perhaps the most touching feature of the house is the small room leading off Wesley's bedroom. This room, simply furnished with a chair, kneeler and a small bureau holding a candle and bible, is known to Methodists as the 'power house', for it is here that Wesley spent the first hours of each day in prayer. The Chapel is a small, but good example of Georgian design, with a porch that was added later, in 1897. Wesley is buried in the chapel graveyard and there is a splendid bronze statue of him by J Adams Acton dated 1891.

Right: John Wesley's House

Handel House

25 Brook Street, W1K 4HB • Tel 020 7495 1685 • www.handelhouse.org • Nearest transport Bond Street and Oxford Circus LU • See website for opening times and admission charges

The great composer George Frederick Handel is understood to have been the first occupant of this house built by George Barnes as part of a four-building, speculative development in this once genteel area of the town. Handel lived and worked here from 1723 to 1759 and since that time the property has had many uses. In the 1970's the freehold was purchased by an insurance company and in 2000 the upper storeys of number 25, where Handel lived, and 23, where Jimi Hendrix briefly lived, were leased to the Handel House Trust and since November 2001 the house has been open to the public.

Now known as the Handel House Museum this house not only tells the fascinating story of this genius composer but gives us a glimpse of what living in an early Georgian house was like. The Trust has been meticulous in restoring this house to its 18th-century state, using a neighbouring property, number 27/29 Brook Street, which retains much of the detail of the original Barnes development, as the model. The plain fireplaces now installed in the Handel House came from properties in Covent Garden, demolished in 1996 to make room for the Royal Opera House extension.

Dennis Severs' House

18 Folgate Street, E1 6BX • Tel 020 7247 4013 • www.dennissevershouse.co.uk • Nearest transport Liverpool Street LU/Rail and Shoreditch High St LU • See website for opening times and admission charges

Not a museum but a living image of how life once may have been within the walls of this house. The house was the brainchild of its late owner, Dennis Severs, an American artist who 'created' a fictional Huguenot family, the Jervis's, placed them in this real 18th-century house and let them fill the space with what might have been. Set in the heart of Spitalfields, Dennis Severs' House is also close to Hawksmoor's Christ Church (see p.95). *Area Map p.8, C:3*

St Pancras Station, see p.154

05

VICTORIAN LONDON

VICTORIAN LONDON

"Oh mine in snows and summer heats. Those good old Tory brick-built streets!" Wilfred Whitten

For much of the 19th century London resembled a giant construction site. Industry, imperialism, philanthropy and 'the coming of the railways' brought massed building projects to the capital and each new institution needed to find an appropriate architectural language. The cottage hospital required a different form of expression to the railway station, music hall or the department store, and on occasion the forms chosen could be controversial.

When the Houses of Parliament burned down in the 1830's the Government decreed, after much debate, that its replacement must be of a Gothic or Elizabethan design. Had the fire happened 20 or 30 years earlier we may well be the proud custodians of a purely Classical building, a form of architecture associated with learning and authority, whilst Gothic said religion, Palazzo meant pomp and Egyptian hinted at something exotic. However a surge of nationalism throughout Europe in the 1820s and 1830s saw some British artists, craftsmen and architects looking back to the medieval Gothic, a style which was seen as 'English' and thus deemed especially appropriate for the Houses of Parliament.

Most of the major railway stations were built between 1836-76, and within that 40 years much of London was carved up as the railway companies vied with each other to acquire land. The cost was not merely a financial one, for example, 7,000 people were rendered homeless when The Great Eastern Railway inched its tracks towards Liverpool Street Station.

The first terminal to be completed to the north of London was Euston station, which took its name from 'Euston Grove', the picturesque nursery garden it was built on. Opened in 1837 the line initially only went as far as Boxmoor, just outside Hemel Hempstead. The following year the line was extended to Birmingham, the 112-mile journey taking just over five hours. In celebration of this feat the railway company commissioned the eminent architect Philip Hardwick (1792-1870) to design a grand entrance to the London terminal. This 'Euston Arch', with four gigantic Doric pillars of stone, 72ft high, was the tallest freestanding structure in London at the time. Sadly this potent symbol of the glory days of the railway was swept away in 1963, despite a great outcry at the time.

King's Cross station opened in 1852 and St Pancras station in 1863, disgorging commuters in their thousands on to New Road (now the Euston Road) to find their own way to office and workshop before the coming of underground trains and a bus network. It is estimated that by the late 1850's just over 200,000 workers went to the City every day on foot, many walking from major railway stations.

'Underground' line trains linking major London stations began operation with the opening of the Paddington to Farringdon branch of the Metropolitan Railway in 1863. By 1884 the route encompassed the centre of London and thus the Circle line was born. Deeper excavations were needed for lines such as The City and South London Railway which ran between Stockwell and King William Street in the City, and which forms part of today's Northern line.

Many villages and small towns around London were swelled by mass housing built for commuters, people who once would have 'lived above the shop', or at least nearby. This is especially so south of the river, where places such as Clapham, Peckham, and Southfields grew rapidly. The population of Streatham, for example, in 1811 was 2,729 – by 1900 it was 70,000, due in the main to the opening of Streatham Hill station in 1856. The plain 'two-up, two-down' house with a garden proliferated in the new suburbs.

During the 19th-century industrialisation and mass production touched almost every aspect of life and this is true of building too. Brick, in particular, became cheaper and more widely available. Red brick was more usual until about 1870 when yellowish-bricks made from

Above: King's Cross Station

London clay, known as London Stock brick, became more popular.

London's population shift was particularly dramatic in the City and Westminster, 123,000 and 241,000 people respectively in 1841 declining to 27,000 and 183,000 by 1901. Those who stayed in the centre of London were generally at either end of the economic scale. The wealthy still built mansions in town, but in far fewer numbers than the century before. The price of building land soared during the 19th century and the mansion block, with large, spacious flats complete with designated servants quarters became practical and fashionable. Many who could afford it lived in the west of London, where the prevailing wind meant the smoke-filled air, polluted by the myriad of belching industrial and domestic chimneys, was, to a certain extent, blown east.

However, during the unusually long, hot and dry summer of 1858 nearly all Londoners had to endure weeks of such a terrible stench that the period has gone down in history as 'the Great Stink'. The source of the ghastly smell was the Thames, into which newly installed sewers discharged their untreated contents. Indeed the windows of the Houses of Parliament were draped with sheets soaked in chloride of lime in an attempt to fend-off illness as it was wrongly believed that outbreaks of cholera were caused by the 'miasma' or bad air. The Stink was not only very unpleasant but was seen to be a health hazard.

Engineer Sir Joseph Bazalgette's massively expensive solution was to construct 83 miles of underground brick sewers to intercept sewage outflows and 1,100 miles of street sewers to regulate the raw sewage which flowed through the streets of London. The outflows were diverted downstream where they were dumped, still untreated, into the Thames. Extensive sewage treatment facilities were built only decades later, see 'Crossness Pumping Station' below.

The very poor existed among the rookeries and slums of Seven Dials, St Giles and the edges of the Fleet Valley, often in close proximity to a festering open sewer. Slum clearance took place when new roads needed to cut through such areas. For example the notorious St Giles, Hogarth's Gin Lane, was pulled apart 1841-47 when a thoroughfare from Oxford Circus to High Holborn became necessary.

The slum problem and continuing outbreaks of cholera led to the publication of the Report on the Sanitary Conditions of the Labouring Classes in 1842, which resulted in various philanthropic organisations taking on the practicalities highlighted by the document. Again, blocks of flats were seen as the solution and from the mid 1840's model dwellings were constructed with various degrees of success. In 1862 American philanthropist George Peabody gave £500,000 of his fortune to a Trust for the provision of 'cheap…healthful dwellings for the poor' and between 1864 and 1890, 5,000 such dwellings had been provided, usually in blocks with five or six floors, fairly close-set and made of striped brick. As a mark of their enduring quality, there are still currently approximately 12,000 Peabody properties on 70 estates of varying size in inner London (see image opposite).

Philanthropy extended to hospital provision and the improvement of existing facilities. In the 1890's wealthy furniture manufacturer John Blundell Maple made a vast donation to University College, Gower Street for a new hospital to be built at, what was then, the only university in England, other than Oxford and Cambridge, to award medical degrees. Architect Alfred Waterhouse designed a

Above: Peabody housing

spectacularly innovative cruciform-shaped building in red brick and terracotta Gothic style, which was in contrast to the Classical form of the rest of the College's buildings. The hospital's offices and operating theatres were placed at the centre with wards suitably isolated in the four 'wings' of the cross pattern. The building is now used by the University's Medical School with no public admission. However it is usually accessible during the Open House weekend, see p.377 for more information.

During the 19th century there were generally two types of hospitals in London – 'voluntary' and 'workhouse'. The former were independent charities established for the

benefit of the 'deserving poor', who, according to contemporary values, were respectable working-class people who had fallen on hard times because of sickness. The latter, the 'workhouse hospitals' were for those who were destitute and had no alternative. Many of these people had been reduced to poverty through either sickness or old age and the workhouses opened hospital wards and even purpose-built infirmaries to treat them. Eminent architect, George Gilbert Scott, whose buildings include the Midland Hotel at St Pancras Station, Albert Memorial, started his career designing workhouses; large, grim buildings.

Local authorities were obliged to at least attempt to provide public libraries funded by ratepayers following the Free Libraries Act of 1850 and public baths were provided to serve a dual purpose, firstly as recreational swimming pools and secondly as baths for those with little or no washing facilities at home. When a new municipal building was erected it was usually built in red brick or terracotta, quite often decorated with the sculptured profiles of inspirational figures, such as Shakespeare and Milton. In Great Smith Street, Westminster Council provided both library and bathing facilities in one building, although both activities were kept quite separate! The building is no longer used for its original purpose and is now a restaurant.

Education was not confined to schools, the notion of 'improvement' was an important Victorian value with large museums built in

Kensington, not far from the Albert Hall, see p.159. The railways made travel not only easier but also relatively cheaper and hotels were required to satisfy this demand. Of particular note are George Gilbert Scott's Midland Hotel at St Pancras Station (see p.154) and the Langham Hotel (see p.292).

Prison planning and construction was of special interest during the 19th century when the number of prisoners rapidly grew as a consequence of the reduction in the number of offences carrying the death penalty or transportation. Pentonville Prison, built 1840-42 by Sir Joshua Jebb, took Jeremy Bentham's Panopticon plan of 1791, which exposed the confined to 24-hour observation, whilst also drawing on models of American provincial prisons and ideas of solitude and silence. The crank, a hard-labour machine, which produced nothing but 'exhaustion of the body and boredom of the mind', was invented at Pentonville.

The Education Act of 1870 ushered in the compulsory provision of schooling for children and necessitated the building of hundreds of schools all over the capital. Church schools naturally favoured designs in the Gothic vein, whilst Board schools preferred red brick and gables. Adult education was encouraged and within the City three charity funded institutes were founded. The most architecturally interesting of the trio is without doubt the Bishopsgate Institute, see p.163.

London in the 19th century was the booming and self-confident hub of an Empire. In 1851 this confidence manifested itself in the Great Exhibition, inspired and championed by the young monarch's husband, Prince Albert. The purpose of the exhibition was to put on a global display of manufactured goods and works of art in order to prove Britain's superiority as a rapidly industrialising country, and by using raw materials from all over the world the Exhibition functioned like a giant shop window.

The event attracted some six million visitors who came to view the wares of 17,000 exhibitors. The event was held at Hyde Park in what became known as the 'Crystal Palace', a structure made from glass and cast-iron, six times the size of St Paul's Cathedral and created not by an architect but by a gardener, Joseph Paxton. He had previously designed and constructed the Palm House at Chatsworth in Derbyshire, but this project was on a much bigger scale – taking nine months to construct, not by conventional builders but by members of the Royal Engineers. The entire 'Crystal Palace' was dismantled and moved to a park in Sydenham, south-east London, but perished in a fire in 1936 and only its name lingers on.

Those who witnessed the array of goods on display at the Great Exhibition wanted to purchase such items for themselves. Purpose-built department stores, such as Harvey Nichols in Knightsbridge, (1889-94) sprang up all over London. Market places have been important throughout history, particularly in large towns and cities and during this period Sir Horace Jones, official architect to the City of London, designed some fine buildings specifically for this purpose including Smithfield Market (see 'Bartholomew Walk' p.264) and Leadenhall Market (see 'Shopping and Architecture' p.359).

London in the 19th century saw massive social change, and not all of it was for the better. One only has to read the novels of Charles Dickens to see that Victoria's London was not always a pleasant place to live and that the hand of philanthropy was often a harsh and cold one. The rise of industrialisation was seen as the death-knell to craftsmanship. Indeed William Morris stated that 'you cannot educate, you cannot civilise man, unless you give him a share in art.' Such sentiment expressed itself in the Arts and Crafts movement, whose principles included the ideals of an original architecture closely linked to nature and of a unity in buildings of the arts of architecture, sculpture and painting. Mass-production was largely rejected by the movement, and its members set about reviving high standards of individual craftsmanship. This included not only woodwork, metalwork, and other decorative arts, but also such things as brick making.

Many people will happily state a preference for architecture of the Victorian era above any other, and yet it was a period of great diversity.

Smithfield Market, see p.264

EXAMPLES OF BUILDINGS FROM THIS PERIOD:

Right: The Victoria Tower, Palace of Westminster. Designed to house the historic records of Parliament, at 325 feet (98.5m) this is the tallest part of the Palace and gives the building its iconic profile

Palace of Westminster & Houses of Parliament
Charles Barry and A W Pugin, 1835-60

Houses of Parliament, Palace of Westminster, SW1 • www.parliament.uk/visiting • Nearest transport Westminster LU • Entrance by ticket – please apply to your local MP or your embassy (apply at least six months ahead), alternatively visitors can queue outside the St Stephen's entrance for admission that day (although not guaranteed), paid guided tours are also available during the Summer Opening, see website for more details

The need for a new Palace of Westminster arose from the fire of October 1834, which destroyed the totally inadequate set of buildings that housed Parliament. It was decided to build a new Houses of Parliament on the same site and what we have as a result is one of the most immediately identifiable buildings in the world.

The Palace had been the site of the principal residence of the kings of England from the 11th century until 1512 when it was first destroyed by fire and the remaining buildings were used as the administrative centre for the Crown. Parliament met in St Stephen's Chapel, sitting in the choir, one group facing the other, and this gave the seating configuration to the chamber of the House of Commons as we see it today.

The only buildings surviving from the 1834 fire are Westminster Hall, the crypt of St Stephen's Chapel, the cloisters and the Jewel Tower. The architect Charles Barry, who won the commission in 1835 following an open competition, cleverly incorporated all of these remains into the design of the new Palace of Westminster.

The government had specified to all those submitting designs that the new building must be in a Gothic or Elizabethan style; only a handful of the hopeful contestants chose the latter. Debate was taking place at the time over the merits of 'Gothic' architecture, seen as English and Christian, versus 'Classic', which was seen, by some, as foreign and pagan. Charles Barry had previously celebrated the 'Classic' in his distinctly Italianate Travellers Club in Pall Mall, so he was a rather odd choice for the commission in that respect. However, Barry employed the talent of A W Pugin, a keen 'Gothicist', who had recently published his 'manifesto' wordily entitled *Contrast or a Parallel between the Noble Edifices of the Middle Ages and the Corresponding Buildings of the Present Day, showing the Present Decay of Taste.*

The partnership appears to have developed well. As a middle-aged, respectable, workaholic architect, Charles Barry had to deal with the grinding tedium of endless battles with numerous committees that were involved in such a huge project. His private practice was to suffer financially as his time and energy were spent working on Westminster Palace. Indeed, he died in May 1860, at the age of 65, just weeks before the building was completed.

Pugin, on the other hand, was an intelligent and exacting young man of 23 when he started work with Barry. An immensely gifted draughtsman, he was employed, initially, to draw the many complex plans for the building. Later he was officially employed to work on the Palace interior as 'superintendent of woodcarving', but with a brief to design everything from the stained glass in the windows to the coat hooks. Pugin too died before the project of Westminster Palace was completed. He was just 40, insane, and a patient at the Bethlem Hospital in south London.

Despite his pitifully short life, Pugin was hugely influential on a whole generation of architects who understood his 1836 statement that 'the greatest test of architectural beauty is the fitness of the design to the purpose it is intended'.

Two towers dominate Barry and Pugin's building. Firstly there is the Clock Tower which was completed in 1852; it is 316 feet high, 40 feet square and the top can be reached by climbing 393 steps. The clock is the largest in Britain and has worked perfectly since 1859. The great bell, known as Big Ben, strikes the quarter hour and each hour and was cast at the Whitechapel Bell Foundry in east London.

The most massive tower is the Victoria Tower at 323 feet tall and it is perhaps this, combined with the long stretch of rhythmic façade, which gives the building its familiar shape. The Gothic detailing of the exterior is so overt the building could easily be taken for a very large English cathedral. The Tower is used for storage and currently holds papers relating to the 1.5 million or so Acts of Parliament passed since 1497.

The interior contains almost 1,000 rooms, including the House of Commons, Commons Lobby, Central Lobby, Lords Lobby, House of Lords, Prince's Chamber, Royal Gallery. There are also 11 courtyards, 8 bars and 6 restaurants (none of which are open to the public). Prince Albert chaired the committee that took responsibility for the interior decorations, helping to choose suitable subjects for the many frescoes as well as the positioning of statues and other details.

The best view of the Palace is probably from a boat on the Thames or, if that is not possible, observe the fine detailing of the south façade by standing in Victoria Tower Gardens. The interior of the Palace of Westminster, and in particular the two debating chambers, need to be seen 'in the flesh', so to speak. Photography and television pictures do not convey adequately the rich, warm and splendid decoration of this surprisingly small space.

For other buildings by Charles Barry, see 'Whitehall Walk' page 320. There are no other examples of Pugin's work in this book, however St Thomas of Canterbury (www.rcdow.org.uk) is considered his best London church.
Area Map p.6, B:1

The Roundhouse
Robert Dockray 1846/
John McAslan & Partners, 2004

Chalk Farm Road, NW1 8EH • Tel 0844
482 8008 • www.roundhouse.org.uk •
Nearest Transport Chalk Farm LU • See
website for opening times and details of
concerts and courses

An outstanding example of 19th-century
industrial architecture, built in 1846 as an
engine-turning shed and designed by Robert
Dockray innovatively using cast and wrought
iron to support the slate roof. Apparently only
used for it's original purpose for a short period
it then became a warehouse for Gilbey's Gin
and then in 1964 playwright Arnold Wesker
established Centre 42, using the space for arts
performances which included Pink Floyd and
Jimi Hendrix. Lack of funds closed the project
in 1983 and the future of the Roundhouse
looked uncertain.

In 2004 the Grade II listed building was
subject to a £29.7 million redevelopment by
John McAslan and Partners architects. The
Roundhouse's circular glazed roof-lights have
been be re-instated, allowing the public to see
interior daylight for the first time in over 100
years. The New Wing built alongside the main
building houses the box office, bar and café,
foyer, offices and an art creative centre, the
Roundhouse Studio, for young people aged
13-25 years.

Banco Commerciale Italiana
Sancton Wood, 1850-52

44 Gresham Street, EC2 • Nearest transport Bank LU • No public access inside
the building

Originally built for the Queen's Assurance
Company in 1850 by Sancton Wood, a pupil of
Smirke, it is now occupied by an Italian bank,
somewhat appropriately given the Italianate
nature of its architecture. The open arcade on
the ground floor has slim Tuscan columns, a
fairly recent innovation in the City at the time,
but one that was to become popular, and the
upper floors have close-set windows, which
occupy most of the stone-faced façade. This
is a fairly early example of the Italianate style
being expressed in office accommodation;
until this date the style had been considered
acceptable for gentlemen's clubs and little else
(for example – Charles Barry's Travellers Club,
Pall Mall, 1832).

The top storey, with its very small windows, is
a fairly recent addition replacing a pitched roof
with large chimneystacks. This was 19th-
century office building of the grandest order
on a prominent corner site and is a welcome
survivor; so many of its contemporaries have
been bulldozed. *Area Map p.8, B:2*

All Saints Church, Margaret Street
William Butterfield, 1841-59 / Ninian Comper, 1911

Margaret Street, W1 • Tel 020 7636 1788 • www.allsaintsmargaretstreet.org.uk • Nearest transport Oxford Circus LU • See website for opening times, services & events

This church was the pioneer building of the High Victorian phase of the Gothic Revival and is perhaps one of the finest examples of eminent architect William Butterfield's work. Just a short step from the consumer chaos that is Oxford Circus, All Saints is the expression of the Ecclesiological Society's movement to restore Catholic privileges (before the 19th century the celebration of the Eucharist every Sunday within the Anglican tradition was not practised).

Completed in 1859, Butterfield was able to incorporate the Society's requirements for a church, a choir school and a clergy house on a plot that is a mere 100 feet square. He did this by placing the church at the rear with the school and house at the front, level with the street, and arranged around a small courtyard. The spire is 227 feet high and was influenced by the great spire of St Mary's, Lubeck; with the nave 63 feet in length and 73 feet in height. Controversially, but with great success, Butterfield chose to build in pink brick (at the time more expensive than stone) in a bold chequered pattern; the first major building on such a scale to be built from brick rather than stone.

Walking from the outside into the spectacular interior is an experience not to be missed as one is greeted with a riot of colour and patterning in granite, alabaster, marble and tiles. The Lady Chapel (1911) designed and decorated by the architect and artist Ninian Comper in a richly decorated, late Gothic style is of particular note.

William Butterfield's other surviving major church in the centre of London is St Augustine, Queens Gate, Kensington.
Area Map p.4, C:1

Right: The Lady Chapel, All Saints Church. Designed and decorated by (Sir John) Ninian Comper. Noted for his superb altar screens, or reredos, Comper's work was always well rooted in both liturgy and history

Albert Memorial
George Gilbert Scott, 1863-72

Kensington Gardens, SW7 (opposite the Albert Hall) • Tel 020 7495 0916 • www.royal-parks.gov.uk • Nearest transport Knightsbridge LU • The memorial can be viewed at any time, see website if you would like to book a guided tour

When Queen Victoria's consort died in December 1861 at the age of 42 it was mooted by the Lord Mayor of London and others that a national memorial should be erected in Prince Albert's honour. Various plans by some of the country's most eminent architects of the day were submitted and the Queen chose Sir George Gilbert Scott's design. The whole project was to be funded partly by national subscription and a massive £50,000 donation from the Government.

Scott's work stands tall at 175 feet and at its centre is a larger than life bronze statue of the seated Prince holding a copy of the catalogue from the 1851 Great Exhibition; the overseeing of this event was thought to have been his proudest achievement. There are a further 175 life-size statues arranged at different levels and these groups of marble figures represent the four continents of the world; agriculture; manufacturing; commerce; engineering; architects; poets and musicians; painters; sculptors; astronomy; geology; geometry; rhetoric; music; astrology; medicine; physiology; faith; hope; charity; temperance; justice; fortitude and prudence. In addition there is a host of bronze angels. All these figures, which are the work of leading British

sculptors of the day, are housed under an iron-framed canopy raised on a flight of stone steps.

The whole project was completed in 1872 and was hailed as 'a fitting memorial to our blameless prince' as well as being dismissed as 'vulgar'! Sir George Gilbert Scott considered it to be his finest piece of work and certainly the whole memorial is a testimony to High Victorian Gothic architectural taste and values.

During World War I the original gilding from the memorial was removed lest enemy Zeppelins were attracted by its shine and was only restored during an £11 million, four-year restoration programme completed in 1998.

Other buildings by George Gilbert Scott:

- **Midland Grand Hotel**, see p.154
- **Foreign and Commonwealth Office**, see p.328
- **St Mary Abbots**, on the corner of High Street Kensington and Church Street, is a good example of Scott's London churches – Early English Gothic interior and notable, fine spire.

Holborn Viaduct
William Haywood, 1863-69

Holborn Viaduct, EC1 • Nearest transport Farringdon LU/Rail or City Thameslink Rail

Being stuck in London's traffic is nothing new and even before mass car ownership the capital's roads were often at a standstill. The Holborn Viaduct was built in 1863-69 as part of a congestion relief measure and to form a link between the West End and the City. It was designed by William Haywood, the City Surveyor and spans Farringdon Street, which runs part of the course of the Fleet, now trickling down to the Thames in pipes under the road.

The most noticeable element of the Viaduct is the cast iron bridge, being 1400 feet in length and 80 feet wide resting on granite hexagonal piers. The marvellous open ironwork is painted red and gold and looks much better than it sounds. The parapet has four bronze statues representing 'Science' and 'Fine Art' on the north side and 'Commerce' and 'Agriculture' on the south.

The Viaduct is best viewed from Farringdon Street but there are staircases at either end of the bridge to access the upper level.

Linley Sambourne House
Joseph Gordon Davis, 1868-71

18 Stafford Terrace, W8 7BH • Tel 020 7602 3316 • www.rbkc.gov.uk/linleysambournehouse • Nearest transport High Street Kensington LU • See website for opening times and admission charges

This house gives us a marvellous opportunity to see the interior of a late Victorian house which has been preserved rather than 'recreated'. It was the home of Edward Linley Sambourne (1844-1910), chief political cartoonist at Punch magazine and is full of his work and collection of photographs. He lived here from 1874 until his death in 1910.

The house was built 1858-60 of brick with good quality stucco enriching the exterior and is part of the grid of streets in the popular Holland Park area of London (Phillimore Gardens and Essex Villas complete this small complex). The interior is a picture of cluttered Victorian domesticity with heavy drapes, some original William Morris wallpaper still in situ and a downstairs lavatory the quality of whose workmanship needs to be seen to be believed!

Arab Hall, Leighton House

Leighton House
George Aitchison, 1866

12 Holland Park Road, W14 • Tel 020 7602 3316 • www.rbkc.gov.uk/leightonhousemuseum • Nearest transport High Street Kensington LU • See website for opening times and admission charges

From the outside, this unassuming house with its red brick façade gives nothing away about its quite extraordinary interior. Architect George Aitchison (1825-1910) designed the body of the house in 1866, but the interior is a pure reflection of its owner's highly aesthetic taste. Lord Frederick Leighton was a highly successful and respected artist, the first professional painter to be knighted, one-time President of the Royal Academy and who counted Queen Victoria as one of his customers.

Lord Leighton had travelled extensively abroad since early childhood and his house was a marvellous backdrop to his extensive collection of paintings and memorabilia. At the centre of the house, both physically and spiritually is the Arab Room, believed to be based on the chamber of the 12th-century Islamic Palace of La Zisa at Palermo. The walls and floors are decorated with Leighton's unique collection of Moorish tiles with additions by William de Morgan. In the middle of this room is a pool and fountain. A 'Silk Room' was added in 1895 to house part of Leighton's collection of paintings and to this was added a zenana, originally a place where women could watch proceedings but remain unseen, which overlooks the Arab Hall and adds to the

sensuous air of exoticism. It is in the Arab Hall where Lord Leighton held his famous soirées at which he entertained the great and the good. However in order not to encourage the outstaying of any welcome, Leighton had only two bedrooms in this large house.

Visitors to the house can see Lord Leighton's studio and paintings by his contemporaries such as John Millais, Edward Burne-Jones, and of course some of his own pictures.

The House has recently undergone a £1.3 million refurbishment which has restored the house to its original spectacular appearance, recreating Leighton's private 'Palace of Art' as it appeared at the time of his death.

Royal Albert Hall
Captain Francis Fowke, 1867-71

Kensington Gore, SW7 • Tel 020 7589 3203 • www.royalalberthall.com • Nearest transport South Kensington & High Street Kensington LU • See website for opening times & events

Prince Albert had suggested that profits from the very successful Great Exhibition of 1851 should be used to build museums, schools and, in particular, a central hall containing a library, concert and exhibition rooms. Following the Prince's death in 1861 it was hoped some of the money raised in 1851 would be used to build such a hall, but funds proved inadequate. However in 1863 the idea was conceived to finance the building by selling 999-year leases on seats in the hall and over 1,300 were sold at 100 pounds each. This allowed the purchasers free entrance to every concert – an arrangement still in existence today, but modified to allow owners access to just 80 concerts a year.

With a capacity of 8,000 people, this huge elliptical hall (not round, as most casual observers believe), was designed by Captain Francis Fowke (1823-65). His design was based on the work of Gottfried Semper, a close friend of Prince Albert and architect of the renowned Dresden Opera House. The foundation stone was laid in 1867 by Queen Victoria, who unexpectedly announced that the building was to be called 'The Royal Albert Hall'; until then it was known as the 'Hall of Arts and Sciences'. The Prince of Wales officially opened the Hall four years later; his mother felt the occasion 'too emotional' to attend.

The brick domed building is decorated in marble and terracotta, the latter being in profusion in the area, such as the neighbouring blocks of flats and Alfred Waterhouse's Natural History Museum built nearby. Four double height entrance porches and a balcony encircle the building as does the magnificent frieze entitled 'The Triumph of Art and Letters'.

The interior of the main hall has three tiers of boxes, stalls and a huge gallery, but the acoustics were dreadful and a problem for many years. The eminent conductor Sir Thomas Beecham said that the Hall could be used for a hundred things – but music was not one of them! In the late 1960's a solution was found for the notorious echo by suspending huge fibreglass diffusers from the ceiling, which look like giant fungi but do the job.

The Hall hosts many varied events but none more famous than the annual festival of music 'The Proms', which run from July to September.

Crossness Pumping Station
Sir Joseph Bazalgette, 1865

The Old Works, Crossness S.T.W., Belvedere Road, Abbey Wood, SE2 9AQ • Tel 020 8311 3711 • www.crossness.org.uk • Nearest transport Abbey Wood Rail, a bus runs from the station to the Crossness site at half hourly intervals • See website for opening times and admission charges • There is a museum and refreshments are available

The Crossness Pumping Station was built by Sir Joseph Bazalgette as part of the London sewage project, opened by the Prince of Wales in 1865.

Of truly outstanding architectural interest is the Beam Engine House, a Grade 1 Listed Industrial Building constructed in the Romanesque style in gault brick made from a mixture of a heavy clay soil and sand from the south east of London. The interior features some spectacular ornamental Victorian wrought and cast ironwork. It also contains the four original pumping engines, one in each corner of the building, possibly the largest remaining rotative beam engines in the world, with 52 ton flywheels and 47 ton beams. Although modern diesel engines were subsequently introduced, the old beam engines remained in service until work on a new sewage treatment plant commenced in the mid 1950's, and this building was eventually abandoned, and the engine house left to decay. The original spectacular 207 foot chimney has been demolished.

Work commenced on the Pumping Station's restoration by a group of volunteers in 1985 and in 1987 the Crossness Engines Trust was established to replace the original Preservation Group in order to put the enterprise on a sound business and legal basis.

Crossness is a unique part of Britain's industrial heritage and an outstanding example of Victorian engineering and architecture, and it is a privilege and a pleasure to be able to visit such an unlikely gem.

The other major pumping stations built as part of Bazalgette's scheme were at Deptford (1864), Erith, Abbey Mills (River Lea) (1868), and Chelsea Embankment (1875).

The German Gymnasium
Edward Gruning, 1865

26 Pancras Road, N1C 2TB • 020 7837 4292 • Nearest transport King's Cross & St Pancras LU & Rail

National Olympian Games; an annual event until the first modern Olympic Games were held at White City in 1908. After this date the building was sold to the Great Northern Railway who added flooring at the gallery level to maximise the space for office use. Since that time the building has had a variety of uses; art depot, gallery, dance venue although its survival was in doubt until 1976 when its importance was recognised and was listed Grade II.

The recent redevelopment of the area has seen its neighbours felled and the gym is now a free standing structure with a new skin of brickwork, made to mirror the original decorative detailing. It now sits proudly between St Pancras and King's Cross stations with it's original wooden roof trusses, to the same design as those covering the first train sheds at King's Cross, still in situ.

The German Gymnasium or Turnhalle, thought to be the first purpose-built gymnasium in Britain, was designed by Edward Gruning as part of a terrace of shops on the Pancras Road constructed in 1865. The following year the gym hosted the indoor events of the first

Currently used as the marketing suite for the asset management team for the King's Cross development, with full public access during office hours, it is hoped that the building will be used as a restaurant or something similar in the future.

German Gymnasium

St Pancras Station and The Midland Grand Hotel
W H Barlow, 1865 (St Pancras)
George Gilbert Scott 1866 (Midland Grand Hotel)

St. Pancras International, Pancras Road, NW1 2QP • Tel 0207 304 3921 (for tours information only) • Nearest transport King's Cross & St Pancras LU & Rail

St Pancras Renaissance London Hotel (formerly The Midland Grand) • Euston Road, NW1 2AR • Tel 020 7841 3540 • www.marriott.com

A frequent response to the question 'What is your favourite building in London?' is often 'St Pancras Station'. The station is undoubtedly a wonderful feat of engineering, but what most people think of as St Pancras Station is in fact the Midland Hotel, an entirely separate building.

At the beginning of 1866 Sir George Gilbert Scott's design for a hotel to mark the extension of the Midland railway to a London terminus was chosen by the Directors, even though his design was larger and more expensive than other plans submitted.

There is hardly any relationship between Scott's hotel and the terminus, designed by W H Barlow. Barlow's plan for the south end of the train shed was adapted to include a second gable and glazed screen, thus protecting the hotel from the noise and pollution of the station. Barlow's roof over the platforms is 689 feet long with an unprecedented clear roof span of 245 feet 6 inches across the station. The 25 ribs of channel and plate iron lattice ribs rise some 100 feet to meet in a slightly pointed apex. The ironwork was made by the Butterley Company and originally painted sky-blue. The terminus is listed Grade I.

Grade I listing has also been granted to Scott's hotel which was opened in 1876 to great acclaim: '…obliterating its rivals; making Euston appear the old fashioned muddle it was and King's Cross a very ordinary and austere engineer's building'. It is interesting to note that the contemporary view of Scott's Gothic design made the 30 odd year old Classic Euston Station 'old fashioned' – such was the rapid and violent change of taste in the 19th century.

The frontage of the hotel, 565 feet in length with a 270 feet tall clock tower and a wider 250 feet tall west tower, is a mass of balconies, windows, gables, dormers, ironwork, columns and carving. The interior is richly decorated throughout with finely carved details on capitals, turrets, stringcourses and friezes, much of which is made from honey-coloured Ancaster stone. Columns are of polished limestone, pink from Devonshire and green from Connemara, and much of the detailing of the principal window surrounds is in Red Mansfield sandstone. The wooden panelling is also finely carved. The flooring is either of geometric ceramic tiles made by Minton and Company or specially commissioned Wilton Axminster carpet.

The hotel had 250 bedrooms, a sumptuous curved dining room and a Grand Staircase, which is one of the finest examples of High Victorian decoration. Also provided was a Ladies' Smoking Room, the first in London, which must have been quite shocking when it opened. The hotel was the most opulent in

Former Midland Grand Hotel

London at the time of its opening and at 14 shillings a night, which included breakfast, dinner and a personal attendant, it was considered to be quite expensive.

However, the demand for en-suite facilities and the rising costs of employing an army of staff to run the business smoothly meant that by 1935 the hotel had to close. From that date until the 1960's the building was renamed 'St Pancras Chambers' and used as offices, amid bids for its demolition, it was at this time the building received Grade I listing status.

During the 1980's the building failed its fire certificate requirements making it unusable. During the early 1990's British Rail and English Heritage funded the £10 million structural renovations and exterior cleaning of the building so badly needed. Internally, beneath layers of 'slapped-on' office paint was the original fabulous decoration, just waiting for time and money to be lavished on them once again.

The solution to this problem came when in January 1994 it was announced that St Pancras had become the Government's preferred London terminus for the new route to the Channel Tunnel. St Pancras International, as the station is now known, is also part of a much wider regeneration project that is transforming the King's Cross area. New life was given to the Midland Hotel, when on 5 May 2011, exactly 138 years to the day that the original hotel was opened, the St Pancras Renaissance hotel welcomed customers once

more. The hotel has everything one would expect from a modern five-star establishment; spa, fitness room, whirlpool, meeting rooms, valet parking, luxurious rooms and suites.

Within the original gloriously decorated entrance hall and coffee room is the 'Gilbert Scott' restaurant and bar, run by Michelin star chef Marcus Wareing, open to hotel patrons and the public alike. Designer David Collins has enhanced the marble pillars and lofty painted ceilings with oxblood red walls and gold leaf flourishes, bringing to the project the glamour and romance that was once synonymous with rail travel. *Area Map p.2-3, B:2*

Previous page left: Statue of Sir John Betjeman, St Pancras Station. Betjeman helped to save St Pancras station from demolition in the 1960s
Previous page right: St Pancras station
This page: former Midland Grand Hotel

London Oratory Church of the Immaculate Heart of Mary
Herbert Gribble, 1876-84

Thurloe Place, Brompton Road, SW7 • Tel 020 7808 0900 • Nearest transport South Kensington LU • Please telephone for opening times, services and events

Pevsner called this church 'the most thorough-going 19th-century import of the Italianate style' and indeed one could be forgiven for the feeling of having been transported to Rome when visiting the Oratory.

Completed in 1884, the church was a celebration of the English Catholic revival of the latter-half of the 19th century and was the first Catholic church of substance built in London since the reformation. It was designed by the young Herbert Gribble, himself a Catholic convert, who was a mere 29 years old when he was given this huge commission. However it was not until 1896 that the west front and dome, which give the church its familiar face of today, were added.

The interior has a broad nave, some 50 feet in width, giving an impression of spaciousness. Instead of aisles Gribble built side chapels. The whole building is light and richly decorated with some striking altarpieces and statues.

In the nave there are huge marble statues of the Apostles carved by Giuseppe Mazzuoli between 1679-1695 for Siena Cathedral. Also of particular note is Rex Whistler's altarpiece of the English Martyrs in the Chapel of St Wilfred. Completed in 1938, this triptych shows St Thomas More and St John Fisher (both of whom had been canonised in 1935) on the side panels with a depiction of executions at Tyburn at the centre. A fine First World War memorial by L Berra is grouped with an Italian marble pietà.

It is rumoured that during the Cold War era the London Oratory was used by the KGB as a dead letter box – one can only congratulate them on their excellent choice of building!

Natural History Museum
Alfred Waterhouse, 1872-81 / C F Moller Architects, 2009

Cromwell Road, SW7 5BD • Tel 020 7942 5000 • www.nhm.ac.uk • Nearest Transport: South Kensington LU • Admission free • See website for opening times

Following on from the success of the Great Exhibition of 1851, it was felt that a more permanent building was required to show-off the British made goods that had been displayed to such an advantage. A plot of land was found in South Kensington and the young Captain Fowke of the Royal Engineers, who was to go on to design the Royal Albert Hall, was engaged as architect. Unfortunately the project did not draw the crowds and the building, described as 'the ugliest building in London', was rapidly demolished. It was decided to replace it with a museum housing the natural 'curiosities' collected by Sir Hans Sloane, the bulk of whose vast collection was held at the British Museum.

A competition was held to design this new Museum of Natural History, with entries submitted anonymously. Captain Fowke won, much to the despair of the judges, many of whom had been critical of the earlier building. Unfortunately, Fowke died before the work had begun and Alfred Waterhouse was appointed as architect in his place.

Building work began on this huge project in 1872 and the first phase of the Museum was opened in 1881. The exterior is completely made from terracotta, with beautifully carvings

of extinct and extant animals and plants to the left and right of the main door respectively. The main façade of the building is huge with two tall, slim towers topped with spires. The rounded arches of the grand entrance were

Grand entrance hall, Natural History Museum

apparently inspired by basalt columns at Fingal's Cave on Staffa in Western Scotland. Waterhouse had earlier travelled to Southern Germany and was evidently inspired by the Romanesque churches he saw there. Indeed the museum has often been likened to a large cathedral, with one enthusiast at the time of it's opening declaring it 'the animal's Westminster Abbey'. However, one critic commented that 'a serious mistake has been made in the erection of a building with such elaborate and ornate internal decorations for museum purposes'.

For many years the front of this building was dulled by the grimy, polluted London air but has recently been the subject of a major cleaning project and now looks wonderful.

The internal layout of the museum was heavily influenced by Richard Owen, expert naturalist and superintendent of the Natural History collection during its move from the British Museum to South Kensington. He and Alfred Waterhouse worked together on the best way to harmonise the architectural decoration with the exhibits.

One of the most memorable parts of the building is the grand entrance hall, where the glass of the roof, the exposed iron structuring and the grand staircase to the upper floors dominate. As with the exterior of the building, the interior is decorated extensively with sculptured forms depicting nature; animal, vegetable and mineral.

Above: Grand entrance hall detail

In 1985, the Museum incorporated the nearby building belonging to the Geological Society, in Exhibition Road, designed 1914 by Sir Richard Allison, and this is now part of the 'Red Zone', where visitors can take the escalator up through the giant Earth sculpture made from iron, zinc and copper.

The latest addition to the Museum is the Darwin Centre, opened in late 2009. Designed by the Danish C F Moller Architects, the structure is an 8-storey 'cocoon', the largest sprayed-concrete, curved structure in Europe. Its cool whiteness contrasts brilliantly with the older part of the Museum (see p.248).

St Mary's Church
John Francis Bentley, 1877-82

Cadogan Street, SW3 2QR • Tel 0207 589 5487 • www.stmaryscadoganstreet.co.uk • Nearest transport Sloane Square LU • See website for opening times, services & events

The rather unexciting exterior of this church belies its lovely interior. John Francis Bentley, architect of Westminster Cathedral, designed St Mary's 1877-82 to incorporate the mortuary chapel designed by A W Pugin in 1845 and a chapel of 1860 by Edward, Pugin's eldest son, both of which had been added to an earlier church building.

Holy Trinity Church, Chelsea
J D Sedding 1888-90

Sloane Street, SW1X9DF • Tel 020 7730 7270 • www.holytrinitysloanesquare.co.uk • Nearest Transport Sloane Square LU • See website for opening times, services & events

Former Poet Laureate Sir John Betjeman referred to Holy Trinity Church as the 'Cathedral of the Arts & Crafts Movement' and indeed it is! This is a fine example of an Arts and Crafts church designed in 1888-90 by J D Sedding, a pupil of Norman Shaw. Sedding believed that the building should be 'wrought and painted over with everything that has life and beauty – in frank and fearless naturalism'.

Sedding was an enthusiastic member of the Art Workers Guild, a society of artists, craftsmen and designers with a common interest in the interaction, development and distribution of creative skills, based in London. Other members at the same time included architect C F A Voysey, who built the Sanderson Wallpaper Factory, Chiswick, and William Lethaby, architect and academic, who worked in the office of Norman Shaw..

The great east window of 48 small panels, designed by Edward Burne-Jones, was the largest ever made by Morris & Co.

Left: East window by Edward Burne-Jones and William Morris, Holy Trinity Church

Bishopsgate Institute
Charles Harrison Townsend, 1892-94

230 Bishopsgate, EC2M 4QH • Tel 020 7392 9200 • www.bishopsgate.org.uk • Nearest transport Liverpool Street LU/Rail

During the last decades of the 19th century, some Arts and Crafts influenced architects were developing a style of building with its roots firmly in the British vernacular past but whose expression would be typical of only its own time. One of the most celebrated proponents of this style was Charles Rennie Mackintosh, who worked mainly in Scotland, and it was for Charles Harrison Townsend to give London some of the best examples of this free style of design. Like his contemporary J D Sedding, Townsend was a member of the Art Workers Guild.

Townsend has, happily, provided us with a trio of good buildings to consider. The terracotta façade of the Grade II listed Bishopsgate Institute, is covered with stylised leafy trees and topped by two turrets. The interior has an impressive clerestoried Great Hall, panelled Boardroom and glass-domed Library, much of which has been recently restored as part of a £7.1 million refurbishment programme. The Bishopsgate Institute is entered through a wide, arched way, quite Romanesque and yet highly original at the same time. *Area Map p.8, C:3*

Horniman Museum
Charles Harrison Townsend, 1898-1901

100 London Rd, Forest Hill, SE23 3PQ •
020 8699 1872 • www.horniman.ac.uk •
Nearest transport Forest Hill LU & Rail •
Admission free • See website for opening
times & exhibition details

Wealthy tea merchant F J Horniman decided
to put his anthropological collection on
public display and engaged Charles Harrison
Townsend to design a suitable building. As
with his other buildings, Townsend gives the
wide arched entrance a welcoming feel, but
with admittance to the building at almost street
level, there is no intimidating grand staircase
to climb. The clock tower to one side of the
building has a lovely play of squares and circles.
This building is one of the best buildings of its
age and perhaps the finest examples of Art
Nouveau architecture in London.

Since its completion in 1891, the Museum has
been expanded, first with a library and lecture
hall added in 1910 by Townsend himself and
more recently with further galleries, a shop and
a café. There are 16 acres of gardens and a
huge Victorian conservatory to explore.

*Right: Horniman Museum. The huge decorative
mosaic panel at the entrance by Robert Anning Bell
is titled 'Humanity in the House of Circumstance'*

Whitechapel Art Gallery
Charles Harrison Townsend, 1899-1901

77-82 Whitechapel High Street, E1 7QX • Tel 020 7522 7888 • www.whitechapel.org • Nearest Transport Aldgate East LU and Liverpool Street LU/Rail • Admission free • See website for details of opening times and exhibitions

The Art Gallery built 1899-1901 was a smaller affair than Townsend had originally designed four years earlier. Financial constraints were also blamed for the exclusion of the planned mosaic by Townsend's fellow Art Workers Guild artist, Walter Crane, entitled 'Art attended by Labour, Time, History, Poesie, Truth and Beauty' which would have adorned the front of the building.

The recent acquisition of the red brick and terracotta Passmore Edwards Library next door has increased the Gallery's exhibition space considerably. The Library had been built at the same time as the Gallery by architects, Potts, Son & Hennings, and designed in the free classical style known as Queen Anne, which had strong associations with liberal philanthropy. Much of the original interior furnishings, staircases etc have been beautifully preserved in both buildings, whilst the overwhelming feel of the place is of quiet, ordered space.

Senate House, see p.196

06

EDWARDIAN LONDON &
THE RISE OF MODERNISM

EDWARDIAN LONDON & THE RISE OF MODERNISM

"If you're blue and you don't know where to go to
Why don't you go where fashion sits – Puttin' on the Ritz..."
Irving Berlin

The Edwardian period was short, Edward VII was monarch for a mere nine years, from 1901-10, and yet the very term 'Edwardian' conjures a powerful image of ladies in large hats, boating parties, amusing automobiles and ponies in paddocks. False though this image may have been for the majority, the economic climate around 1900 meant that architects such as the eminent Edwin Lutyens were commissioned by clients whose new-found wealth from retail, coal and textiles afforded them picturesque houses and a small stake in the land. What they really wanted, but couldn't quite afford, was a country house and pedigreed estate, so their desires were satisfied with oversized stairwells and room layouts which gave odd vistas but still felt informal. The exteriors tended to be vaguely Tudor with hipped gables and tall chimneys.

Referred to as the 'Domestic Revival' movement, Lutyens translated some of this emotion to his London buildings and the office blocks he designed were treated to his genius for composition and balance. However, Lutyens soon became unfashionable, being seen as a self-flaunting Victorian who failed, or refused, to 'move with the times'.

The Edwardian period may well have been a short one but in reality it saw the introduction of a plethora of styles and movements; Post-impressionism, Fauvism, Expressionism, Cubism. These new conceptual themes and philosophies in building were more popular on the Continent at the beginning of the century and it would take time and the catastrophe of a war to bring such radical ideas to Britain to any serious degree. Even then they usually remained as ideas rather than anything material.

Art nouveau, which had been expressed as far back as the mid 19th century in decorative forms such as the ornamentation on the capitals of Blackfriars Railway Bridge and Holborn Viaduct, was still popular. So too was the Arts and Crafts Movement although there are now few examples of its architecture in London.

Familiar Gothic Revival forms were still used for church building while large scale public buildings were more often than not of a 'Wrenaissance' form – a sort of grandiose baroque in the mode of Wren and Vanbrugh. The French form of classical baroque, as taught by the influential Ecole des Beaux Arts in Paris, was also deemed a suitable form for large scale buildings such as banks. The distinctive Venetian form of baroque was used for the ground breaking Methodist Central Hall (see p.180) which at once marked its independence from forms of Anglican church building.

Advances in technology at the dawning of the 20th century affected architecture. The advent of electric lighting, first installed in the City at the now demolished Lloyds Bank in Lombard Street in 1887, meant that by the turn of the century the provision of natural light within buildings became less of an issue. The first passenger lifts were introduced in 1890 and this together with the introduction of concrete and steel framed buildings ten years later, meant that larger, taller buildings were possible.

This was good news for the City in particular where numbers pouring in each day increased dramatically in the first quarter of the century; 364,000 people in 1911 compared to 437,000 in 1921. The City was the financial capital of the Empire and prospered year on year. Even when industry and manufacturing no longer boomed, as they had done in the previous century, the City was still 'doing nicely' and had fully recovered by the early 1920s from the dark days of the 1914-18 war. However, the Great Depression of the early 1930's shook the very foundation of the City.

Westminster was very much aware of its place as the capital of the Empire. Street widening schemes took place as much for aesthetic reasons as for the accommodation of the

motor car. Gentlemen's clubs were built and thrived. Shopping occupied happy hours for those who could afford it, and it appeared that more and more could do so. When Nash built his Via Triumphalis, he made provision in Regent Street for small shops which gave customers a personal service or sent staff out to their houses, and where haute couture was usual. By the beginning of the century these arrangements were seen to be wholly inadequate by shopkeepers who complained about the lack of space for the stock to satisfy this new army of shoppers.

Mr Gordon Selfridge opened his department store in Oxford Street on 15 March 1909, bringing to London his brand of Chicago consumerism and in Knightsbridge Harrods was expanding at a pace that required new premises to be built and in 1905 the first part of its terracotta emporium was opened (see 'Shopping and Architecture').

Hotels and restaurants also saw business booming. The Ritz Hotel, built on Piccadilly, was of a pioneering design as well as the byword for glamour (see 'Eat and Drink Architecture') whilst, at the other end of the scale, the now defunct Lyons tea-rooms were also doing well and in 1909 the first Lyons Corner House was opened in purpose built premises in Coventry Street. The novelty of 'brand' architecture, good, value for money fare and waitresses nicknamed 'nippies', because of their speed of service, served a truly classless clientele. Indignation ensued recently among acquaintances of mine of a certain age when Lyons was favourably compared to the McDonalds Restaurant chain; it was rather like having one's favourite aunt compared with a harlot.

Cinema and theatre audiences grew steadily. This was the era of Frank Matcham who built the magnificent Coliseum in 1902-04 (see p.176) the Hackney Empire in 1901, both the subject of recent major renovations, and the London Palladium, in 1910.

Certainly much of the impetus for the Edwardian love of outings to shops or cinemas was the ease of transport within the capital. In 1900 the opening of the Central line took passengers from Bond Street to the Bank of England in what seemed like no time at all.

Car ownership soared during this period. In 1900 there were only 8,000 cars in the whole country, but by 1920 the number of driving licences issued to London addresses alone numbered 100,000 and rose to 261,000 by 1930. The 1920s saw the first traffic-control measures appearing in central London in the form of manually operated traffic lights and white line road markings. Garages and car parks became necessary, a few examples of which are still with us – see former Lex Garage p.190.

However, this cosy vision, false or not, of Edwardian life as expressed in its architecture was to come to an end with what was then called the Great War, the European conflict of 1914-18. The mood of those involved in the

world of the arts throughout Europe had been changing, perhaps from the end of the 19th century and certainly from the beginning of the 20th. This change was characterised by a consistent rejection of tradition and a self-conscious effort to explore other possibilities of living. The fact that such philosophies were being considered by a wide swathe of the arts, painting, literature and music as well as architecture, in a Europe-wide forum, is significant. Notwithstanding the above, this was seen by some as the response to the carnage of World War I and the subsequent rise of social equality. Such changes may simply have been the response to photography, to have access to images which previously could only have been seen by the very few privileged enough to travel must have had an impact on many levels.

The term 'Modernism' has been given to this shift in thinking and was particularly important in the field of architecture and is most properly identified with the Modern Movement. This was the 20th-century European movement which desired architecture appropriate to modern society and which used all the technical advances at its disposal, such as the reinforced concrete frame.

The first wave of the Modern Movement in architecture was by 1917 already being defined by a small group of Dutch artists, designers and architects, named after their influential magazine, De Stijl. This movement was dedicated to clean, uncomplicated

Above: Selfridges, see p.360

Any idea of a supposed resonance with the Arts and Crafts and William Morris can be scotched by the fact that the Modern Movement did not look back to a golden age of medieval craftsmen for its inspiration but instead explored all the possibilities available through modern technology. The breaking-down of social and cultural barriers was also of concern to Modernist architects.

However, those who commissioned building works in London, and Britain as a whole, had been traditionally suspicious of anything foreign, including architecture, unless it had a Roman or Greek pedigree. Nonetheless émigré architects such as Erno Goldfinger succeeded in bringing the Modern Movement to London during the 1930s (see '1-3 Willow Road' p.197).

abstract purism and a fondness for straight lines. The early Modern Movement can also be closely identified with the setting up of the Bauhaus school in Germany in 1919. This groundbreaking unit thrived until repressed by the Nazis in 1933. The first Bauhaus director was Walter Gropius (1883-1969) who taught the ideal of the committed craftsman knowing his place in the arts. However it was the ideal of functionality in architecture that was the main Bauhaus message whereby practical considerations and not aesthetics determined the form of a building. At its heart was the desire to improve the material conditions of modern society through good, honest design.

Britain never did develop its own Bauhaus equivalent, adapting instead an Arts and Crafts aesthetic. Mock Tudor, 'Tudorbethan' and Jacobean-style was the order of the day, particularly in domestic building from the 1920s onwards. Buildings were, typically, half-timbered with a mix of brick and pebble dash and featured wooden framed windows with iron casements and a generous dose of stained glass, with, perhaps an elaborate chimneystack or a slate hung roof.

Despite the economic depression of the 1930s house building continued apace. Speculative builders lined the roads heading out of town with ribbon developments and filled the suburbs with houses, usually in semi-detached pairs and these more often than not were owner-occupied rather than rented. In 1919 there were approximately eight million homes in Britain but by 1939 there were 12 million.

Generally smaller than the houses of the previous generation these 1930s houses are often mocked and derided. The perceived bastardisation of designs such as the afore-mentioned Arts and Crafts resulted in the less-decorated style of the 1930s semi with large bay windows and generous use of chrome. However, given the level of privacy these houses afforded, combined with the luxury of indoor plumbing, they must have seemed like a glimpse of heaven itself to their owners.

One particular style seems to have summed up the mood of post Great War Europe and was called variously 'Moderne', 'Jazz-Moderne' or, 'Domestic Cubism', but which we know better as 'Art Deco' a term understood to have been coined by the historian Bevis Hillier in the late 1960's. However the style was perhaps inspired by the 1925 Paris exhibition known as the 'Exposition internationale des arts décoratifs et industriels modernes'. The dominant style of the twenties and thirties, its exuberance and eclecticism were reactions to the austerity of the war years. In many ways the exhibition consisted of 'modern' versions deriving from earlier periods, e.g. Egyptian or Roman, but given a less ornate, almost geometric style as could be seen in the 20th-century art movements: Cubism, Futurism.

Hillier referred to 'Art Deco' as the last of the total styles and from ocean-going liners to handbags, glamorous cinemas to Bizarre Ware pottery designed by Clarice Cliffe there seemed to be something for everyone.

One of the best exponents of Art Deco architecture in London was Charles Holden. He was commissioned by Frank Pick, the head of London Transport during its glory years of the 1920s and 30s, to design more than 50 London Underground stations. Holden was also the architect of the London Transport Headquarters as well as other major projects such as Senate House and Zimbabwe House.

Then came World War II and from the 7th September 1940 the enemy Blitzkrieg relentlessly pounded London killing thousands and reducing many of her buildings to rubble. When the war ended and the damage was surveyed what, everyone asked, would lift London's spirits now?

Euston Fire Station
W E Riley & LCC Architects Department, 1901-02

Euston Road, NW1 • No public access to the interior

A lovely example of an Arts and Crafts influenced building in the style adopted by London County Council. There are two similar such buildings in Hampstead but this one must surely be one of the most overlooked gems in this area. Situated to the east of the Euston Station complex, the top floor of the building was designed as the residence for the Chief Fire Officer of the station.

This remarkable fire station is built from red brick and Portland stone. Note the tall, plain chimneypieces and the stylised lettering over the doors facing the Euston Road.
Area Map p.2-3, A:2

173

Westminster Cathedral
John Francis Bentley, 1903

42 Francis Street, SW1P 1QW • Tel 020 7798 9055 • www.westminstercathedral.org.uk
• Nearest transport Victoria LU/Rail • See website for opening times, services & events

Westminster Cathedral is the principal Roman Catholic church in England. Cardinal Vaughan had been the instigator of the building of a cathedral here and wanted something built as quickly as possible, but a shortage of funds was always going to hamper any project that was too ambitious. Nonetheless, John Francis Bentley, a Roman Catholic convert, was appointed architect and his inclination was to design something Gothic in nature. This was thwarted by Cardinal Vaughan who felt an early Christian basilica would compete less with nearby Westminster Abbey.

Bentley was dispatched to do his own 'grand tour' of Italy, and it was a visit to St Vitale in Ravenna that 'really told me all I wanted'. On his return work started almost immediately and by the time Bentley died in 1902 he had witnessed the completion of his cathedral, apart from the

tower. Ironically, the first service in the cathedral in 1903 was the funeral of Cardinal Vaughan.

The cathedral nave is made up of three great domed bays each 60 feet in width, with chapels set to either side. At the east end a fourth domed bay serves as the Sanctuary. The cathedral's exterior form is dominated by a spectacular campanile 284 feet high and the whole building is strikingly faced in red brick with bands of Portland stone. Much of the interior is derived from Italian sources, such as the pulpit which is in an appropriately early Christian style by Aristide Leonori, dating from 1899. The 14 Stations of the Cross,carved in low relief by Eric Gill between 1914-18, decorate the piers of the nave and are worth a visit alone. Look out for the inscription at the foot of the Sanctuary steps marking the Mass celebrated here by Pope John Paul II during his visit to London in 1982, the first to be celebrated in England by a reigning Pope.

This is one of the more surprising and memorable buildings in London. On entering the nave, the eye is drawn to the colourful, sparkling myriad of mosaics that adorn the walls of the nave and side-chapels. However, the undecorated domes are like black voids awaiting their decoration, when funds allow, which makes the building all the more interesting to visit.

Westminster Cathedral

Coliseum Theatre
Frank Matcham, 1904

St Martin's Lane, WC2N • Tel 020 7836 0111 • www.eno.org • Nearest transport Charing Cross LU & Rail • See website for details of tours of the building and access

The Coliseum Theatre was designed by Frank Matcham for the impresario Oswald Stoll as a variety house. Its proscenium stage, a revolving one at that and the first in England, has been graced by the talents of Ellen Terry, Sarah Bernhardt and Diaghilev's Ballet Company. At its opening it had the largest audience capacity (2,358) in London and was pure Edwardian (some at the time said elephantine) baroque, with touches of Renaissance, Louis XVI and Italianate styles for good measure. It can be safely said that Matcham's designs were 'eclectic'. The architecture may well have been looking to the past for it's inspiration, but this was a steel-framed construction with lifts and telephones. The exterior has a terracotta façade with a domed short column on top, supporting a huge globe that once revolved until Westminster City Council made it stop, for reasons that would baffle us ordinary mortals.

Since 1968, the theatre has been the home of the English National Opera and has been a popular and well-patronised venue. However, the interior had always been a little awkward and the facilities for staff and patrons had become outdated by the time a four-year programme of improvements was begun in 2000. A certain amount of restoration to

Matcham's original design, which had been re-built over the years, was also included.

The £40 million project was completed almost on time and has been praised by critics and audiences alike. The glass barrel roof to the St Martin's Lane façade has been reinstated and the improvements to the public facilities, including better front of house and foyer arrangements are a joy. All patrons now enter from St Martin's Lane, whereas before, those in the 'gods' had to negotiate the daunting flight of stairs from the door in the adjacent alleyway.

The auditorium is an essay in red and cream 'plush', the seats are comfortable and no longer squeak; the number of ladies' lavatories has been doubled; a silent, air-cooling system has been installed and even the roof-top globe, albeit a replica of the original, spins again.

During his long career as an architect, Frank Matcham designed 82 new theatres and was responsible for the reconstruction of 78 others. Interestingly, another of Matcham's London gems, the Hackney Empire, has also benefited from a massive and recently completed programme of improvements.
Area Map p.6, B:3

38 & 39 Cheyne Walk
C R Ashbee, 1904

38 and 39 Cheyne Walk, SW3 • Nearest transport Sloane Square LU • Private dwellings – no public access

These properties are important examples of the work of the influential Charles Robert Ashbee (1863-1942), Arts and Crafts architect and designer par excellence. Although he was heavily influenced by William Morris and John Ruskin as well as the principles of Socialism, Ashbee's house building was confined to the upper end of the artisan class. These houses are the only two remaining from a group of eight, one having been demolished as late as 1968 to make way for some frankly rather boring flats.

The detailing on these houses, the ironwork railings for example, was the product of Ashbee's influential School and Guild of Handicraft, a cooperative group of craftsmen.

Ex Country Life Offices
Sir Edwin Lutyens, 1904

Country Life Offices, 2-10 Tavistock Street, WC2 • Nearest transport Covent Garden LU • Private offices – no public access

Lutyens built these offices as a new head office for his friend and client Edward Hudson who had founded the magazine 'Country Life' in 1897. This was his first commission in London but was followed by many more.

Wren's work at Hampton Court Palace is clearly echoed here in the flat front, sash windows and carved stone decoration. The quirky window placed within the entrance pediment is a nice touch. The chimneystacks have looked a little insignificant since windows were added to the attic level in the mid 1950s.
Area Map p.6, B:3

Edwardian London & the Rise of Modernism

Central Criminal Court (Old Bailey)
E W Mountford, 1907

Old Bailey, EC4M • Tel 020 7248 3277 • www.cityoflondon.gov.uk • Nearest transport St Paul's LU • See website for opening times and details of tours of the building

Designed by E W Mountford (1855-1908) and completed in 1907, the building's most dominant feature is its dome, which was inspired by the one at the Royal Naval Hospital Greenwich and which also echoes the huge dome of nearby St Paul's Cathedral.

Considered to be the finest example of Neo-English baroque inspired by Wren, Vanbrugh and French classicism it was built on a solid base of Cornish granite with Portland stone facing on the upper part of the building, the material favoured by this movement.

The original building contained four courts and 90 holding cells but this has been extended to 19 court rooms over the years. The richly decorated marble Grand Hall and Lower Hall have lunettes painted by Gerald Moira with scenes from the Old Testament and English history. The building's most famous feature is the 12 foot high statue of Justice cast in bronze and covered with gold leaf which stands on top of the dome. In her right hand she bears the sword of retribution and in her left hand she holds the scales of justice. Interestingly this Justice is not blindfolded, but all-seeing.

Built on the site of the notorious Newgate Prison and place of public execution since at least the second half of the twelfth century, the Court has tried many famous cases – including William Penn, Daniel Defoe, Oscar Wilde, William 'Lord Haw Haw' Joyce, Dr Crippen, and the Kray brothers. *Area Map p.8, A:2*

Zimbabwe House
Charles Holden, 1907-08

429 Strand, WC2 • Nearest transport Charing Cross LU & Rail • No public access

These offices were originally built for the British Medical Association and sold to the Southern Rhodesian High Commission in 1930.

Pevsner described this building, an early work by the architect who went on to design Senate House and underground stations for London Transport, as 'virile'. Indeed Holden has here succeeded in making the classic form solid without being overly clumsy and used a variety of classic devices, such as blank arches and columns, to great effect.

However, the building is probably more noted for being the sculptor Jacob Epstein's first large commission. The figures he carved into the Portland stone were highly controversial in that their 'manhoods' were deemed to be excessively large. Such was the offence caused the neighbouring property was obliged to use frosted glass in windows that overlooked Holden's building. Some thought that these figures were mutilated in the 1930s, but frost damage is more likely to have caused the said appendages and heads of the figures to drop off. See Whitehall Walk for more information, p.320. *Area Map p.6, B:3*

Edward VII Galleries – British Museum
Sir John Burnet, 1904-11

British Museum, Great Russell St, WC1B • Tel 020 7636 1555 • www.britishmuseum.org • Nearest transport Holborn and Russell Square LU • See website for opening times and details of special exhibitions

We have considered the familiar front façade of the British Museum in a previous chapter and this is the 'back entrance' in Montague Place. A neoclassical approach to this building was made by Burnet using a giant order of three-quarter engaged Ionic columns. This is of course a nod to Smirke's colonnade and yet its composition as a whole owes much to Burnet's education at the Ecole des Beaux-Arts, and gives the composition an edgy flourish. It's worth having a wander through the museum and out of the rear exit to have a look.

This extension to the museum was part of the plan to clear Bloomsbury of many of its residential properties and create an area that would be associated with scholarship. Within a few years Charles Holden was to build Senate House for the University of London opposite Burnet's work.

Methodist Central Hall
Lanchester and Rickards, 1905-11

Storey's Gate, SW1H • Tel 020 7654 3826 • www.methodist-central-hall.org.uk • Nearest transport St James's Park or Westminster LU • Tours of the building are available by booking in advance – see website for service details, events and opening times

This is one of those buildings which from its exterior is hard to imagine exactly what it is used for as it gives no visual clues as to its purpose. It seems too isolated to be a bank and it certainly doesn't look like a church; the eminent architectural historian Nikolaus Pevsner said it could easily be mistaken for a very substantial casino! It is in fact a Methodist Hall, a multi-purpose building which functions as a Methodist church, a conference and exhibition centre, an art gallery, and an office building.

It was constructed on the site of the Royal Aquarium, which had been built as recently as 1876 as a place of entertainment for London's intelligentsia who, alas, stayed away in their droves. However, sights had to be lowered to attract a different, hopefully paying, clientele but the tone plummeted so much that the Aquarium was obliged to close and sell-up in 1903. The building was demolished to make way for the Methodist Hall.

Funds to build the Hall were raised by a 'one million guineas from one million Methodists' campaign and building begun in 1905 to a design by Henry Lanchester and Edwin Rickards. They chose the baroque style as a suitable foil to the nearby Gothic Westminster Abbey and Houses of Parliament. However it was not the 'Wrenaissance' baroque influenced by the works of Wren and Vanbrugh being practised elsewhere in London, but an even more flamboyant style from Austria.

The building is framed in concrete and steel with brick arches and the huge main meeting hall, which seats 2,353 people, is almost square, as is the impressive dome that tops the construction. The interior has a sumptuous staircase, which sweeps visitors up to a spacious landing with smaller meeting rooms off.

There is very impressive sculpture on the exterior by Henry Poole, who collaborated with Lanchester and Rickards on other projects. One contemporary described the architects' work as 'combining opulence and taste with a touch of refined swagger'. No wonder guessing the building's identity was so hard!

Also see 'Eat and Drink Architecture' page 340. *Area Map p.6, B:1*

Cadogan Hall,
Formerly the First Church
of Christ Scientist
R F Chisholm, 1908

5 Sloane Terrace, SW1X 9DQ •Tel 020
7730 4500 • www.cadoganhall.com •
Nearest transport Sloane Square LU • See
website for opening times & events

The architect, R F Chisholm, had previously
worked in India and this could account for the
exotic touches to this lovely building. Despite
its bell tower, the passer-by may be surprised
to learn that this building was a place of
worship. The light ashlar exterior is beautifully
maintained; the interior has a barrel vaulted
ceiling, a large balcony running around three
sides and is free of columns. The furnishings
are of a very high quality and include windows
of handmade opaque glass.

When the congregation became too small to
sustain this building in the mid-1990's, it was
acquired by Cadogan Estates. It now serves
as a music venue, renamed as the Cadogan
Hall and is the home of the Royal Philharmonic
Orchestra, who gave their first concert here in
November 2004.

Left: Cadogan Hall

181

Former County Hall
Ralph Knott, 1909-1933

County Hall, Westminster Bridge Road, SE1 7PB • www.londoncountyhall.com • Nearest Transport Waterloo Station LU & Rail • Limited public access, see website for details

Knott was a pupil of the eminent architect Sir Aston Webb and worked in a similar Edwardian Baroque manner. The construction of this building was very protracted with delays caused by, among other things, the finding of a Roman boat in 1910 during the excavations for the concrete raft on which County Hall is built. Parts of the timbers were destroyed before their presence was recognized, but what was left of the boat was carefully lifted, treated with preservative and deposited in the London Museum, where it can still be seen. At the time it was thought to have been a Roman galley, but experts in nautical research have concluded that her timbers were too lightly jointed for a sea-going vessel and that she was probably a ferry boat, plying to and fro across the river.

Work on the building stopped again in 1916 owing to the war, but was resumed in 1919, and the building was opened on 17th July, 1922, though the northern section was not completed until 1933. Indeed Ralph Knott was only 29 when he won this prestigious commission, but died in 1929, four years before it was finished.

The six-storey County Hall is planned round a number of internal courtyards with the council chamber placed at the heart of the building. The enclosing blocks form an approximate rectangle whose slightly tapering long sides face westwards to the river and eastwards to Belvedere Road. The continuous river facade is relieved by the broad sweep of the colonnaded crescent, while in the middle of the Belvedere Road front an imposing feature is made of the ceremonial entrance.

The building served its purpose as the head quarters of the local authorities in London for just over 60 years before the Thatcher Government abolished the Greater London Council in 1986. It now houses two hotels, an aquarium, the London Eye ticket office, food outlets and various other ventures.
Area Map p.6, C:2

Former County Hall

Port of London Authority

Port of London Authority
Sir Edwin Cooper, 1912

10 Trinity Square, EC3 • Nearest transport
Tower Hill LU • No public access to interior

This is one of those rather imposing buildings
on a corner plot that the Edwardian builders
seemed to love so much. The columns and
indeed the whole building is rather chunky and
busy, considering that the obvious influence of
the Beaux-Arts is usually expressed in a lighter
tone. Six huge Corinthian columns stretch from
ground level to the entablature that runs around
the whole building. Of interest is the proliferation
of sculpture on the exterior from Father Thames
lording it in the stepped tower to sea horses and
galleons further down. These were designed by
Albert Hodge and worked by C Doman.

The Port of London Authority came into being
in 1909 by Act of Parliament to control bad
practices in the London docks and to oversee
physical improvements on the river. By 1971
there were no docks left in London to speak of
and the Authority moved to a small office in St
Katharine Dock.

The building is now the London office of Willis-
Faber. Architecture fans may recall that in 1967
Willis-Faber commissioned Norman Foster to
build an office complex in Ipswich, a town not
previously known for its innovative architecture.
However, thanks to Foster's huge glass fronted
reflective block, which is listed, it now enjoys
international acclaim. *Area Map p.8, C:2*

Britannic House
Sir Edwin Lutyens, 1921-25

Britannic House, corner of Moorgate and Finsbury Circus, EC2 • Nearest transport Moorgate LU & Rail • No public access

This is one of Lutyens' largest London buildings at seven storeys tall with a lovely curved frontage to Finsbury Circus. A rusticated ground floor and small, very deep set windows give the building a solid appearance with the top three floors flanked by giant Corinthian columns and rounded windows, echoing the ground floor fenestration. This building was made, with almost no expense spared for the British-Persian Oil Company, which later became BP.

Rebuilding of the interior took place in 1987-89 by Inskip and Jenkins who tactfully retained the original marble floors and staircase. The building was eventually sold by BP in 2005.

Now deemed too small for a head office function, the building has become 'multi-occupancy'. Gaunt Francis architects saw that the solution was to radically replan the centre of this Grade II Listed building, introducing a new lift core and enhanced atrium space with a spectacular new atrium roof. Six new glass lift cars are included in a shaftless lift lobby arrangement. The historic Lutyens interiors were carefully restored and the new works carefully integrated into them. The project was shortlisted for the BCO Awards in 2009 and won the City Heritage Award in 2009.

Britannic House is located in Finsbury Circus, which was laid out to a design by Dance the Younger in 1802. For some of Dance's other work see Chapter 4, 'Restoration to Georgian', page 117. Previously this site was occupied by the Bethlehem Hospital, known as 'Bedlam', but is now a green oasis in the City with a bowling green laid in 1909. *Area Map p.8, B:3*

Carreras Cigarette Factory (Greater London House)
M E and O H Collins, 1926-28

Hampstead Road, NW1 • Nearest Transport Mornington Crescent LU • No public access – but the best of this building is its colourful exterior

Built within a few years of Howard Carter's discovery of Tutankhamun's tomb, when anything and everything Egyptian became the height of fashion, mix this with Art Deco ideals of clean lines and large areas of glass and we begin to see how this astonishing building came into being.

One of the first factories in the country to be constructed from pre-stressed concrete, the building no longer serves its original purpose, but since the 1960s has been known as Greater London House and is used as a mixed-tenancy office complex.

However, the main entrance is still guarded by a pair of large black cats, the black cat being the logo of Carreras Cigarettes and is also represented in a series of reliefs along the façade of the building – look closely and you will see they have yellow eyes and wire whiskers.

This is, I understand, the only Egyptian temple in North London.

Right: Carreras Cigarette Factory

Freemasons' Hall (United Grand Lodge of England)
Ashley and Newman, 1927-33

60 Great Queen Street, WC2B • Tel 020 7831 9811 • www.ugle.org.uk • Nearest transport Covent Garden LU • The building, Masonic Museum & Library are all open to the public (see website for details)

This is the third Masonic Hall on this spot. The first dated from 1776 and was by Thomas Sandby (1721-98), whose Great Hall was much admired and preserved through subsequent rebuilding until irrevocably damaged by fire in 1883, a few remaining sections are held at the British Museum.

This late 1920s building by Ashley and Newman, neither of whom are credited with any other London buildings, bears an uncanny resemblance to the Port of London Authority building (see previous page). Built from Portland stone, the Hall copes well with its awkward corner plot and exudes an air of gravitas, like the head office of a bank. Indeed its entrance façade was used recently in the BBC television series, 'Spooks', pretending to be MI6 Headquarters.

The overtly Art Deco interior is certainly worth a visit with a grand marble staircase, vaulted corridors and exquisite, massive bronze doors that lead to the 62 feet high Grand Hall, with seating for 1,700 people. The building is now Grade II listed. *Area Map p.2-3, B:1*

London Transport Headquarters

London Transport Headquarters
Charles Holden, 1927-29

55 Broadway, SW1 • Nearest transport St James's Park LU • No public access

For this building, described by one admirer as 'a sophisticated essay in massing', Holden used a clever cruciform grouping to gain optimum natural light. To appreciate this building one must think back to what sort of impact it made at the time of its construction, when its 'step back' form was seen as pure New York.

The HQ was built at a time when small, privately owned transport companies were being consolidated into a London Passenger National Transport Board and it is possible to read the confident, American style architecture of 55 Broadway as propaganda, persuading often reluctant transport companies of the merits of merger.

This great ziggurat of a building of Portland stone boasts fabulous carved statues by Eric Gill, depicting the South Wind on the north block east side of the building and the shockingly explicit male and female figures denoting 'Day and Night' by Jacob Epstein. The 175 feet tall central tower of the building houses utilities such as stairs, lifts and lavatories.

The building, which cleverly incorporates St James's underground station at its basement level, is now used by Transport For London. *Area Map p.6, A:1*

Bank of England
Sir Herbert Baker, 1921-37

Bartholomew Lane, EC2R 8AH • Tel 020 7601 5545 • www.bankofengland.co.uk/museum • Nearest transport Bank LU • No public access to bank (see website for opening times of the museum)

Architecturally speaking, the glory days of the Bank of England were from the 1780s to 1808 when Soane's new Banking Halls were the talk of the City. Alas these were swept away in an enlargement programme in the 1920s and 30s with just Soane's retaining wall truly left intact. With the electric light now commonplace, the Bank no longer needed to rely on Soane's ingeniously top-lit halls and could build higher and wider thus creating more interior space, which was at a premium in such a restricted area.

Baker's main entrance sits well with the existing perimeter wall and the ample portico of coupled columns lines up with the colonnade giving the building its familiar form of today.

The most interesting aspect of the building is the Bank of England Museum, which is entered via Bartholomew Lane. The museum is set around a faithful recreation of Sir John Soane's Bank Stock Office of 1792-93 (by Higgins Gardner 1986-88), and it certainly gives the visitor a flavour of what was regarded as the finest neo-classic interior in Europe. This is the only part of the bank that can be entered by the general public. *Area Map p.8, B:2*

Rudolf Steiner House
Montague Wheeler, 1926-37

35 Park Road, NW1 • Tel 020 7723 4400
• www.rsh.anth.org.uk • Nearest transport
Baker Street LU • See website for opening
times and details of exhibitions and courses

Expressionism in architecture found a voice in
Germany and the Netherlands circa 1905-
30 and was the antithesis of Modernism.
Expressionism was concerned that buildings
should not be merely functional but creative,
free and powerful sculptural forms in
themselves. Probably the most notable building
of this type is the Goetheanum in Dornach,
Switzerland built by Rudolf Steiner in 1928.

Rudolf Steiner House near Baker Street is the
only example of Expressionist architecture
in London, and is a pretty tame one at that.
The stone-faced building is perhaps rather
inconspicuous but nonetheless it is a well
used building with a theatre, bookshop and a
particularly good library with a host of archive
material relating to the construction of the
building. Of particular note is the very fine
curved staircase. *Area Map p.4, B:2*

Former Lex Garage
J J Joass, 1929

NCP, (Formerly the Lex Car Park) • 32
Brewer Street, W1F 0ST • Tel 0870 606
7050 • www.ncp.co.uk • Nearest Trans-
port-Piccadilly Circus LU

One of the first ramped multi-storey car
parks in the country, and was Grade II Listed
by English Heritage in 2002 to save it from
imminent demolition, citing it as an important
example of early motoring history.

It was designed by John James Joass, an
advocate of Edwardian Baroque, and also
responsible for several London buildings
including Whiteley's store in Bayswater.
Originally the car park offered waiting rooms for
chauffeurs and changing rooms for ladies, but
sadly these facilities are no longer available.

Recently refurbished, the car park is
administered by NCP and the site was entered
for the British Parking Association awards in
2009 as part of NCP's London focus sites
which were awarded a Special Commendation
in the Best Refurbishment Category.
Area Map p.6, A:3

Phoenix Theatre
Giles Gilbert Scott, Bertie Crewe and Cyril Masey, 1930

Charing Cross Road, WC2H 0JP • Tel 0844 871 7627 • www.phoenix-theatre. co.uk • Access to the interior for patrons only • See website for details of productions and ticket prices

Built on a rather awkward plot at the junction of the busy Charing Cross Road and Flitcroft Street where the main entrance has been placed. The corner position lends itself to the circular entrance lobby, above which is a shallow rotunda with four columns and the attic level has small square windows. The interior was the work of Theodore Komisarjevsky, émigré Russian theatre director and designer, who furnished the Phoenix in gilt and red plush with ornate ceilings and shapely doors. He commissioned fellow countryman Vladimir Polunin to paint panels placed above the theatre boxes in the style of Tintoretto, Titian and Giorgione. Polunin went on to produce artwork for London Transport posters during the 1930s.

The senior architect of this project, Giles Gilbert Scott, was the grandson of George Gilbert Scott and was responsible for some iconic structures such as the Battersea Power Station and the one time ubiquitous K3 red telephone boxes. Bertie Crewe was a pupil of Frank Matcham and had enjoyed a long career designing theatres and later cinemas. *Area Map p.6, B:3*

Arnos Grove Underground Station
Charles Holden, 1930

Bowes Road, N14 • www.tfl.gov.uk • Open normal London Transport hours

When the Piccadilly line was extended in 1930 Frank Pick, the legendary head of London Transport, gave Charles Holden the task of designing the new stations. Pick believed that nothing was too good for the travelling public and he felt aesthetics were as important as the trains and buses running on time. Pick commissioned a calligrapher to give London Transport its own typeface, artists to design posters and, a designer to provide a logo –still in use today! 'The best' also ran to architecture and Holden's stations are classics. His Piccadilly line extension stations, are all unique and yet are variations on a theme – built from exposed brickwork and concrete, using simple forms such as cylinders and rectangles with ceramic tiles to add colour. Holden designed everything – lighting, kiosks, ticket machines, platform seating and even the clock faces and litterbins.

Holden and Pick had travelled to parts of northern Europe for inspiration. Indeed the Arnos Grove building is reminiscent of the much-admired Stockholm City Library of 1928. Arnos Grove has a drum-shaped ticket hall, whose large windows let light flood in during the day; at night electric light shines out. Southgate station is a rectangular version of this station.

Unilever House
J Lomax Simpson, with Burnet, Tate and Lorne, 1931

New Bridge Street/Victoria Embankment, EC4 • Nearest transport Blackfriars LU & Rail • No public access

This building is on the site of the once renowned De Keyser's Hotel a very successful enterprise started by Sir Polydore de Keyser, a waiter from Belgium, who eventually opened his 400 room hotel in 1874. De Keyser became Lord Mayor of London in 1887, the first Catholic since the Reformation to do so and his hotel closed at the end of World War I and the land sold to Unilever in 1921.

Sited on a busy corner where traffic roars along Victoria Embankment and over Blackfriars Bridge, this impressive stone building is windowless on the ground floor, presumably to help eliminate some of the noise from the road. From the fourth floor of this lovely curved building is a parapet from which a row of giant Ionic columns stretch upwards. The roots of the design of this building are undoubtedly classical but with more than a hint of Art Deco.

It is a worthwhile building to contemplate for its form alone, despite the traffic. However the real treat is its display of sculpture with huge figures taming sinuous horses, representing 'Controlled Energy', by William Reid Dick and other figures by Gilbert Ledward and Nicholas Munro. During the evening the façade of the building is particularly well lit.

In a six-year programme of refurbishment that ended in 1983, Unilever House was renovated and expanded by the addition of an eight-storey wing. The new wing had to be low enough so that it did not violate the long-standing edict of London planning authorities that no building should be high enough to block the view of St Paul's Cathedral from Waterloo Bridge. *Area Map p.8, A:2*

Daimler Car Hire Garage
Wallis Gilbert & Partners, 1931

McCann Erickson, 7-11 Herbrand Street,
WC1N 1EX • Private with no public access

Designed by the architectural practice that
produced grand projects such as the Hoover
Factory and the Victoria Coach Station, this
building, which must have been one of their
smallest, first served as a Daimler Garage,
then as a taxi garage before starting its new
life in 2000 as the London office of the highly
successful advertising agency McCann
Erickson.

Under its flat roof, the pristine white building
has a rectangular office block, tall central
tower housing the stairwell, lit by a long
window, which links to what was a curved car
ramp and is now a 50 foot well-lit atrium. As
with nearly all works from this partnership, this
building is in an Art Deco style. The building is
Grade II Listed. *Area Map p.2-3, B:1*

*Right: Daimler Car Hire Garage. One of Wallis Gilbert
& Partners smaller projects – they also designed many
large industrial buildings such as the iconic Hoover
Factory in west London*

St Olaf House
H S Goodhart-Rendel, 1932

Tooley Street, SE1 • Nearest transport London Bridge LU & Rail • Private office, no public access

Built as the head office for the nearby Hay's Wharf in 1931-32, see 'South Bank Walk', St Olaf House, which almost abuts London Bridge, is an Art Deco gem faced in Portland stone. The building has curved sides and a lively use of windows and those on the central four floors have bronze frames. The huge lettering over the entrances on both sides of the building is in a stylised, triangulated Art Deco form.

The staircase is a notable example of the Art Deco style, with a zigzag balustrade – worth pressing your nose against the entrance door to have a peep. *Area Map p.8, B:1*

Odeon Cinema
Mather and Weedon, 1937

Leicester Square, WC2 • Nearest transport Leicester Square LU • Access as patrons, cinema times vary • Wheelchair access available

The profile of this building is an Art Deco dreamscape, built in uncompromising black granite with a huge square tower to one side. Renovations by Stephen Limbrick in the late 1980s have gone a long way to redress the damage caused by a mid-1960s refit, when much of the Art Deco interior was lost. However, there is still not that much to draw one into the interior unless you want to see the latest Hollywood blockbuster of course.

This building is at its best in the evening, when it is bathed in blue neon light.

Probably one of the best surviving Art Deco cinema interiors can be found at the former Hounslow Odeon, now Mecca Bingo, London Road, Hounslow, Middlesex.
Area Map p.6, B:3

Left: St Olaf House

Senate House
Charles Holden, 1937

The University of London, Malet Street, WC1 • Tel 020 7862 8000 • Nearest transport Goodge Street LU • No public access, however Senate House usually participates in the London Open House scheme (see p.377)

The plan for this fabulous building was conceived in 1927 with the purchase of a ten and a half acre site from the Bedford Estate to provide buildings for the University of London, which having been formed in 1836 was in need of more space. The proposal was to provide administrative offices, a library, ceremonial hall, students' union, five institutions and two schools; a massive undertaking.

Architect Charles Holden was selected on the strength of his London Underground stations and 55 Broadway, which had recently opened. His masterplan was duly approved and the

start of work on the Senate House and Library was completed by 1937. However lack of funding and the intervention of World War II saw the rest of Holden's plans thwarted.

Holden designed this building with the overall massing based on a pyramidal form for stability, thereby giving Senate House its slight Aztec temple flavour. Holden chose not to use the fairly new technology of steel-framing for his building, although it is used in the floor construction and there is steel framing within the tower to support the many book stacks.

London's first true skyscraper is faced in Cornish granite on the ground floor with Portland stone used on the upper floors. It is thought that the exterior was intended to receive carved figures and ornamentation, but these were never realised and, perhaps, the building is better for it.

Great care has been lavished on the interior. The Ceremonial Hall, where graduates of the University receive their degrees, is double-height and lined with travertine marble. The same material is used on the exquisite staircase which has a notable wrought iron balustrade. *Area Map p.2-3, B:1*

1-3 Willow Road
Erno Goldfinger, 1937-39

Hampstead, NW3 • Tel 020 7435 6166 • www.nationaltrust.org.uk • Nearest transport
Hampstead or Hampstead Heath LU • See website for opening times & admission charges

This small housing project by the Hungarian-born architect Erno Goldfinger is one of the most important examples of the Modern Movement in London. Having worked in Paris, where he mixed with avant-garde artists and architects, he settled in London in 1934.

Goldfinger encountered immense hostility from local conservation groups who saw his proposal for the terrace as being out of step with the rest of Georgian Hampstead. Nonetheless planning permission was eventually granted and the building of the three-house terrace went ahead.

Each of the houses within the terrace has a slightly different internal plan. Goldfinger took the centre house, the largest, as a home for his young family. Mindful of such a family's needs, Goldfinger incorporated a large amount of interior flexibility – whereby walls were moveable so that one large nursery could become two bedrooms when the need arose.

The terrace is three floors high at the front and four at the rear, each house has an integral garage, and is constructed from reinforced concrete with brick-faced walls. Concrete was also used for the framing of the first floor windows and for the ground floor columns.

Such unifying motifs make this terrace appear to be one large house and thus it fits well with its Georgian neighbours.

Erno Goldfinger was an immensely influential architect and his other London work includes the French Government Tourist Offices at 66 Haymarket (designed in 1958) and their further offices at 177 Piccadilly (built 1963); Alexander Fleming House at Elephant and Castle (1966); Haggerston Girls School (1967) and the much admired Trellick Tower, details of which can be found in the next chapter (see p.210).

Goldfinger's own house, No 2, has been in the care of the National Trust since 1994 and is open to the public. The house is filled with furniture designed by Goldfinger and his art collection is on display including works by Bridget Riley, Max Ernst and Henry Moore. There are also some family photographs on show, one particular favourite being a picture of Goldfinger with his aged mother when she came to live in Willow Road – along with her incredibly heavy-looking, solid Hungarian furniture, that looks remarkably at home in such a Modernist setting. There is also an opportunity to see a short film on Erno Goldfinger and his work, which is most worthwhile.

Canary Wharf Station (foreground), Norman Foster (see p.281)

07

1945 TO THE 21ST CENTURY

1945 TO THE 21ST CENTURY

"Architecture should speak of its time and place, but yearn for timelessness." Frank Gehry

In 1951 Britain set aside post-war austerity for an all too brief moment of celebration and fun. One hundred years after the Great Exhibition, the Labour government, who had ousted Churchill in the general election of 1945, threw economic caution to the wind and decided to allow frivolity and a modicum of excess to replace the rationing and monotonous drabness which had followed in the wake of peace.

The means the government chose was an exhibition which they called a festival, to distinguish it from the instructive exhibitions held during the war and which had been deadly serious by necessity.

The primary medium the enlightened socialists chose for their festival was architecture. Every major city in the United Kingdom had been ravaged by the Blitz so the idea of reconstruction and redevelopment was in itself a tonic to the nation.

A parcel of land on the south bank of the River Thames between Waterloo and Hungerford Bridges, just north of Waterloo Station, was set aside as the London site of the festival and a young architect, Hugh Casson, was appointed Festival Director.

The Festival of Britain, ran for five months, attracted almost ten million visitors and was the nursery for all British post-war modern architects. It was here that Casson and team coined an exceedingly British version of Modernism, that could be said to have been 'contemporary', rather than 'Modern'. Influences were drawn from Scandinavia as well as from French and German sources. Indeed many of the architects employed were European émigrés who had arrived in London in the late 1930's with ideas formed by Gropius and Corbusier. Even some of the humble exhibition kiosks were designed by Erno Goldfinger and the landscape enhanced with works by Epstein, Hepworth and Moore.

The nation loved the whole thing with its bright colours, strange shapes and challenging new ideas about how the British home should be decorated.

Sadly, however, when Winston Churchill regained power in the general election of 1951, he decided in a fit of pique to clear the whole thing away with the exception of the Royal Festival Hall. The Dome of Discovery, the Skylon, the Homes and Gardens Pavilion were all unnecessarily demolished and Britain returned to the realities of austerity.

The architects that had so proved their worth during the Festival now set about the business of rebuilding the country. They designed housing, hospitals, schools and shopping centres, rebuilt derelict churches and repaired bombed-out houses. Their buildings in the brave new British Modernist style became symbols of the recently established Welfare State. In time the Festival mood returned as new towns and new housing created new homes that were as different from the pre-war norm as was Dior's 'New Look' from the uniform-like fashions of the 1940's.

Reinforced concrete replaced brickwork in the same way that steel had replaced timber at the beginning of the century. Government instruction to the architectural profession was quite clear – build, and build fast. But, on a fateful morning in May 1968 this architectural euphoria came to an end, shattered like the pre-cast concrete panels that so dramatically crashed to the ground when the 23 storey tower block of flats that was Ronan Point in Newham, East London collapsed. Clearly it was no longer safe to trust the architectural and engineering vision which housed families in the high-rise apartment buildings that had become symbolic of Britain's post-war renaissance. Critics began to argue that Modernism was a deeply flawed architectural philosophy and that Britain's architecture should return to vernacular roots for safety and sanity's sake. Britain, their reasoning went, was historically a country of brick and stone, not concrete and steel, its buildings in the main were low-rise and had pitched roofs.

Above: Lloyd's of London, Richard Rogers, see p.214

Meanwhile across the English Channel young architects Richard Rogers and Renzo Piano had completed the mind-bogglingly audacious high-tech Pompidou Centre in Paris of 1976, which was immediately voted the 'Most Popular Building in France'. The aspirations of British architecture would not bow down in the face of popular yearning for an unnecessary romanticism. Then in 1978 against all the odds Rogers was appointed by the insurance organisation Lloyd's of London, one of the most conservative institutions in the notoriously stuffy City of London, to design its headquarters. This building is considered, to this day, to be one of the most daring and futuristic in the world.

The American architect Robert Venturi had published his seminal book 'Complexity and Contradiction in Architecture' in the 1960's when his views suddenly became fashionable. In his so-called Postmodern world, the deep roots of the psyche could only be satisfied by a complex, not rational, environment which carried with it subconscious references to architectural languages of the past. Office buildings built of brick needed to have references to Classical architecture to satisfy the hunger in the human mind for reassurance from the past. The Postmodern architectural movement came with a rich, albeit fraudulent, philosophical system which appealed to a large number of architects. The American Modernist Philip Johnson changed his spots overnight and designed the AT&T building in Manhattan with a Chippendale style split pediment where it reached sky. James Stirling designed the over-complex building at No1 Poultry and in 1983 Terry Farrell gave a popular twist to Postmodernism with his building in Camden for TV AM with its jokey coloured boiled eggs on the canal elevation and a steel work keystone classical arch over the car park entrance.

Terry Farrell went on to complete three further grand projects in the Postmodern manner. The MI6 building at Vauxhall, Embankment Place over Charing Cross Station and Alban Gate which spans London Wall in the City.

In 1984 Prince Charles, the Prince of Wales, was guest of honour at a dinner hosted

Above: No1 Poultry, James Stirling

by the Royal Institute of British Architects at Hampton Court Palace to celebrate the Institute's 150th anniversary. The Prince was there to represent the Queen, the Institute's patron, and to present the Royal Gold Medal. The Prince used the opportunity afforded by his speech to attack British architecture and specifically the proposals for an extension to the National Gallery designed by Ahrens, Burton and Koralek (ABK). The Prince touched a popular nerve and was praised by tabloid and broadsheet alike for taking a brave stand against an arrogant and out of touch profession. The ABK scheme for the National Gallery was dropped and was eventually replaced with a Postmodern concoction by the ringmaster of the philosophy Robert Venturi, with Denise Scott Brown.

On Saturday 19 November 1994 the British people experienced their first National Lottery draw. Twenty-eight per cent of the profits from the Lottery are set aside for 'good causes'; to date this has amounted to over a staggering £25 billion. The 'good causes' include those which require building. The Arts Council Lottery Fund was to finance art galleries and museums while the Heritage Lottery Fund was there to repair and enhance the nation's historic building stock and the Millennium Fund had bulging coffers to help the nation celebrate a change in date through architecture. The architectural profession had been unprepared for the extent of this new bounty.

Architects at this time were to become dab handed at new computer aided design technology, so out went the drawing boards and in came electronic hardware. However, architectural computers did more than replace the T square, set square and Rotring pen. They afforded a new freedom to the architectural imagination liberating it from the previous constraints which were in effect linear geometry. When plans were drawn by hand using the T square and set square, buildings over the fullness of architectural history had tended, in the main, to be rectilinear and right-angular. A computer, however, could turn the strangest lines, shapes and forms into concrete reality. For structural engineers the computer meant more finely honed calculations resulting in new structural systems. Colour photocopying meant that the architect's palette needed no longer to be monochrome – if Mondrian could paint it, architects could now draw it, reproduce it and specify it. The new language was shape and colour.

Herzog and de Meuron's transformation of the Bankside power station into the Tate Modern and the extension and renewal of Tate Britain were paid for by the Lottery. Outside the capital London architects were busying themselves with Lottery-funded projects throughout the length and breadth of the country. Nicholas Grimshaw designed the spectacularly popular Eden Project in Cornwall, whilst Nigel Coates produced the fatally unpopular Popular Music Centre in Sheffield. Leeds got the Armoury Museum by Derek Walker, and the list continues on, illustrating the Lottery's considerable benefit to British architects and British architecture.

In the main Lottery funded projects are at the forefront of neo-Modernism, a contemporary language that rejects both the vernacular and Postmodernism.

Most of the Lottery funded projects have been immensely popular with one costly exception – the ill-fated Millennium Dome designed by Richard Rodgers. The idea of celebrating a mere change in date was always suspect, if for no other reason than the ludicrous prospect of central government organising a national party! However, the previous, Conservative, government had committed themselves to the Dome and their successors, Tony Blair's New Labour, saw the venture as a symbol of all that the party stood for: new, daring, big and brash. The millennium itself may have gone off like a damp squib with the devastatingly unpopular Dome as its symbol, but in fact Richard Rogers' structure is as fine a work of architecture as you'll find anywhere in the world.

Thankfully the Dome underwent a change of management and interior re-configuration and emerged in 2007 as the 02 Arena, now one of Europe's most popular music venues.

As British architecture entered the new millennium fuelled by public enthusiasm and the continuing generosity of the Lottery, Norman Foster emerged as the most successful architect of his generation. London plays host to dozens of buildings by the maestro, including the architecturally challenging Greater London Authority headquarters, on the south bank of the Thames next to Tower Bridge, and the so-called 'gherkin' (the Swiss Re building) in the City of London.

One of Norman Foster's most iconic works, and probably the one most members of the public encounter, is the Great Court project at the British Museum. Indeed, reinvention with the help of good architecture has opened up many spaces in London that were once rather forbidding. For example, recent work at St Pancras and King's Cross has given us the opportunity to view parts of the structures that were hidden before and in Chelsea an army barracks transformed into an art gallery.

21st-century London has a plethora of interesting new buildings too; Renzo Piano producing Europe's tallest building at London Bridge and one of its most colourful at St Giles; Will Alsop delighting most and infuriating some with his innovative Peckham Library and Palestra in Southwark; the much awaited first London building by Zaha Hadid at the Olympic Park; and although Daniel Libeskind's much discussed 'Spiral' extension to the Victoria and Albert Museum has never materialised, he has built one small project at the London Metropolitan University.

British architecture, particularly in London is as strong, if not stronger, now than it was during the triumph of the Festival of Britain. Architects now seem as unstoppable as were those Victorians who wrought the new London.

Royal Festival Hall
Martin and Matthew et al, 1951 / Allies & Morrison, 1992-2007

Southbank Centre, Belvedere Road, SE1 • Tel 020 7960 4200 • www.rfh.org.uk • Nearest transport Waterloo LU & Rail • See website for opening times and details of events, tickets and wheelchair access

Designed in 1948 by a team led by Sir Leslie Martin (1908-2000) and Sir Robert Matthew (1906-75) the Royal Festival Hall was finished in time for the 1951 Festival of Britain, for which it was a showpiece. For visitors to the Festival and passing Londoners this was a taste of what modern architecture could be – solid, functional and accessible.

The exterior is a display of glass and Portland stone, the river elevation having been extended forward during major renovation work in the early 1960s. The interior is a series of intersecting levels with a pleasing use of wood, marble, lighting and textiles throughout. The concert hall is a revelation, Leslie Martin having stipulated from the start that 'the egg of the concert hall should be surrounded by a box of structure'. The acoustics had been taken seriously at the design stage so the problems that dogged the Royal Albert Hall and even the much more recent Barbican Hall, were eliminated. The auditorium, designed by Peter Moro, accommodates 2,600 in seating arranged in one large stalls area, a substantial balcony, and four tiers of boxes. At the hall's opening one critic carped that the boxes looked like 'drawers pulled out in a hurried burglary raid'; Corbusier thought they were

a joke 'but a very good joke'. Now they are seen as amusing, pleasing on the eye, are exceedingly comfortable to occupy and have been copied many times since.

The architects Martin and Matthew, both employed by the enlightened London County Council at the time of the Festival, went on to enjoy fairly distinguished careers, especially Sir Leslie Martin who was acknowledged

Hayward Gallery, South Bank Centre

as a leading light in the Modern Movement. He designed some quite major additions to various Oxford and Cambridge colleges as well as the celebrated Royal Concert Hall in Glasgow. In addition to being a practising architect he was an academic, enjoying the role of Professor of Architecture at Cambridge University for over 40 years.

The Hall, being the first new concert venue to open in post-war Europe, was a focus for musicians, but needed to adapt over time to new demands from performers and audiences. Since 1992 the Hall has been the subject of ongoing refurbishment by the architectural partnership of Allies and Morrison; no mean feat given its Grade I listing. With a budget of £110 million, the Hall has been restored to its original elegance and vitality. By moving all the administrative offices into a new office building between the hall and the railway, many of the internal spaces previously used as offices are now available as public areas. On the river façade, a dingy service road has been transformed into an elegant parade of restaurants and shops.

Refurbishment of the Hall was completed by May 2007 when it once again became a centre of London's cultural life.

Close by and part of the 'South Bank Centre' along with the Festival Hall are the Queen Elizabeth Hall, the Purcell Room and Hayward Gallery, built in 1964 by Sir Hubert Bennett and Jack Whittle for the London County Council. This group of buildings is a marvellous example of New Brutalism, with its admiration of the work of Le Corbusier and its use of huge blank walls of rough concrete. These buildings have been much criticised not least for their interconnecting walkways which are difficult for the able-bodied to negotiate and totally impossible for people with any form of mobility restriction and, worst of all, appear to be unnecessary. On paper the design for this group must have seemed bold and exciting but given its location next to a grey Thames and under an often dull London sky some observers comment that the buildings seem out of place.

The interiors of the Queen Elizabeth Hall, seating 1,000, and Purcell Room, seating an intimate 368, feed off the same foyer and whilst they appear to be the smaller siblings of the Festival Hall both are less satisfactory.
Area Map p.6, C:2

Commonwealth Institute
Robert Matthew, Johnson-Marshall and Partners, 1962

205 Kensington High Street, W8, Nearest transport High Street Kensington LU

Good things come to those who wait. In the case of the modernist monument that is the former Commonwealth Institute building this comes in the shape of Terrance Conran, who has chosen the long-redundant building as the site for an enlarged Design Museum which will move here from its current home on the South Bank (see p.344) in 2014.

Set back from the western end of Kensington High Street, on the edge of the lovely Holland Park, the building will retain its original distinctive tent-like copper hyperbolic-paraboloid roof. Designed during the period of post-war optimism, very much in the Festival of Britain spirit, it was completed in 1962. Its primary function as an exhibition space for British foreign interests was redundant within 20 years and the building has been threatened with demolition, despite its Grade II listing.

Conran has injected a lot of money into this project, with architect John Pawson, king of minimalism, responsible for the main conversion and the design of the surrounding area given to Rem Koolhaas, whose work always excites and divides.

The Economist Building
Alison & Peter Smithson, 1964

The Economist Building, 25 St James's Street, SW1; Nearest transport Green Park LU (Victoria, Piccadilly, and Jubilee lines); No public access

An office block of 1960's vintage which still looks fresh and relevant. The building consists of three towers of differing heights arranged around a shallow pedestrian plaza. The four-storey smallest tower directly faces St James's Street and was originally designed as bank premises. The tallest tower of 15 storeys is the home of The Economist magazine, the commissioning client of the project, and the third block is an eight-storey residential tower.

The towers are made from concrete with Portland stone spandrels and pilasters with aluminium window frames. The whole building sits well with its neighbours such as Boodles Club of 1765 without a hint of imitation or mockery. This was the first 1960s building to be Grade II listed. *Area Map p.6, A:2*

B T Tower

BT Tower
Eric Bedford, 1961-1965

60 Cleveland Street, W1T 4JZ • Tel 020 7432 5970 • Nearest Transport Goodge Street and Warren Street LU • Limited public access, please telephone for details

The Tower, which can be seen from all over the Capital, combines an office block with the function of a telecommunications tower. The structure is immediately unsettling to the eye, being thinner in the middle than at the top and bottom. This wasp waist effect has always had style and may look futuristic in some ways, but at the time it was built it was an astonishing architectural statement.

The Tower was the first purpose-built tower to transmit high frequency radio waves. Until the construction of the NatWest Tower in the City in the early 1980's, this 620 foot (189m) tower of concrete, steel and glass was the tallest building in London. Its cylindrical form reduces wind resistance and improves stability.

From the time of its opening the public were allowed to ride one of the two high-speed lifts, travelling at some 6 metres a second (22 km/h), taking 30 seconds to reach any of the three observation floors or up to the 34th floor restaurant which was built on a 3 metre wide (9ft 10 inch) revolving segment, spinning through 360 degrees every 22 minutes. The restaurant closed in 1980 amid security worries. *Area Map p.2-3, A:1*

Centre Point
Richard Seifert & Partners, 1966

101 New Oxford Street, WC1 • Nearest transport Tottenham Court Road LU • No public access

At the time of its construction this building aroused strong hostility and the public was critical of the London County Council's decision to grant planning permission for what was a private speculative project. Concerns regarding the building's intended use as offices rather than as living accommodation were also aired. Ironically in the light of such complaints this particular office block stood unoccupied for nearly ten years until converted to flats in 1975.

The structure's size, at 398 feet high and with 34 storeys, was also seen as being out of scale with its surroundings. Notwithstanding the controversy in which it was built, Centre Point is an extraordinary construction. Exceedingly slim, when viewed from the south and north, its glass within a frame of pre-cast concrete sections give it an individual surface texture that heralded the type of building with which Richard Seifert was to grace London, such as Tower 42 (formerly NatWest Tower) in the City, and Space House (formerly Aerial House) in Kingsway.
Area Map p.2-3, B:1

Trellick Tower
Erno Goldfinger & Partners, 1972

5 Golborne Road, W10 • Nearest transport Westbourne Park LU • No public access.

One of Goldfinger's first projects when he arrived in London as an émigré from Hungary, was to build a house for his family in Hampstead; details of this which be found at the end of the previous chapter. His post-war commissions included the Daily Worker Building in Farringdon Road of 1946 (still there but sadly not in it's original state and now serving as a furniture showroom), a four-storey block of flats in Regent's Park Road of 1954 and a small office building in Albemarle Street of 1956.

He won his most ambitious commission in 1959 to reconstruct five sites owned by the London County Council at the Elephant & Castle road junction in south London, providing housing, a shopping centre, offices and leisure facilities for local residents as well as a traffic interchange destined to become an important gateway into London. The project was a bold and unashamedly brutal scheme that the purists loved and others, particularly those who had to live there, hated.

Nevertheless, the rest of Goldfinger's working life was taken up with two massive public housing projects, both for the London County Council. The first was the Balfron Tower (1963-68) in Rowlett Street Poplar, east

London, which, at 27-floors high, was one of the tallest dwellings in Europe at the time. On completion, Goldfinger and his wife moved in to flat number 130 on the 26th floor for eight weeks, assessing the experience and listing the points raised by their fellow tenants. The problems, such as two lifts not being enough, were taken into account at the next major housing project – Trellick Tower.

This was under construction as Ronan Point tumbled down and public opinion was very much against high-rise living. Goldfinger argued that Ronan Point had been constructed using a prefabricated concrete system, which he felt was flawed, whereas he employed a poured concrete method.

Trellick Tower consists of 217 dwellings in a mix of nine different types of flats and maisonettes, all of which are 'through' apartments with windows on both sides, with the block facing south/north. The slab is 31 storeys high with a separate lift/stair tower and bridges to the main block at every three floors à la Le Corbusier's 'Unité d'Habitation' in Marseilles. Goldfinger paid meticulous attention to detail, for example, windows pivoted for cleaning; soundproofing and double glazing and the entrance hall was marble-lined. The views across London from the upper floors are stunning.

Despite the architect's best efforts, this was not a place where people wanted to live. Goldfinger had employed Le Corbusier's philosophy as set out in 'Villa Redieuse', or the

Trellick Tower

Radiant City, of 1935. However, the *Radiant City* was based on the abandonment of class based stratification; a philosophy not readily attainable in the contemporary city. With housing assigned according to family size, not economic position, the reality was that it was those who had once endured the terraced slum dwellings that Trellick Tower replaced, who lived in what the tabloid press dubbed 'The Tower of Terror'. The block was repeatedly and seriously vandalised and the tenants were hardly comforted by the blockbuster film of 1974 *The Towering Inferno* or J G Ballard's novel of 1975 *High Rise*, in which he describes tower blocks as 'architecture built for war'.

However Trellick Tower is still there, Grade II listed no less, and is now a desirable address. Thatcher's 'Right to Buy' policy enabled some tenants to purchase apartments, and subsequently sell thus allowing a mix of occupant, although many apartments are still allocated to those with social-housing needs. A door entry intercom system and the employment of a concierge were initiated in the mid-1980's and an active residents association campaigned for a number of changes to the building and housing policy over the years, including the better security and only placing people there who want to go there.

The Trellick Tower 'gentrification' has led the way for other projects such as Denys Lasdun's Keeling House in Bethnal Green. Originally built in 1957, it was emptied of council tenants in the early 1990's and eventually sold to a private developer; having received a Grade II Listing which in part prevented its demolition. During 1999/2000 architects Munkenbeck and Marshall converted the block into luxury apartments.

Although Trellick Tower has no public access, it is often included as part of the Open House scheme, see p.377 for details.

Danish Embassy
Arne Jacobsen, 1969-1977

Royal Danish Embassy, 55 Sloane St, SW1X 9SR • Tel 020 72351255 • Nearest Transport: Knightsbridge or Sloane Square LU • Not open to the public, but often part of the Open House scheme (see p.377 for details)

Amongst the Belgravian mansion houses, mostly built in a style that cartoonist and architectural enthusiast Osbert Lancaster dubbed 'Pont Street Dutch', sits the Danish Embassy. Sufficiently different from its neighbours to turn the heads of passengers on the buses that pass by, the Embassy was designed by Arne Jacobsen.

Jacobsen's original design specified bronze and black granite cladding on the front façade, but the cost was prohibitive and painted aluminium and concrete were used instead. On the recessed ground floor of the front facade the simple geometry of the painted metal cladding is complemented by an abstract, geometric concrete mural by the Danish painter and sculptor Ole Schwalbe.

For something so startlingly contemporary, the Embassy sits comfortably with its more mature neighbours. Sadly the architect died before completion of this work.

Arne's other British work of note is the now Grade I listed St Catherine's College, Oxford, although he is equally noted for his chair designs. As with his architecture, his

furniture combines modernist ideals with the Scandinavian love of simple, natural design. His 'Swan', 'Egg' and 'Number 7' chairs are now considered classics of design; the latter being forever associated with model Christine Keeler who posed naked on one.

Lloyd's of London
Richard Rogers Partnership, 1978-86

71 Fenchurch Street, EC3M 4BS • Tel 020 7709 9166 • Nearest transport Monument LU
• No public access – but often part of the Open House scheme, see p.377 for details

In need of further office space to accommodate its growing business, Lloyd's sought the talent of Richard Rogers, now Lord Rogers of Riverside, to design a new building which is surely the most striking modern building in London.

Lloyd's, a society of insurance underwriters, originated in Edward Lloyd's coffeehouse in Tower Street in the mid 1680s. Ship owners, merchants and ships' captains beat a path to Lloyd's coffee house in order to obtain marine insurance. However, by 1769 new larger premises were established in Pope Head's Alley, but within two years these too had been outgrown. Business growth dictated several further moves to more spacious accommodation until the 1890s when Thomas Edward Collcutt created a bespoke office block

at 71 Fenchurch Street. This is now a Grade II listed building and so could not be demolished to make way for the new construction and neither could the façade of Coronation House, the next door building also owned by Lloyd's; both had to be incorporated into Richard Rogers' design.

In the early 1970s Richard Rogers and the internationally acclaimed architect Renzo Piano won the commission to design and build the new Pompidou Centre in Paris. Theirs was a radical design, with over half the site given over to a public piazza, and some of the features of the Lloyd's building can be traced back to design elements employed in Paris.

The most notable feature is that all the vertical structures and services are placed on the outside of the building, thereby leaving uninterrupted floor space within. Consequently the 'Room', as the ten-storey glazed atrium is modestly called, could expand or contract, by means of a series of galleries around a central space. Escalators and external glazed lifts provide easy access between floors, thereby making the best possible use of the space available with minimum impact on Collcutt's building and the surrounding streets.

With its exterior components and the main lifts and escalators in full view behind full-height glazing there is little need for ornamentation. The ten-storey glazed atrium is a sight to behold and much of this can in fact be seen from the outside.

On the ninth floor of this glass building, sitting within a free-standing stone box is the Board Room, designed by Robert Adam! Indeed it was a complete room salvaged in the early 1950's from Bowood House, Wiltshire, placed within the previous Lloyd's building and accommodated within Richard Roger's masterpiece.

Just as interesting is the beautifully preserved interior of Collcutt's building, particularly the richly decorated Library, with its sumptuous use of wood and the General Committee Room with its barrel-vaulted ceiling painted by Gerald Moira (1867-1959).

The Link Gallery, originally part of Collcutt's General Office provides a transitional space between the two buildings and is lined with paintings, several of which are by the eminent Sir Frank Brangwyn RA (1867-1956).

It is worth making a visit to the City in the evening just to see this building glowing ingeniously with coloured lighting designed by the Imagination team in 1988.
Area Map p.8, C:2

Lloyd's of London

The Circle
CZWG Architects, 1987-89

Queen Elizabeth Street, SE1 • Nearest transport London Bridge LU & Rail • No public access

Included here for its striking use of colour – cobalt blue, and lots of it, the project takes its name from the rounded forecourt in front of the flats, of which there are 302. In addition there are eight office suites, a health club with swimming pool, a small restaurant and some retail units. The Circle is part of the now exceedingly fashionable area of Shad Thames.

The blueness of the building comes from glazed tiles used on the entrance façades; the rest of the building is of stock brick. Attention to detailing such as diagonal glazing bars and the deployment of balconies makes this an attractive development. Concern as to the Circle's appeal over time has been voiced and suggestions that the use of such a single strong colour was somehow 'gimmicky' are, more than 20 years on, as yet unfounded.

The CZWG group have been responsible for some other notable housing projects such as Cascades (built 1987-88) on the Westferry Road and the China Wharf mix of flats and offices (built 1986-88) in Mill Street on the south bank of the Thames. *Area Map p.8, C:1*

Right: The Circle

Lord's Cricket Ground

St John's Wood Road, NW8 • Tel 020 7432 1000 • www.lords.org • Nearest transport St John's Wood LU • See website for details of tours of the grounds

'The home of cricket' since 1814 can certainly boast of some very interesting and innovative architecture, much of it is late 20th century and plans are afoot for further work. However one of the most notable buildings dates from the Victorian era and is called the 'Pavilion', with its famous Long Room; the 'Holy of Holies' where members watch the game and players go out to defeat or victory. Built in 1889-90 to a design by Thomas Verity, more associated with London theatre architecture, the Pavilion is now Grade II Listed.

Since its bicentenary, in 1987, the Marylebone Cricket Club has spent over £50 million on improving Lord's. This includes the refurbishment of the Pavilion and construction of the Media Centre and Grand Stand: the installation of permanent but retractable floodlights; the development of an Indoor Cricket School & Cricket Academy with an analysis suite, gymnasium, sports injury clinic and treatment rooms. Future development will include the construction of an additional new real tennis court to enable Lord's to host top-class international real tennis competitions and the creation of a purpose-built museum to house MCC's outstanding collection of cricket art and artefacts.

RECENT IMPROVEMENTS INCLUDE:

Mound Stand
Michael Hopkins, 1985-7

The brick arcade of the original 19th-century stand was retained and extended, making the underside an attractive and usable public concourse. The seating tiers on the mound were renewed. A new steel superstructure, supported on six slim columns thereby minimising disruption to views are linked by a plate girder, from which lattice trusses cantilever out forming the skeleton of a three – storey structure. Private boxes and dining rooms hang below the skeleton and a tier of raked seating backed by open-air restaurants and bars sits on top.

The six columns continue up to become masts supporting a flamboyant canopy of PVC-coated, polyester fabric. The whole structure is held back by tension members anchored to the ground and strapped to brick piers below to stiffen them. This spectacular pavilion is, as the architect points out, a modern reinterpretation of the traditional village green marquee.

Cricket School
David Morley, 1993-6

A mould breaking building in that it is the first indoor facility to utilise natural light for the playing area. Detailed analysis of light was carried out to ensure that the ingress of light into the hall wouldn't have a detrimental effect on play. A bespoke blind system was designed, employing sail fabric, and has resulted in reduced running costs of some £30,000 every year. It was acclaimed as the best Sport and Leisure building in the UK in 1996, and was runner-up for the Stirling Prize.

Media Centre
Future Systems, 1995-8

Architects Jan Kaplicky and Amanda Levete designed this truly unique building – a single-shell aluminium monocoque structure which was made, prefabricated in 26 sections off-site in a Cornish boatbuilder's yard and assembled at Lord's. As futuristic as it first appears, the Media Centre fits well with the other structures at the Ground and, indeed, is the same height, 49 feet or 15 metres, as the Nursery Pavilion (David Morley, 1999) directly opposite, across the square. The Media Centre has space for 100 journalists plus television and radio commentators – this is where 'Blowers' and Aggers', and other stalwarts of the BBC's 'Test Match Special' broadcast from. The Media Centre was awarded the prestigious RIBA Stirling Prize in 1999.

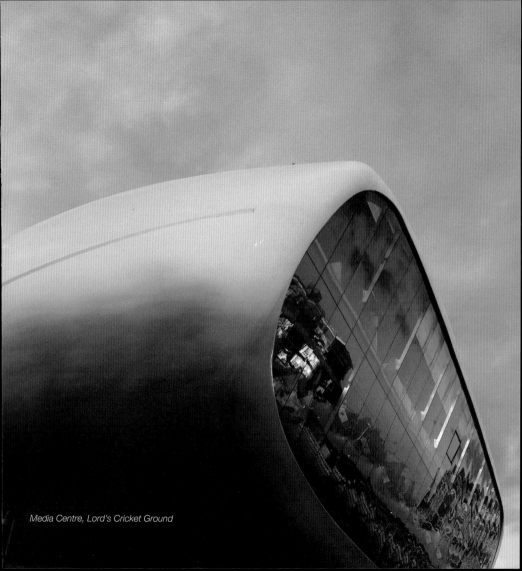

Media Centre, Lord's Cricket Ground

Imagination
Ron Herron, 1989

25 Store Street, South Crescent, WC1E 7BL • Tel 020 7323 3300 • www.imagination.com
• Nearest transport Goodge St LU • No public access (apart from occasional exhibitions)

Originally this six-storey Edwardian building was two schools. Girls occupied the building to the front, whilst the boys were taught in an almost identical one at the rear with a narrow laneway, open to the elements, dividing the two. Various uses were made of the building after the schools closed but it was left in a state of dilapidation until 1988 when the premises were acquired by Imagination, the global communications agency.

The refurbishment project was handed to their in-house architect Ron Herron, who had worked on the conception of the South Bank Centre in the early 1960s and who had been

part of the ground-breaking Archigram group of designers responsible for some interesting but unrealised projects. Their vision of disposable, flexible and thus easily extended buildings was very influential from the mid 1960s to mid 1970s. Some of their philosophy can be traced in the Imagination building.

Viewed from the street it's impossible to envisage what lies behind the red brick and hanging green ivy of the façade. The original building space has been given a high-specification and smart appearance, but it is the treatment of the 23 foot wide space between the original buildings that is the most astonishing feature. This once dead-end alley, the walls of which have had their bricks painted white, rises six storeys. White steel and aluminium bridges, link the two buildings and criss-cross the space between them and the whole is roofed by a network of suspension rods that push-up gigantic umbrellas of Teflon-coated PVC fabric.

Throughout the building the predominantly white and natural aluminium decoration has a remarkably calming effect, whilst the use of walkways and the light from the atrium space gives the whole a sense of drama. The refurbishment of the building has won many awards including the 1990 Royal Institute of British Architects 'National Award for Architecture'. In the same year at the BBC Design Awards Sir Norman Foster said of the building 'I was so full of enthusiasm, I couldn't stop talking about it. I was stopping people, I was phoning people, I thought it was really wonderful'.

The remarkable Imagination building combines the old and new so successfully that it influenced many subsequent buildings, particularly given the stringent new conservation policies and advances in construction technology.

Although this is a workplace with no public access every year the company 'dresses up' the façade of the building for the festive season. In 2010 some 16,000 twinkling LED lights were involved, and is certainly worth a detour to see!
Area Map p.2-3, A:1

Left: Façade, Imagination Right: Atrium, Imagination

Sackler Galleries at the Royal Academy of Arts
Foster Associates, 1991

The Royal Academy of Arts, Burlington House, Piccadilly, W1 • Tel 020 7300 8000 • www.royalacademy.org.uk • Nearest transport Piccadilly Circus or Green Park LU • Admission free – except for special exhibitions) • See website for opening times

Climb the sweep of glass stairs to the Sackler Galleries, past what used to be the exterior walls of the old building taking in the sheer beauty of the former façade that may have gone unnoticed until given this opportunity to be seen on its own level. This tends to happen with Foster's buildings in that, wonderful as they are in themselves, they also open up the surroundings, whether it be a view, another part of the building or simply the sky.

You may prefer to take the glass-walled lift to the Galleries, but whether by lift or stairs, when you arrive you will be greeted by the bright space and clean lines of the top-lit ante room which beautifully displays some of the Academy's best sculpture, including Michaelangelo's Virgin and Child with the Infant St John. As at the 'Imagination' building, the void between two buildings was used to house new service structures;(,) in the Royal Academy's case providing the space for the stairs, lift and ante-room to the Sackler Galleries (which were formerly the isolated, and seldom visited, Diploma Galleries).

Norman Foster's fusion of the old and the new here has been universally acclaimed as nothing short of a masterpiece in itself, sitting very well within Burlington House, one of the few surviving 18th-century mansions in this part of London. The Royal Academy moved to these premises, so much larger than its cramped quarters in the Old Somerset House, in 1868, the 100th anniversary of its foundation.
Area Map p.6, A:2

Sackler Galleries, Royal Academy of Arts

Vauxhall Cross
Terry Farrell, 1982-92

Albert Embankment, SE1 • Nearest transport Vauxhall LU/Rail • No public access

Seen at its best from the opposite bank of the Thames with one's back to Tate Britain, Vauxhall Cross was designed and built to house the headquarters of the British Secret Intelligence Service, otherwise known as 'MI6'. Gone are the days when Secret Service employees worked in nameless Government blocks, for there is nothing anonymous about this ostentatious building. Indeed, the exterior has made a splendid backdrop to many films, notably James Bond in 'The World is Not Enough', where we see 007 taking part in a speed boat chase on the river Thames outside. The building even incorporates a public riverside walkway; however the windows are so incredibly small that peeping-in is impossible!

Its stepped construction, not unlike a ziggurat – hence its nickname of 'Babylon on Thames' – is emphasised by the use of the contrasting materials of pale concrete cladding and dark wall glazing.

Unsurprisingly, Vauxhall Cross, for all its 'openness', is very much a modern-day fortress with banks of security cameras, inside and out, and walls, doors and windows that repel electronic eavesdropping and jamming and are bullet and bomb proof.

Embankment Place
Terry Farrell, 1985-1990

Charing Cross, WC2 • Nearest transport Embankment LU or Charing Cross LU & Rail • Public access along walkways to Hungerford Bridge and Charing Cross Station but no public access to Embankment Place

Embankment Place was built to take advantage of 'air rights' over Charing Cross Station, rising nine storeys over the railway tracks, providing office and retail space, the latter at various points around the complex.

Constructed from red brick and polished black stone with a huge curved roof and stone clad towers, Embankment Place is arguably one of London's finest examples of Postmodernist architecture – witty, neo-eclectic and in absolute contrast to the bland concrete blocks of previous decades. *Area Map p.6, B:2*

Opposite page: Hungerford Bridge, linking the South Bank of the Thames with the West End via Embankment Place. Two footbridges either side of a 19th-century railway bridge, each has a slender concrete deck attached by cable stays to a series of inclined steel pylons. Designed by Lifschutz Davidson 2003

The Channel 4 Headquarters
Richard Rogers Partnership, 1991-94

124 Horseferry Road, SW1 • Nearest transport St James's Park LU, Victoria LU & Rail • No public access • Full wheelchair access

The Horseferry Road is not an area noted for its innovative architecture and yet, amid a number of bleak buildings stands, bold and brave, Richard Rogers' Channel 4 Headquarters and transmission centre. This was the architect's first work after the success of Lloyd's of London. The building project is a mixed-use site with only half the complex being used by Channel 4, the other half, that is the south and east sides, being residential units.

The five-storey office wings extend back at right angles with a glass tower at their centre containing the stairs and external glass-box lifts. The large, rather strange looking objects on the lift-tower are not some avant-garde piece of art but the transmission antennae.

The walls of the building are in the main of glass and grey steel with a surprising use of ochre-red at intervals and apparently the same colour as the Golden Gate Bridge in San Francisco. Those passing by can see the curved glass and steel entry atrium without too much difficulty. *Area Map p.6, B:1*

The British Library
Sir Colin St John Wilson, 1978-97

96 Euston Road, NW1 • Tel 020 7412 7332 • www.bl.uk • Nearest transport Euston LU & Rail and King's Cross/St Pancras LU & Rai • Wheelchair access available • See website for opening hours, details of tours, exhibitions and public lectures

Originally part of the British Museum, the space given over to the British Library in Smirke's building was totally inadequate by the 20th century. The commission to design a new library was first awarded to Sir Leslie Martin, architect of the Royal Festival Hall, in 1962. It took ten years to find a plot of suitable size and a further twenty to construct the library, by which time Wilson, Martin's pupil and eventual associate had inherited the project. The delays and hiccups were mostly financial. In 1978 Wilson's plans were to provide storage for 25 million books and seating for 3,440 readers but by 1988 funding for the project was dramatically slashed. As a result what actually is provided is space for 1,176 readers and storage for 12 million books.

Of course, one problem with such a protracted project is that tastes change. During the decades of implementation and what looked fresh on paper in the late 1970's now resembles an out-of-town shopping centre with its red bricks and pitched roof, chosen initially to blend with its neighbour Gilbert Scott's Midland Grand Hotel. Even the brave attempt at a city piazza in front of the library somehow fails to entice the unsuspecting passer-by and it is not a universally loved building.

However the fact that the exterior leaves a lot to be desired is a shame for it detracts from the interior space which is worth seeing by the casual visitor and is a joy to use for the readers who pass through the building every day. It is perhaps the finest public space created in the 20th century, with tall, square pillars faced with white Travertine marble and the floor paved with Portland and Purbeck stone. The foyer displays some fine modern works by British artists such as R B Kitaj's tapestry inspired by T S Eliot's *The Waste Land*. The exhibition galleries are comfortable to use and have such gems on display as a copy of the Magna Carta and the lyrics of a Beatles song written on the back of an envelope.

There is a pleasing use of light from clerestory windows incorporated wherever possible throughout the building and the reading rooms are calm, light spaces with well-crafted furniture of American white oak. Books are stored and retrieved, via motorised rollers and paternosters, from the four-storey basement. However, a large section of stock is still held off-site because of the already inadequate facilities at the library and the reading rooms are often at capacity. *Area Map p.2-3, B:2*

British Library

Shri Swaminarayan Mandir
Chandrakant B Sompura/Triad Architects Planners, 1995

105-115 Brentfield Road, NW10 • Tel 020 8965 2651 • www.mandir.org • Nearest transport Neasden LU, Wembley Park LU then PR2 bus • Please telephone for wheelchair access information) Visitors are welcome, see website for opening times, services & events

Neasden, in north London, is not the most attractive area in town and yet, turning the corner on Brentfield Road, you will be forgiven for believing your eyes are deceiving you as you behold the most important and spectacular Hindu temple outside of India. The Mandir (the Sandskrit word for temple) has seven white pinnacles and seven white domes, standing out above the neighbouring red brick Victorian terraces.

In the Hindu faith the Mandir is not just a religious building but a part of god manifest on earth. Consequently no man-made materials are allowed in its construction, so the conventional ingredients of a modern building – steel, glass, aluminium, concrete cannot be used. Only natural materials are permitted. Certain types of sandstone were ruled-out because of the English weather conditions and the onslaught of the pollution from the London traffic. The solution was found in 2,828 tonnes of cream-coloured Bulgarian limestone for the outside of the Mandir and 2,000 tonnes of white Carrara marble for the interior – the same type of marble Michaelangelo used for his sculptures.

The stone was shipped to India where 1,500 sculptors worked for two years creating their masterpiece in accordance with the ancient shilpashaastras – a treatise on ancient temple architecture. Their labour was given voluntarily.

All this work was shipped to England and assembled like a massive jigsaw puzzle within three years and at a cost of £12 million; surely one of the new wonders of the western world.

Sadler's Wells Theatre
Arts Team @ RHWL with Nicholas Hare Architects, 1998

Roseberry Avenue, EC1R 4TN • Tel 020 7863 8198 • www.sadlers-wells.com • Nearest transport Angel LU • Wheelchair access • See website for opening times and tickets

This is the sixth theatre on the site. The last was built in 1931 and was fondly remembered but not easy to use with cramped facilities. However with a Grade II listing most people assumed that little could be done, but when pressed English Heritage confirmed that Sadler's Wells was listed for its historical significance rather than its architectural merit and therefore what we have now is an almost brand new theatre.

Technical and operational facilities were given a badly needed update and an 85 foot fly-tower was built and stands proud – in both senses of the word – above the rest of the theatre. The bar, ticketing and WC facilities are all excellent, as is the provision for wheelchair users. The auditorium has one of the best dance stages anywhere and one only has to note the amount of world-class companies who include Sadler's Wells on their performance itineraries since refurbishment for evidence of its success.

Importantly the whole foyer area, now feeling like one single space from the ground floor almost to the roof with its exciting use of light and sheer glass front wall, makes the theatre feel accessible to those who might otherwise find a visit to such a temple of culture rather daunting. The whole project cost £30 million, funded from the National Lottery. *Area Map p.2-3, C:1*

Tate Modern

Tate Modern
Giles Gilbert Scott, 1947-1963 / Herzog and de Meuron, 2000

Bankside, SE1 • Tel 020 7887 8888 • www.tate.org.uk • Nearest transport Southwark LU • Admission free (apart from major exhibitions) • See website for opening times, exhibitions, events and wheelchair access

As one of London's most visited art galleries, the Tate Modern building itself is perhaps as much a draw as the exhibits it contains. This magnificent landmark on the south side of the Thames started life as the Bankside Power Station when post-war London required more energy than it was then producing.

Architect Giles Gilbert Scott, grandson of George, won the commission in 1947 amid great controversy as Londoners were appalled at the thought of something as utilitarian as a power station being constructed directly across the river to the iconic St Paul's Cathedral. Indeed Lord Lewellin made an impassioned plea in the House of Lords against the project stating 'However good the architect, ...it will be rather like introducing an alligator into the water-lily pond in one's garden.'

Nonetheless building went ahead and the oil-fired power station was constructed, but not completed until 1963. The construction is of brick-cladding over a steel frame with a centrally placed chimney which was limited to a height of 325ft (99m), just shorter than the dome of St Paul's, thus complying with the architectural etiquette of London.

The rapidly rising cost of oil rendered Bankside uneconomical and was closed in 1981, its future under threat until 1994 when Nicholas Serota, the far-sighted director of the Tate Gallery, chose this building to display its collection of international modern art. The competition to oversee the £134 million scheme, (much of the funding came from National Lottery money), was won by the Swiss architects Jacques Herzog and Pierre de Meuron, who, whilst leaving the visible exterior, including the chimney, almost untouched, fashioned the interior into galleries from the iron industrial architecture. The turbine hall, measuring 550ft (155m) long, 75ft (23 m) wide and 115ft (35m) high, provides a perfect space for hosting large-scale temporary exhibitions. Herzog and de Meuron won the prestigious Pritzker Architecture Prize for this project.

Tate Modern opened in May 2000 and during its first decade an estimated 45 million visitors have been awed by this fabulous building. There are several places to refuel within, see 'Eat and Drink Architecture' page 332, and there is a large bookshop with an extensive range of books on art and architecture.
Area Map p.8, A:1

The Great Court, The British Museum
Robert Smirke, 1823-47 / Foster and Partners, 2000

British Museum, Great Russell Street, WC1 • Tel 020 7636 1555 • www.britishmuseum.
org • Nearest transport Holborn, Russell Square or Tottenham Court Road LU • See
website for opening times and details of special exhibitions

When the British Library moved to its new premises in St Pancras in 1998, the Round Reading Room and its surrounding space was taken into use by the British Museum. Before the Reading Room had been built by Sidney Smirke in 1855, the area had been an open courtyard, albeit not one that had been held in affection, having been called a 'miserable-looking space'. Norman Foster and his team have given the courtyard back to the public in spectacular fashion.

The Round Reading Room forms the core of the space, retaining its original function but now serving as a public reference library, whilst a staircase wraps around its exterior giving access to the restaurant (some of whose tables have fabulous views into Smirke's Reading Room) and to the upper galleries via a short walkway.

The whole Great Court area, the largest covered public space in Europe, is covered by a lightweight roof with 3312 glass panels – each one a different size. The roof structure rests on the perimeter walls and slender columns hidden beneath the skin of the Reading Room. The area feels somehow lighter than out of doors with the only slight irritation being the noise-level. However, even that cannot spoil the overall effect, especially when one can look up and see clouds scudding across the London sky or when the sun shines through the glass and casts shadows on the creamy marble beneath.

Judging by the crowds of people who now use this piazza this is one of the most successful and universally popular architectural and engineering feats of the modern age.

The Great Court has a bookshop, a gift shop, lecture theatres and WCs as well as two cafés and improved access to galleries on the ground floor. *Area Map p.2-3, B:2*

Great Court, British Museum

The Wallace Collection
Joshua Brown et al, 1776-1807 / Rick Mather Architects, 2000

Hertford House, Manchester Square, W1 • Tel 020 7563 9500 • www.wallacecollection.org • Nearest transport Bond Street LU • Admission free • See website for opening times, details of tours and exhibitions

The Wallace Collection is home to one of London's best preserved art collections. It used to be possibly one of the city's best kept secrets – no matter when one visited it was never crowded and yet it all felt a bit stuffy and overbearing.

Rick Mather's work at the Collection, in celebration of its Centenary, has magically opened up the heart of this Georgian house, allowing in light and space to brighten the whole experience of this unique place.

Expansion beyond the walls of the museum was logistically impossible so the architect opened up former basement levels as galleries, spaces for storage, lecture theatre and education centre.

The use of glass for the sides of staircases and roofing works well with the fabric of the original building. The central courtyard has also received a glass roof and is now home to a splendid café, an oasis of calm in the West End. Among the treasures on display are works by Rembrandt, Joshua Reynolds, Romney, Gainsborough, Van Dyck, Titian, Poussin and Frans Hals. *Area Map p.4, B:1*

Royal Opera House
E M Barry, 1858 / Dixon & Jones Building Design Partnership, 2000

Covent Garden, WC2E 9DD • Tel 020 7304 4000 • www.roh.org.uk/org • Nearest transport Covent Garden LU • Wheelchair access • See website for opening times, productions, tours and tickets

By the closing years of the 20th century, the facilities at E M Barry's 1858 Opera House had become inadequate for both audience and performers alike. Refurbishment of this Grade I listed theatre and an increase in the general arts space to advance the Opera House as both a national and internationally renowned facility was seen as vital. Public access was also an issue and the powers that be at the Royal Opera House wanted to exorcise the myth that their building was only for the elite. The whole scheme also needed to take into consideration the replacement of the long-lost façades of Inigo Jones's Covent Garden piazza (at the rear) and to this end the architects created a stripped-down classical reinterpretation, rather than a mere replica, of what had been there before.

The focus of this notion of public access was the restoration of the 1860 Floral Hall, using a clever combination of clear glass and mirrors to cultivate a feeling of light and space which was to be enjoyed by ticket-holders and casual visitor alike. The need for a major service entrance on Bow Street meant that the Floral Hall had to be elevated above its original position and however stunning this new space undoubtedly is, trying to access it is not for the unadventurous, which has been the main criticism of this particular project.

Nonetheless the rest of the Royal Opera House has benefited greatly from the £140 million spent. The Grade I listed auditorium has better acoustics and sightlines; the backstage technology, scenery storage, workroom and dressing room space has been improved and the addition of a much needed 400-seat Studio Theatre used for rehearsals, chamber concerts and educational projects has been a resounding success. *Area Map p.6, B:3*

City Hall
Foster and Partners, 1998-2002

The Queen's Walk, SE1 2AA • Tel 020 7983 4000 • www.london.gov.uk/gla • Nearest transport London Bridge LU & Rail • City Hall is open to the public • See the website for opening times, events and exhibitions

This building is part of the 67 acre development in the area to the west of Tower Bridge on the south bank of the Thames, known as More London. The City Hall provides four acres of space on ten levels to house the offices of the Mayor of London, 500 staff members and the assembly chamber for the 25 elected members of the London Assembly.

The curiously shaped glass building is entered either at the ground level or, better still, through a large, slightly sunken amphitheatre, paved with rather nice blue limestone and the focus of outdoor events. The amphitheatre entrance leads the visitor into a public café and on to an elliptical exhibition space where a dramatic, yet gently rising, ramp takes visitors up through the building affording fantastic views of London out of the windows; or should we say walls? Visitors can see into the assembly chamber, which is also open to the public, and which provides 250 seats for visitors and members of the press.

Beyond the assembly chamber level the ramp curls on past the Mayor's Office to the public space at the top of the building. This area is known as 'London's Living Room' and has an external terrace encircling the whole of City Hall.

The form of the building is derived from a geometrically modified sphere which provides the greatest volume with the least surface area, thereby minimising heat loss and thus saving energy. The building leans back towards the south where the floor plates step inwards to provide natural shading for the offices beneath. Energy saving schemes are employed throughout the building. Typical is the cooling system which uses cold ground water pumped from the water table and passed through beams in the ceilings, reducing, by approximately one quarter, the annual energy consumption. City Hall was the first building completed in the 'More London' complex – please see 'South Bank Walk'. *Area Map p.8, C:1*

City Hall

Swiss Re Headquarters

Swiss Re Headquarters
Foster and Partners, 1997-2004

St Mary Axe, EC3 • Nearest transport Liverpool Street LU & Rail • Private offices, no public access

When the architecturally noted Baltic Exchange in the heart of the City was damaged beyond repair by an IRA bomb in 1992, those with an interest in such matters waited with bated breath to see what would replace it. What Norman Foster and his team have produced exceeds expectation for amid the rectangular and pointed City skyline emerged this rounded bullet-shaped building.

The 41 storey, 10-acre construction has been described as 'London's first ecological tall building'. Part of the low-energy environmental strategy is the provision of air conditioning whereby stale air is drawn into green garden spaces integrated into the workplace and re-oxygenated by the dense planting, and inspired by Buckminster Fuller's theory of the 'Climatroffice'. Mechanical air conditioning is only used in a 'back-up' role and, joy of joys, the windows can be opened! The building's services, lifts and stairs are concentrated in a central core leaving the rest of the floor space free of intrusions. The top two levels accommodate bars and restaurants, with the rest of the building being used for offices.

Opinion is mixed on this building's appearance – it is called the 'gherkin' by some, even worse names by others. However in an age of computer-aided design, architecture does not have to conform to what went before. More importantly, there are sound ecological reasons for curves (see City Hall page 236). Such thought has been put into this structure, including the painstaking aerodynamic modelling of the tower so as to avoid down draughts, thereby ensuring those using the piazza outside are not buffeted by the wind. Tapering at the top into the crown reduces wind resistance further.

The building has 24,000 square metres of glass cladding, but interestingly, for a rounded construction, there is only one curved piece of glass and that is at the very top.

This building was the winner of the 2005 RIBA Stirling Prize. *Area Map p.8, C:2*

Graduate Centre, London Metropolitan University

Graduate Centre, London Metropolitan University
Daniel Libeskind, 2004

London Metropolitan University, 166-220 Holloway Road, N7 8DB • Nearest Transport Holloway Road LU • No public access to the interior but lookout for open days

The three dramatically intersecting blocks clad in embossed coloured stainless steel that make up this Graduate Centre for the London Metropolitan University, look as though they have been dropped into place, rather than constructed, on this rather drab part of north London.

The architect of the Centre, Daniel Libeskind, has used his considerable, imaginative talent on iconic buildings such as the Imperial War Museum North, Manchester and the Jewish Museum in Berlin. He had designed an extension to the Victoria and Albert Museum, the 'Spiral', which one commentator described as 'the Guggenheim in Bilbao turned on its side and then beaten senseless with a hammer'. Wonderful as it sounds, it was rather too much for the powers-that-be and the project was sadly shelved in 2005.

The Graduate Centre gives us a tantalising glimpse of his work here in London. The steel panels on the outside of the building form a shining, ever-changing surface and indeed nothing seems to stand still – doors and windows are irregular as are corridors and staircases.

Young Vic Theatre
Bill Howell, 1970 / Haworth Tomkins, 2006

66 The Cut, SE1 • Tel 020 7922 2922 • www.youngvic.org • Nearest Transport Southwark LU, Waterloo LU & Rail • See website for opening times, productions and tickets

The first theatre, designed in the early 1970's by Bill Howell, cost a mere £60,000. Costs were kept low by such means as ingeniously turning an abandoned Victorian shop into the foyer, but this was always seen very much as a rather haphazard, temporary home, albeit one that lasted thirty-plus years. The brief to update facilities for the 21st century was to double the footprint, add height to the auditorium, thus greatly improving its technical specification, and two studio theatres. The exterior is clad in steel mesh, customised concrete blocks and glass and the whole looks very much at home in its urban setting.

This building is in complete contrast with its blousey, Edwardian cousins in the West End and yet both types are loved and respected by those who frequent them.

The Young Vic was founded by Sir Lawrence Oliver in 1970 for the younger members of his newly formed National Theatre Company. Fledgling directors, designers, actors, writers and technicians gathered to present the great works of world repertoire, alongside new plays, in a relatively informal environment at the lowest possible seat prices. It has become the country's leading home for younger theatre artists, especially directors.

Shortlisted for the RIBA Stirling Prize, RIBA London Building of the Year 2007

Above: Steel mesh exterior illuminated at night

Wembley Stadium
Foster and Partners with HOK S+V+E, 2007

Wembley National Stadium, Wembley, HA9 0WS • Tel 0844 980 8001 • www.wembleystadium.com • Nearest Transport Wembley Park LU • See website for information of tours and events

Built on the site of the original 1923 Wembley Stadium which was constructed for the British Empire Exhibition of the following year with the purpose to 'stimulate trade, strengthen bonds that bind mother Country to her Sister States and Daughters', and became synonymous with football and sell-out rock concerts. The Stadium was closed in 2000 and demolished three years later, when work began on its much-needed modern replacement.

The new Stadium covers almost twice the area of the old, is nearly four times its height and has increased spectator capacity to 90,000 seated in one 'bowl' rather than four separate stands. A new feature is the partly retractable roof which keeps the spectator dry in the event of rain or snow, but does not cover the pitch. The 11-acre roof, weighing some 6,000 tonnes is mostly supported by a giant arch, thereby eliminating the need for pillars inside the stadium and ensuring all spectators have a clear view of events.

The 133 metre tall arch is just as much an iconic feature as the twin towers of the old building, perhaps more so as the new landmark can be seen from all over the capital, especially at night when it is illuminated. Constructed from British-made steel it is 315 metres in length and the longest single roof structure in the world. Facts and figures abound regarding this structure, such as the London Eye could fit between the top of the arch and the pitch, but perhaps it suffices to say that it is a truly amazing construction.

Regular tours of the Stadium are available, which includes the opportunity to hold aloft the FA Cup, albeit only a replica.

City of London
Information Centre
Make Architects, 2007

St Paul's Churchyard, EC4M 8BX • www.
visitthecity.co.uk • Nearest Transport St
Paul's and Mansion House LU • Open daily

Reminiscent of a paper-aeroplane, this
dynamic, contemporary little building is
situated to the south-west of the South
Transept of St Paul's Cathedral and only a few
steps from the Millennium Bridge which is the
pedestrian link from the City to Tate Modern.

The folded metallic envelope is constructed as
a steel frame braced by a structural ply skin
and clad in 220 pre-finished stainless steel
panels; the subtly reflected surfaces of which
contrast superbly with the pale stone of St
Paul's. The interior, lined with a tessellation of
174 vivid yellow panels formed from 'Trespa',
a recycled timber product, is bathed in natural
light from the full-height glazed frontage and
the triangular rooflights.

Constructed off-site in two sections, this
building was craned into place during the
night and finished-off within a couple of days.
The rainwater that falls on the roof is collected
to irrigate nearby planting and to flush the
building's toilets. *Area Map p.8, A:2*

*Right: City of London Information Centre with
St Paul's Cathedral in the background*

245

Maggie's Centre
Rogers Stirk Harbour and Partners, 2008

Charing Cross Hospital, Fulham Palace Road, W6 8RF • Tel 020 7386 1750 • www.maggiescentres.org • Nearest Transport Baron's Court LU

The new Centre, the first to be built in England, is open to anyone affected by cancer in the capital. Built at the front of Charing Cross Hospital, it is an oasis of calm where people with cancer, their family and friends can access the support they need free of charge.

The Centre is named for the founder of the movement, Maggie Keswick Jencks, writer and designer who collaborated with her husband, architect Charles Jencks, on a number of projects. When Maggie was diagnosed with cancer in 1993 she decided to spend her time creating a place where people would be helped not just to cope with the disease but to fight it – as she did. The first Centre was opened in Edinburgh in 1996, with two more built in Scotland, designed by internationally renowned architects, Frank Gehry and Zaha Hadid, and many others are in the planning stage around the country.

Very much in the spirit of their founder, the organisation strives to create spaces that are non-institutional and domestic in scale, but which are also unique. Architects are asked to design buildings where people feel safe and valued and also to create an atmosphere that stimulates their imagination. Richard Rogers has risen to the challenge of an awkward plot facing a busy road and has designed an uplifting building consisting of a double-height kitchen, three sitting rooms, as well as other smaller spaces for more private conversations, and a courtyard garden. Light floods into this little cheerful-looking orange-red building from the glazed walls at the first floor level and roof lights.

Richard Rogers and his team won the ultimate accolade of being awarded the prestigious RIBA Stirling Prize for 2009.

Saatchi Gallery (Formerly the Duke of York's Headquarters)
John Saunders, 1800 / Allford Hall Monaghan Morris, 2008

Duke of York's HQ, King's Road, SW3 4SQ
• www.saatchi-gallery.co.uk • Nearest Transport Sloane Square LU • Admission free • See website for opening times

Built originally circa 1800 as the Royal Military Asylum by John Saunders, it later became a Drill Hall for the Territorial Army and now houses the Saatchi Gallery. The interior was stripped back to its bare stock-brick walls, a small rear extension was added and fifteen separate, but interconnecting galleries were formed with stark white walls; the perfect backdrop for displays of contemporary art. The entrance to the building is through the portico with its four Doric columns. The work was undertaken by architects Allford Hall Monaghan Morris.

Cremorne Riverside Centre
Sarah Wigglesworth Architects, 2008

Cremorne Gardens, Lots Road, SW10 0QH
• No public access, but the interesting exterior is easily viewed

The centre consists of two rusting Cor-Ten steel-clad boxes, united by a grille-work platform that leads to the river. The buildings which are designed to be demountable in case of flooding, sit perfectly between leisure gardens and post-industrial wasteland.

The building, which replaces an old Portakabin, provides new accommodation for a canoeing facility near Battersea Bridge, with a brief to provide a facility that would accommodate classes of up to 30 children and young people, including those with disabilities.

The walls are insulated with wool from Cumbria, heating is through a ground source pump, made easier by the high water table and a roof planted with grass which provides a habitat for spiders and insects.

At a cost of £580,000, the project was funded by the Big Lottery Fund with match funding from the Royal Borough of Kensington & Chelsea.

This modest, but exciting building project was shortlisted for a RIBA and Prime Minister's 'Better Pubic Building' Award.

Darwin Centre at the Natural History Museum
C F Moller Architects, 2008

Cromwell Road, SW7 5BD • Tel 020 7942 5000 • www.nhm.ac.uk • Nearest Transport
South Kensington LU • Admission free • See website for opening times

The Danish architectural practice of C F
Moller has produced an outstanding solution
to the vexed question of how much admired
landmark buildings of an earlier age can
be sympathetically developed for the 21st
century. The Darwin Centre, named after
the evolutionary theorist Charles Darwin, is
the most significant addition to the Natural
History Museum since it opened in South
Kensington in 1881. The £78 million extension
to Waterhouse's highly decorative Victorian
building (see p.159) takes the form of a 65
metre (210 foot) tall, curved shell of dazzling
white reinforced concrete, resembling a
cocoon and sitting within a massive glass and
steel atrium.

However, this cocoon is no architectural
gimmick – the exposed thermal mass of the
30cm thick, continuous reinforced concrete
shell maintains a stable internal environment,
and minimises energy loading. This regulates
the temperature and humidity thereby reducing
the risk of pest infestations and ensuring that
the collection of 17 million insect and 3 million
plant specimens are protected and preserved.
Take the lift up eight floors to the top of the
cocoon and then follow the sloping spiral path
down, past the exhibits and the workspaces
for the museum's scientific staff.

Darwin Centre, National History Museum

Palestra
Will Alsop Architects, 2009

197 Blackfriars Road, SE1 8AA • See the
London Development Agency website
www.lda.gov.uk for more information

'If you built it, they will come'. In 2000 Will
Alsop's Peckham Library not only won the RIBA
Stirling Prize, it also made a neglected part of the
Borough of Southwark rather funky. There is little
doubt that Palestra is doing the same for this
part of the Borough – this is the sort of building
that stops you in your tracks to say 'wow'!

Built as a speculative office block it actually
serves just two tenants and one of those is the
London Development Agency. On the ground
floor of the building there is an Alsop favourite
– a pod, which the LDA use for exhibitions,
receptions and a place where passers-by can
pop in and pick up information on their work.
Next to the pod is the reception to the building,
sleek and bright with colourful decoration
looking like giant 'Smarties'.

Reminiscent of a Minorcan prehistoric taula
on stilts, the tilted lower part is clad in a
structurally bonded double glazed curtain
walling system, with each panel having a
colour printed full height across one-third the
width of the glazing, giving a patchwork effect.
A highly original piece of architecture.
Area Map p.8, A:1

Left: Palestra, winner of 2007 RIBA National Award

The Shard
Renzo Piano, begun 2009

The Shard, London Bridge Place, SE1 • www.shardlondonbridge.com • Nearest Transport London Bridge LU & Rail

It is perhaps a brave man who continues to design tall buildings post 9/11, particularly one that breaks through the 1000ft barrier, to become nearly twice the height of SwissRe, and, for the time being, what will be the tallest building in Western Europe. However Renzo Piano's designs have always been brave, and beautiful to boot, being responsible for the masterplanning of the rebuilding of Potsdamer Platz in Berlin, designing, with Richard Rogers, the acclaimed Pompidou Centre in Paris and the colourful Central St Giles building off Oxford Street in London.

From the outset, this building has been marked for 'mixed use' containing offices, for, among others, Transport for London, a hotel, housing, a health club and pool on the 52nd floor along with galleries, restaurant, bars and at the very top a viewing gallery open to the public, which it is hoped will become a major tourist attraction.

The Shard, generous at the bottom and narrow at the top, is undoubtedly one of the most exciting buildings to grace London. Built with a sophisticated use of glazing, expressive facades of angled panes reflecting light and the changing patterns of the sky, the form of the building will change according to the weather and seasons. Questions have been raised as to the wisdom of using so much glass but a ventilated double skin façade will considerably reduce heat gain and increase comfort close to the facade. Excess heat from the offices will be used to heat the hotel and apartments and any additional excess heat will be dissipated naturally through a 16-storey radiator at the top of the tower. Winter gardens with operable windows will be located on each floor allowing the occupants to connect with the outside world.

The building is designed to maintain its stability under the most onerous conditions. Its early conceptual designs were among the first in the UK to be realised following the publication of the US National Institute of Standards and Technology report into the World Trade Centre collapse, which has resulted in the global re-evaluation of the design of tall structures.

In addition to the Shard are the long-awaited major improvements to London Bridge station and the surrounding area. *Area Map p.8, B:1*

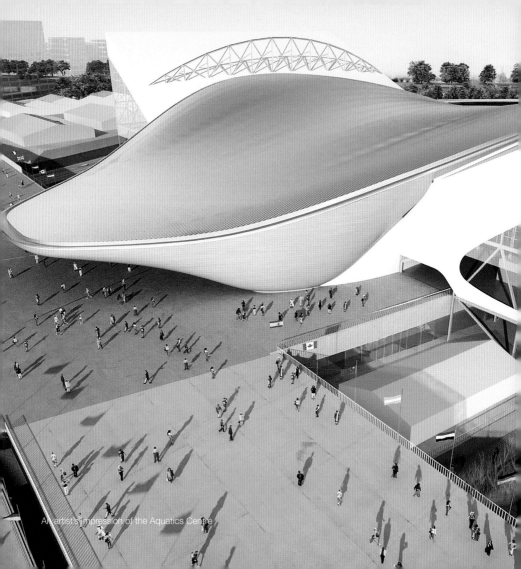

An artist's impression of the Aquatics Centre

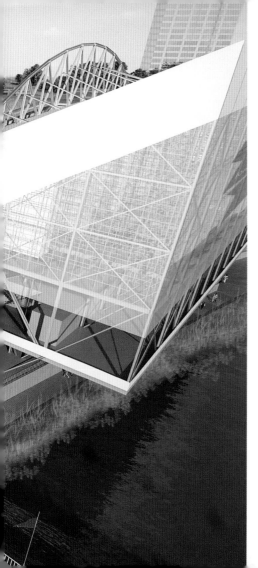

Aquatics Centre, Olympic Park
Zaha Hadid Architects, 2010+

Aquatics Centre, Olympic Park, Stratford, London E15 • Tel 020 3 2012 000 • www.london2012.com • See the website for transport details

Of all the buildings that make up the 2012 Olympic Park, Zaha Hadid's Aquatic Centre has been hailed as the 'Gateway to the Games'. The roof of this iconic building is wave-shaped, the frame of which was made from steel trusses fabricated in Newport from plate rolled in Gateshead, Motherwell and Scunthorpe and rests on just three concrete supports. The construction of this 160m long 2,800 tonne spectacular aluminium-covered roof is thought to be one of most complex projects in the Olympic Park. The ceiling is made of timber-cladding that sweeps outside to cover the northern roof-supports.

During the games the Aquatics Centre will offer a capacity of 17,500 seats for the main competition pool and diving, and 5,000 seats for the water polo venue. After the games, 2,500 temporary seats will be removed and a 'leisure water' facility added turning the Centre into a permanent fixture in the community with facilities that have, until now, been unavailable in London.

London has had to wait a long time to have a Zaha Hadid building of its own, so let us hope this will the first of many from this most exciting of architects.

Trafalgar Square, see p.321

08

WALKING LONDON'S ARCHITECTURE

Walking London's Architecure

Bartholomew Walk 256-265

Fleet Street and Beyond Walk 266-273

Greenwich Walk 274-283

John Nash Walk 284-297

South Bank Walk 298-311

Strand Walk 312-319

Whitehall Walk 320-331

Bartholomew Walk

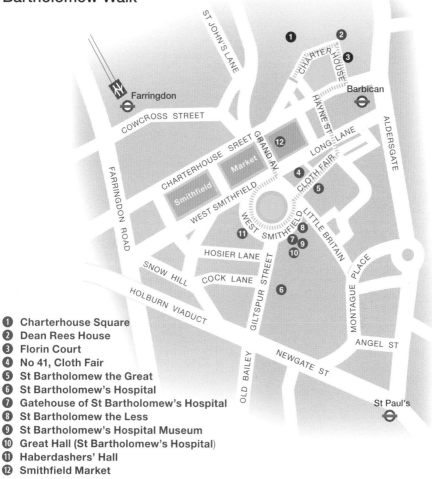

1. **Charterhouse Square**
2. **Dean Rees House**
3. **Florin Court**
4. **No 41, Cloth Fair**
5. **St Bartholomew the Great**
6. **St Bartholomew's Hospital**
7. **Gatehouse of St Bartholomew's Hospital**
8. **St Bartholomew the Less**
9. **St Bartholomew's Hospital Museum**
10. **Great Hall (St Bartholomew's Hospital)**
11. **Haberdashers' Hall**
12. **Smithfield Market**

loyal knight to King Edward III, having fought for his monarch against the Scots and the Flemish.

The purpose of the land purchase was to provide a burial ground for the many victims of the 'Black Death', the term given to a particularly vicious epidemic of bubonic plague that ravaged London and the rest of Europe during the 14th century. Thought to have reached London in September 1348 it had petered out by 1350, but in that short period between 50,000 and 100,000 Londoners, about half the population, suffered an agonising, but blessedly swift, death. Whole families were wiped out and commerce and manufacturing came to a halt when entire workforces perished. In one month alone in 1349 the Abbot of Westminster died along with 27 monks.

De Manny's act of piety did not end there for in 1370 he founded the Charterhouse, a Carthusian priory. Building work began in the following year by Henry Yevele (c1330-1400) who was considered to be the most gifted master mason of his day. Yevele had worked extensively for the King, especially at Westminster Abbey and he was also charged with the design of royal tombs, such as that for John of Gaunt who died in 1399. Work on the priory was finished in about 1414.

Life was hard for the brothers in the priory, living and eating alone except for Sundays and feast days, and where speaking to one another was only allowed after the Sunday

A fairly short walk, in terms of distance, but one which takes in the variety London has always offered. Choose any area in the capital and the curious will find all sorts of half-hidden nuggets of history and architectural gems. There are many places to take refreshment in this area, particularly around Smithfield, as well as the charming café-bar in the C15th cloister of St Bartholomew the Great.

We start this walk in the corner of ❶ **Charterhouse Square** by the entrance gates to St Bartholomew's and Royal London School of Medicine and Dentistry. Where you are standing was once part of the 13 acres purchased in 1348 by Sir Walter de Manny, a meal when they were also allowed a walk outside the priory grounds.

The priory closed at the dissolution of the monasteries in the 1540s and the land was given to Lord North, who demolished the church and much else in order to build himself a fine mansion house. This was bought in the early 17th century by Thomas Sutton who used the premises as a school for 44 poor boys and as a 'hospital' for 80 elderly poor gentlemen. This formed the basis of the famous Charterhouse School, which enjoyed a chequered history until its move to larger premises in Surrey in 1872. Famous pupils of the school include John Wesley, Robert Baden Powell (founder of the Boy Scout movement) and the writer William Thackeray.

For a short while the premises were used by the Merchant Taylors' School, which soon found larger accommodation in Hertfordshire. The site became the Medical College of St Bartholomew's in 1933, but suffered extensive bomb damage during World War II. It is not possible to visit the remains of the priory on a casual basis, but tours are organised between April and August. For information please telephone 020 7251 5002 – but be warned these tours get filled very quickly and must be booked in advance.

As you are standing by the gates of the School of Medicine, the last house in the square closest to you is the ❷ **Dean Rees House**, which dates from 1894; it is quite an ornate building for its size and has French overtones. The house was actually built for the Headmaster of the Merchant Taylors' School, an institute funded by the lively and prosperous livery company of the City of London of the same name.

Walk along the east side of Charterhouse Square, and at numbers 6-9 you will find a block of flats named ❸ **Florin Court**. This lovely, curved building, recessed at the centre, opened in 1936 and was designed by Guy Morgan. The residents of this handsome ten-storey block enjoy a roof garden with wonderful views and there is a swimming pool in the basement. The architectural historian Nikolaus Pevsner described Florin Court as being 'poised between modernism and Art Deco'. Fans of Agatha Christie's 'Poirot' television series, starring David Suchet, will recognise this building as being the home of the dandified detective.

Moving on, cross Charterhouse Street, bear right and take the narrow Hayne Street, cross Long Lane, and take the narrow alleyway next to the 'Red Cow' public house. This brings us to **Cloth Fair**.

Building first took place on this land when it passed from nearby Bartholomew's Priory to Lord Rich at the dissolution of the monasteries. Although the Priory was not completely closed, much of its property was confiscated. Until the mid 20th century, houses were packed on both sides of this fairly narrow street, giving a flavour of how much of London looked at the time of

5 *St Bartholomew the Great*

the Great Fire. Take a look at the red brick, four storey **4** **No 41**, which is a private residence, an almost unique example of a 17th-century City merchant's house. The house is hard to date precisely and it could be as early as 1614 when the first land lease was released although the building conforms to post Great Fire regulations. Nos 39-40 date from about 1830.

The curious name of the street is derived from the cloth merchants who settled here and because of the area's association with the Bartholomew Fair; an annual three day affair which always started on the feast day of St Bartholomew, 24th August. Begun in 1133 this fair was an important source of income for the Priory of St Bartholomew, whose canny founder Rahere had instigated the Fair as a way of making money for his hospital. A Royal Charter authorising the Fair had been granted by Henry I to Rehere, whom, it is believed, was at one time minstrel to the King.

The Fair soon became a cloth specialists' market, where merchants from all over England and the Continent would flock to sell and buy their wares. During the 17th century wrangling arose over who was to receive the largest portion of the Fair's revenue and the Fair was threatened with closure. Nonetheless diversions – fire-eaters, magicians, tight-rope walkers – abounded here for a good many years more until 1855 when public disorder, probably related to the vast quantity of drink consumed, was blamed for its eventual closure. Ben Jonson's play 'Bartholomew's

Fair' is an apparently accurate vignette. This street was also the birthplace of the architect Inigo Jones, his father being a cloth merchant.

After exiting Cloth Fair at West Smithfield bear left where you will shortly arrive at the Tudor gatehouse of the church of ❺ **St Bartholomew the Great** (see p.34 for more details).

On leaving St Bartholomew the Great, walk through the gatehouse again and along West Smithfield, past the entrance to Little Britain and along the perimeter wall of ❻ **St Bartholomew's Hospital**. Often as not there are bunches of flowers left on the ground under the plaque on the wall commemorating the 300 or so Protestants burned at the stake near this spot between 1553 and 1558, during the reign of Queen Mary; a deed which earned her the nickname of 'Bloody Mary'.

The name 'Smithfield' is probably a corruption of 'smooth field', meaning flat land. Jousting tournaments took place here as did public executions until about 1400 when they were moved to Tyburn.

Now we move onto the ❼ **Gatehouse of St Bartholomew's Hospital**. This nice little building dates from about 1700 and has a bust of Henry VIII in a niche at the centre of the pediment. The carved figures representing Lameness and Disease are contemporary with the building.

Walking past the gatehouse into the Hospital grounds on your left is the church of ❽ **St Bartholomew the Less**. Some of the church dates from the 15th century, namely the south tower and the vestry but the rest dates from 1823-25 and is by Thomas Hardwick to a plan by George Dance the Younger. This is a lovely little octagonal, brick-built church with small windows placed high up to give a dramatic light effect. Although the church is now parochial, rather than exclusively for the Hospital, the link can be seen in its early 20th-century stained glass window, depicting a nurse and which was the gift of the Worshipful Company of Glaziers.

This building suffered severe bomb damage during World War II but was sympathetically restored by Lord Mottistone of Seely and Paget, who was responsible for much of the post-war restoration work in the City. The church is open every day from 7am to approximately 8pm.

When you have finished at the church make your way to the 'North Block' where sign posts will direct you to ❾ **St Bartholomew's Hospital Museum**. This small museum has a collection of surgical instruments and illustrates the fascinating history of the Hospital and the changing roles of the staff. Make your way through the museum to the door that leads to the ❿ **Great Hall**.

This building was designed by James Gibbs (1682-1754), also responsible for St Martin-in-the-Fields and St Mary-le-Strand, in about 1730. Gibbs gave his services to the Hospital for free. Security will not permit you going very far into the Hall, but far enough to allow a look at the wonderful murals painted on the walls of the staircase by William Hogarth in 1735-37. The paintings represent Christ at the Pool of Bethesda and The Good Samaritan. The figures are larger than life size and the artist is said to have used hospital patients for his models. Hogarth did this work without charge, perhaps as an act of pure charity for he had been born nearby and his sister and mother still lived there. He may also have seen the gesture as an opportunity to show that British artists could paint as well as the Italians whose work was being brought home as souvenirs by the wealthy from their Grand Tours. Indeed it is rumoured that an Italian artist had been offered the commission at the Hospital, for which a large fee would have to have been paid, when Hogarth stepped in. To get a better look at the whole work join one of the Friday tours (2pm at Henry VIII Gate).

Many historic events are associated with the hospital, which is not surprising given its location. One of the most famous was in 1381 when Wat Tyler, leader of the Peasants' Revolt, was brought to St Bartholomew's Hospital having been stabbed in the back by the Lord Mayor of London, William Walmouth, as Tyler went to speak peaceably to the King. However before he could be treated he was dragged outside and beheaded by the King's men.

After visiting the museum you may like to walk through to the Court, also designed by James Gibbs as are the buildings to the left and right. The impetus to build separate ward blocks was justified by Gibbs as a precaution against fire, but the elimination of the risk of cross-infection may have been a factor.

Go out of the Hospital grounds and to your left follow West Smithfield, crossing Giltspur Street and Hosier Lane. Still in West Smithfield, at number 18 is ⓫ **Haberdashers' Hall**.

The Worshipful Company of Haberdashers is one of the 108 City Livery Companies. These City Companies are in many ways like clubs. Their members are called freemen or liverymen and officers are elected to a committee or court chaired by the Master, usually for one year. Livery companies date back to the middle ages, when they were founded to promote and protect the crafts which their members practiced. The livery companies probably had their origins in this country before the Norman Conquest of 1066 and are similar to the fraternities and guilds (or mysteries) that flourished throughout Europe for many centuries. The term 'mystery' is still in use and derives from the Latin 'misterium' meaning 'professional skill'.

Livery was the term used for the clothing, food and drink provided for the officers and retainers of great households, such as those of bishops, barons, colleges or guilds. The term then became restricted to mean just the distinctive clothing and badges which were

the symbols of privilege and protection. Since the members of each guild were distinguished from one another in this way, the guilds gradually became known as livery companies. It is still their custom to wear ceremonial dress on official occasions.

The earliest record of livery activity is a Royal Charter granted to the Weavers' Company in 1155. Members paid to belong and the word 'guild' is derived from the Saxon 'gildan' meaning 'to pay'. These guilds controlled services and the manufacture and selling of goods and food within the City of London. This prevented unlimited competition and helped to keep wages and working conditions steady. Customers, employers and employees were protected by checks for inferior work that did not meet the guild's standards. Fines and other penalties could be severe – including expulsion, which meant the loss of livelihood. Disputes were settled by arbitration at the guild's hall, which also served as a meeting place for their particular trade. Many street names within the City of London have trade-derived names, such as Bread Street, Milk Street, Ironmonger Lane and, of course, Cloth Fair. Many of the trades and crafts have now diminished in importance and the modern livery company concentrates its energies on charitable and educational activities.

The first Haberdashers' Hall was built in 1458-61 in Maiden Lane, later re-named Staining Lane, in the City and was destroyed in the Great Fire. The second Hall was built

1667 on the same spot but was destroyed during enemy bombing in World War II and the last was built 1954-56 as part of an office complex. In April 2002 the Company moved to its new bespoke premises here in West Smithfield. Her Majesty the Queen attended the opening ceremony.

The West Smithfield façade of the new building is made up of shops and residential units with offices to the rear. The Livery Hall, associated offices and meeting rooms are arranged on two floors around a central courtyard. The Livery Hall, where the official business takes place, has a high vaulted ceiling and oak panelled walls. Designed by the eminent architect Michael Hopkins, it has modern stained glass and bespoke furniture by David Linley (the son of the late Princess Margaret). This is a lovely, light, modern, yet classic building. Tours of this building are rare, only four per year at the moment (tel 020 7246 9988 for further details).

Walking on, past the interestingly named Bishop's Finger pub, cross the road and head for Grand Avenue, which dissects **⑫ Smithfield Market**. A cattle market was formally established on this site in 1638, and during the early 18th-century tales of unruly cattle and even more unruly herdsmen abounded. The beasts were herded into conditions that were totally inadequate and were slaughtered in the market with blood and waste running into the nearby Fleet River. Some of the streets about the market bear witness to this market, such as Cowcross Street.

Sir Horace Jones (1819-87), City architect, was charged with designing a building that would be suitable as the chief meat market for London. The site was enlarged to about ten acres to accommodate Jones's huge building, 631 feet in length and 246 feet wide. Nikolaus Pevsner, said of the building that 'it is of an uncertain style', but without any architectural precedent, finding a suitable 'style' must have been a nightmare for Jones.

Jones used red brick with Portland stone decorations and cast iron – lots of it. As you stand in the Grand Avenue note the cast-iron railings, gates and decorations. Also of note is the rather touching war memorial. In 2005 the market underwent a £70 million renovation in which all the paintwork has been restored to its original colours, these are unexpectedly vibrant deep blue, red and green with a lavish sprinkling of gold stars. Sir Horace Jones went on to design Leadenhall Market, parts of the Guildhall and Tower Bridge.

In order to see Smithfield Meat Market in full working mode one has to get up very early as the trading 'day' finishes by 8am. Some pubs in the area have a 6am licence, the only place in London where this is so. Obviously it must be thirsty work.

When the market is at rest, the many cafés, bars and restaurants in the area come alive, and a lovely view of the illuminated dome of St Paul's can be enjoyed from many of the establishments.

More Information:

St Bartholomew the Great
6 Kinghorn Street,
West Smithfield, EC1A 7HW
Tel: 020 7606 5171
www.greatstbarts.com
Transport: Barbican LU,
Farringdon LU, St Paul's LU

Cloister Café
St Bartholomew the Great,
6 Kinghorn Street,
West Smithfield, EC1A 7HW
www.greatstbarts.com
Transport: Barbican LU,
Farringdon LU, St Paul's LU
Open daily

St Bartholomew the Less
Smithfield Gate,
West Smithfield, EC1A 7BE
Tel: 020 7601 8066
www.stbartstheless.org.uk
Transport: Barbican LU,
Farringdon LU, St Paul's LU

St Bartholomew's Hospital Museum
West Smithfield, EC1
Tel: 020 3465 5798
Transport: Barbican LU,
Farringdon LU, St Paul's LU

Fleet Street & Beyond Walk

1. St Bride Church
2. Reuters building
3. St Bride Printing Library
4. Daily Express building
5. Daily Telegraph building, (now Peterborough Court)
6. The Cheshire Cheese (public house)
7. Dr Johnson's House
8. Whitefriars Monastery
9. Hoare's Bank
10. St Dunstan in the West
11. Prince Henry's Room
12. Temple Church
13. Inner Temple
14. Middle Temple
15. Middle Temple Hall
16. Temple bar

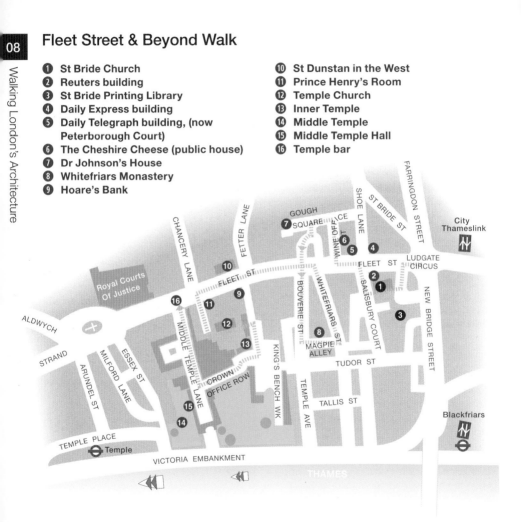

We start our walk at the Ludgate Circus end of Fleet Street. The street is named after the River Fleet which once flowed down what is now Farringdon Street and New Bridge Street and on into the Thames. What is left of the river today trickles through pipes under the road.

Our first stop is Sir Christopher Wren's beautiful church of **① St Bride** – note the magnificent steeple (see p.69 for more information). As you leave St Bride and rejoin Fleet Street note the building to your left, the **② Reuters Building** (85 Fleet Street). This is the former Headquarters of Reuters and The Press Association and was designed by Sir Edwin Lutyens in 1935. One may be forgiven for thinking the three-storey 'pavilion' was an afterthought, but it was very much part of Lutyens' plan. The building is no longer occupied by Reuters, whose departure from the area in 2005 marked the end of the newspaper publishing era in Fleet Street. Since the time of Wynkyn de Worde, about 1500, the street and the surrounding alleyways have had an association with the printed word. During its early days the Crown and the Church viewed the printed word with suspicion and strict censorship prevailed and an unsuspecting printer could find himself in prison.

If you are particularly interested in the printed word there is a superb little library, **③ St Bride Printing Library** tucked away behind St Bride church. This is a good source of books and periodicals relating to the history and techniques of printing (for details see p.273).

The first London newspaper, the Daily Courant, was published on 11 March 1702 and others followed such as The Morning Chronicle and The Diary, all published in Fleet Street. Until recently Fleet Street, and the surrounding area, was primarily concerned with the publication of daily national and provincial newspapers. Even now people of a certain age refer to the press as 'Fleet Street', long after the newspapers had decamped to more convenient premises in Canary Wharf.

However, the departing newspaper industry has left behind a couple of fabulous buildings, the first of which you will see now. Having crossed Fleet Street opposite the Reuters Building you should now be on the corner of

Shoe Lane, in front of you will be the gleaming, unmistakable rounded form of the former ❹ **Daily Express Building**. Designed by Sir Owen Williams and built 1930-33, this was the first curtain walled building in London, with distinctive banding in glass and black Vitrolite set in chromium strips. The printing of the newspaper took place in the basement and at the rear of the building (this part was demolished in 1990). As it is now a private office there is no public access, but by pressing your nose against the reception door you will be able to see into the fabulous Reception Hall; note the ceiling and the concealed lighting arrangement – pure Art Deco. The building is usually part of the 'Open House' scheme (see p.377 for more details).

Just a few paces on is the former ❺ **Daily Telegraph Building**, (now Peterborough Court) built 1928-31 by Elcock and Sutcliffe. This massive stone building with six vast columns from the third storey and stepped-back roofline exudes confidence and self-importance, but must have felt old-fashioned within just a couple of years of the opening of the Daily Express building. The huge projecting Art Deco clock is something of a landmark. This building is now a private office and there is no public access.

Now we can take a diversion from Fleet Street. Stay on this, the north side of the road and you will soon find yourself at a narrow alley way called Wine Office Court and, on entering, you will see to your right ❻ **The Cheshire**

Cheese public house. Parts of this building date back to 1667, the original pub having perished in the Great Fire of 1666. This very atmospheric building still has its 18th-century room arrangement intact, so there are lots of cosy corners to hide in. This was the haunt of Dr Johnson and his circle, which in turn made it a focus of pilgrimage for writers such as Mark Twain and Charles Dickens.

Further on along Wine Office Court and to the left is Gough Square. One of the first things you will see is a small statue of a cat called 'Hodge', the companion of Dr Samuel Johnson who lived in the Square for a number of years. His house, number 17, is his only surviving home and is particularly significant in that it was here, in the attic, that he wrote his Dictionary of the English Language. **❼ Dr Johnson's House** is open to the public and a visit is a most worthwhile experience and gives a good flavour of 18th-century life (see p.127 for details).

Make your way back to Fleet Street and cross to the south side into Bouverie Street and then left into Magpie Alley; this will bring you to the rear of the offices of the prestigious City law firm Freshfields. Have a look over the railings into the glass-clad basement where you will see the preserved remains of a tiny fraction of **❽ Whitefriars Monastery**. The Whitefriars were so called because they wore a white mantle over a brown habit, but were really Carmelites, named for Mount Carmel where their mother church was located. A priory had

been built for them in this area in the mid 13th century. On the dissolution of the monasteries all the buildings were confiscated, the hall being made into a playhouse.

Back to Fleet Street, turn left and walk on until you arrive at number 37, **❾ Hoare's Bank**. One of the last remaining private banks in London, it has been in business for over 400 years and is therefore older than the Bank of England. Hoare's has occupied this building since 1830. The bank took the then unusual decision to trade from a bespoke building rather than a converted house, as was the custom. However this building has accommodation to enable a Director of the bank to be always in residence.

The building is made from Bath stone with a wrought-iron balcony, a 1930s addition. The Banking Hall has a circular bronze stove at the centre and polished wood counters.

Just a few yards along Fleet Street, on the opposite side (north) of the road is the church of **❿ St Dunstan in the West**. Not surprisingly there is another St Dunstan in the City, to the east. The foundation of St Dunstan in the West can be traced back to the 13th century but this present building dates from 1830-33. The plan of the church is a Gothic octagon, unusual for such a late building. The number of interesting external features go some way to compensate for very restricted public access opportunities. To the right of the church, as you are viewing it, is a statue of

Elizabeth I, dating from 1586. As she died in 1603, this statue was made in her lifetime and the question arises whether it is an accurate likeness? It was made to stand at Ludgate (demolished in 1760) as were the statues of King Lud and his sons, which are inside the church. The Northcliffe monument on the exterior of the church commemorates the life of Alfred Harmsworth, 1st Viscount Northcliffe, the journalist and newspaper magnate. He started his career by editing his school magazine and went on to found such publications as Comic Cuts (1890), the Daily Mail (1896) and the Daily Mirror (1903). The huge clock dates from 1671 with two figures, sporting gold loincloths, who strike the quarter-hours with their clubs; they could well be Gog and Magog, the giants of legend who roamed the City.

Proceed along the south side of Fleet Street, until you arrive at the alleyway named Inner Temple Gate. There you will find the building known as ⑪ **Prince Henry's Room**. One of the last remaining timber-framed houses in London, it dates back to at least 1610 and therefore survived the Great Fire of 1666 which ended its path of destruction only a few yards further down the road. The building also survived the threat of demolition in the late 19th century and the Blitz of 1940-41. The building contains interesting interior wooden panelling contemporary with the building and further 18th-century panelling and fireplace. There is also a very nice plaster ceiling decorated with motifs including the Prince of Wales's feathers. The building probably takes

its name from its time as a tavern rather than with any royal associations.

Walk down Inner Temple Lane and you will arrive at the west end of one of the most exquisite churches to be found anywhere. This is the ⑫ **Temple Church** (see p.52).

When you exit the Temple church, look around at the buildings in the immediate vicinity. These buildings make up the ⑬ **Inner Temple** and the ⑭ **Middle Temple**, which represent two of the four Inns of Court of London – the others being Gray's Inn (entrance in Gray's Inn Road, telephone 020 7458 7800 for information) and Lincoln's Inn (accessed from Lincoln's Inn Fields, telephone 020 7405 1393 for information).

The four Inns, or Honourable Societies of Barristers, each fulfil the same function but have different traditions, rather like collegiate universities. According to custom, which dates back many hundreds of years, any law student training to be a barrister in England must join one of the Inns of Court and dine there at least 24 times, as well as passing written exams, before becoming officially qualified.

The maze of courtyards and buildings that make up the Inner and Middle Temples seem like something from another era, especially in the evening when the area is still lit by gas light. With your back to the Temple Church make your way right towards ⑮ **Middle Temple Hall**. Built between 1562-73 this Hall saw the first performance of 'Twelfth Night' in February

15

1602 and it is thought its author, William Shakespeare, acted a small part in it. Of note is the magnificent hammerbeam ceiling and the 29 foot table, made from a single oak tree from Windsor forest and presented as a gift by Elizabeth I.

Follow Middle Temple Lane back out to Fleet Street and look for the ⑯ **Temple Bar** (see right) in the road. This marks the boundary between the City of London and London general. Until its removal in 1878, the old Temple Bar was a stone tri-arched affair thought to have been designed by Wren. It had to be taken down and something a little more modest put in its place to ease the flow of the ever-increasing traffic. It is now on display in Paternoster Square, next to St Paul's Cathedral. Since its placement in the 1670s the Temple Bar had seen a lot of activity, not least the custom of displaying the heads of executed traitors on it, the last being that of Francis Townley the Jacobite, in 1746.

The present Temple Bar is made of granite and coloured stone with statues of Queen Victoria and the future Edward VII, topped by a fierce looking griffin rampant. Sir Horace Jones, City architect, who was also responsible for Leadenhall Market, Smithfield and Tower Bridge and other projects, designed the Bar in 1880.

This is where the City and this particular walk ends. If you are feeling energetic you could carry on with the Strand walk which, quite conveniently, starts right here (see p.312).

More Information:

St Bride Printing Library
*St Bride's Institute,
Bride Lane, EC4
Tel: 020 7353 460
www.stbride.org.
Transport: Blackfriars
or Aldwych LU*

Dr Johnson's House
*17 Gough Square, EC4
Tel: 020 7353 3745
www.drjohnsonshouse.org
Transport: Chancery Lane,
Aldwych or Blackfriars LU*

St Dunstan in the West
*Bride Lane, EC4
Tel: 020 7405 1929
www.stdunstansinthewest.org
Transport: Blackfriars or
Aldwych LU
Admission free*

Prince Henry's Room
*17 Fleet Street, EC4
Tel: 020 7953 4522
www.cityoflondon.gov.uk
Transport: Temple or
Aldwych LU
Admission free*

Temple Church
*Temple, EC4Y 7BB
Tel: 020 7353 3470
www.templechurch.com
Transport: Temple or Aldwych LU*

Inner Temple
*Middle Temple Lane, EC4
Tel: 020 7797 8250
www.innertemple.org.uk
Transport: Temple or Aldwych LU*

Middle Temple
*Middle Temple Lane, EC4
Tel: 020 7427 4800
www.middletemple.org.uk
Transport: Temple or Aldwych LU*

16 *Temple Bar*

GOING·TO·S.ᵗ PAULS FEBRUARY·27·1872

Greenwich Walk

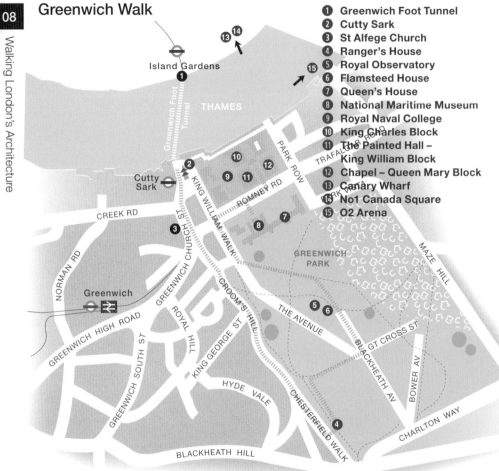

1. Greenwich Foot Tunnel
2. Cutty Sark
3. St Alfege Church
4. Ranger's House
5. Royal Observatory
6. Flamsteed House
7. Queen's House
8. National Maritime Museum
9. Royal Naval College
10. King Charles Block
11. The Painted Hall – King William Block
12. Chapel – Queen Mary Block
13. Canary Wharf
14. No1 Canada Square
15. O2 Arena

As much as you will enjoy this part of London there is no need to kiss the ground as Johnson and his friend James Boswell did! Arrive by Docklands Light Railway at the Cutty Sark station to start the journey or alight a stop earlier, at Island Gardens station and take the ❶ **Greenwich Foot Tunnel** and have the unique experience of walking under the Thames.

This tunnel is 1,217 feet in length and built exclusively for pedestrians. Opened in 1902 the tunnel replaced the ferry which had been in operation since the mid 17th century and allowed workers from south London to walk to work in West India and Millwall Docks.

With an internal diameter of only 11 feet this is not an experience for those who suffer with claustrophobia. At each end of the tunnel there are circular shafts with domed glass roofs that house stairs and lifts (for more details see p.283)

On arrival at Greenwich a small diversion can be made by take a look at the ❷ **Cutty Sark**, the world's only surviving tea clipper from the 19th century. She was launched in 1869 and won the prestigious clippers' Shanghai to London race in 1871 making the voyage in only 107 days. Her last voyage was in 1938 and she has been here in dry dock since 1957 but was badly damaged by fire in May 2007. The Cutty Sark Trust has undertaken extensive repairs in order to save and restore the ship.

The first building we are going to look at is ❸ **St Alfege Church** at the junction of Church Street and Greenwich High Road. This splendid Georgian church is named after the Archbishop of Canterbury who was murdered near this spot by Danish invaders in 1012 and stands in replacement of a much earlier church in which the future King Henry VIII was baptised in 1491.

Designed by Nicholas Hawksmoor and built between 1712-18 after its predecessor had collapsed in a storm, this was the first church to be built under the Fifty New Churches Act of 1711, funded from a coal tax. Hawksmoor's church is rectangular with a flat ceiling and the east façade, which faces Greenwich High

Road, has a shallow apse and behind which rises the main portico with four Doric pilasters at the sides and two massive columns in the middle supporting a pediment surmounted by three huge urns. The south and north sides carry giant pilasters and on the west end sits the tower. Designed in the manner of James Gibbs, the tower and steeple were in fact added by John James in 1730.

The interior of the church suffered extensive damage in the Second World War, restoration of which was carried out by the eminent, if somewhat eccentric, architect Sir Albert Richardson, who faithfully reproduced Hawksmoor's work. The beautifully coffered ceiling at the apse and other decoration are in fact trompe l'oeil paintings.

Famous people associated with this church include General James Wolfe, who defeated the French at Quebec and was buried here in 1759 and General Charles Gordon, hero of Khartoum, who was baptised here in 1833. Thomas Tallis, the 16th-century composer was buried in the previous church on the site where he had been the organist. He is commemorated in a south aisle window. The church is open to the public at varying times, see p.283 for details.

On leaving the church head for Stockwell Street, which forms a three-way junction with Greenwich High Road and Church Street. Walk the length of Stockwell Street which becomes Croom's Hill and at the end of which

take the left-hand fork to arrive at Chesterfield Walk. Half way along Chesterfield Walk is ❹ **Ranger's House**. This is one of three houses built in the 1680s by Andrew Snape, the King's Sergeant Farrier, as a speculative venture. One of the houses was demolished in 1815 but the other remaining house of this trio is Macartney House which you would have passed at the start of Chesterfield Walk and which had additions in 1802 by Sir John Soane. It was converted into flats in 1925.

Ranger's House has been the subject of additions over the years to form a very substantial domestic dwelling, one of its owners being Philip, 4th Earl of Chesterfield (1694-1773). The house is seven bays wide of red brick with a stone centre frontispiece, in which sits the main doorway flanked by Ionic columns with a Venetian window above. The wings of the house are in yellow brick and the south wing had a gallery added in 1750. The house has recently been refurbished by English Heritage and is now home to the Wernher Collection, an eclectic collection of more than 700 works of art purchased by mining magnate Sir Julius Wernher 1850-1912 (for more information see p.283).

When you have finished at Ranger's House make your way across into Greenwich Park and head for the ❺ **Royal Observatory** with its distinctive dome. Greenwich Park itself consists of 163 acres set on a hill between Blackheath and the River Thames. King Henry VI enclosed the park in 1433, with its perimeter wall built during the reign of James I. The land is still owned by the Crown. Directly across from Ranger's House and situated in the top of the park in the far corner is a 13 acre enclosure known as 'The Wilderness' in which deer roam – having first been introduced to the park in 1515 for the purpose of hunting.

The name Greenwich is derived from the Anglo-Saxon 'green port' and Saxon remains have been found in the area. From the top of the hill one can take in the splendid views across the Thames towards the skyscrapers of Canary Wharf. If the weather is pleasant you may wish to wander in the park or just sit by the pond, a popular haven for wildfowl. You may also be lucky enough to be serenaded by music from the decorative cast-iron bandstand that dates from 1880. The park is open to pedestrians every day from 6am to dusk, with traffic permitted from 7am to dusk.

King Charles II founded the Royal Observatory at the instigation of the influential Royal Society. The original part of the building dates from 1675 and was designed by Christopher Wren and Robert Hooke, both of whom were active members of the Royal Society. ❻ **Flamsteed House**, as the more 'domestic' part of the Observatory is known, is named after the first Astronomer Royal John Flamsteed who lived and worked here. This was the first purpose-built scientific research establishment in Britain.

Built from red brick with some nice exterior detailing that Wren called 'a little for pompe',

Flamsteed House has one of the best-kept Wren interiors, the splendid Octagon Room and apartments. Flamsteed lived in the four rooms of the ground floor, and worked in the Octagon room above until his death in 1719. The house now contains displays telling the story of time and astronomy. The 28-inch Refracting Telescope in the onion-shaped dome is the largest in Britain and is still used for occasional night viewing. The whole project cost the Crown only £500, but there appears to have been a little 'scratching around' for materials and, splendid as the building is, it does not compare with Perrault's very grand Observatoire in Paris, which Greenwich was trying to emulate.

In 1948 it was decided that the lights of London were too bright and were interfering with accurate readings so the astronomers moved to darkest Sussex and today the Astronomer Royal is based in Cambridge.

The Greenwich Meridian, Longitude 0, an imaginary line joining the north and south Poles, passes through the dead centre of a specialised telescope installed at the Observatory in 1851. A line in the ground marks the position of the meridian. It is a famous feature in the courtyard and it is from where all time zones around the world are measured since international agreement in 1884. This is your opportunity to stand with one foot in each hemisphere of the East and West – everyone does it!

Above Wren's Octagon Room, on one of the two turrets is a ball on a rod. This Time Ball has been dropped at 1pm every day since 1833 so that passing sailors could set their clocks by it (for more details see p.283).

From the Observatory, walk on down the hill towards Inigo Jones's splendid ❼ **Queen's House** (see p.44). Flanking the Queen's House, attached by colonnades are the long rooms, added during the 19th century and now forming the ❽ **National Maritime Museum**.

The National Maritime Museum was formally established by Act of Parliament in 1934 and was opened to the public in 1937. The museum has displays of boats, real as well as models, and the largest collection of marine art in the world. There is also a permanent exhibition entitled 'Maritime London' that uses prints and video installations to present the history of the capital's shipping industry.

At the heart of the museum is Neptune Court a glass-roofed former open courtyard which had previously lain unused but which now houses large display items. It is claimed that this is Europe's largest free-span glazed roof and it is certainly impressive. Rick Mather, an exciting British architect, masterminded this project between 1996-99 together with a general overhaul of the museum and its facilities, which was funded by the National Lottery (for more details see p.283).

After leaving the museum we can now walk down to the buildings of the ❾ **Royal Naval College**, crossing the busy Romney Road directly in front of the Queen's House. Enter the gates immediately in front and you will have arrived at the group of four buildings known as the former Royal Naval College. The College moved from Portsmouth to occupy these buildings in 1873. Its four main blocks were built from 1696 to 1751 to the plan of Sir Christopher Wren and were used from 1704 to 1869 as the Royal Hospital for Seamen.

Greenwich Hospital, as it was universally known, was the naval equivalent of the Royal Hospital Chelsea (see p.91) – a home for needy veterans of the service. The idea was originally mooted by King James II, himself a naval officer at one time, and was developed by his daughter Queen Mary who founded the Hospital by Royal Charter in October 1694.

The group of buildings stand on the site of the demolished Tudor palace of Placentia and is set around a Grand Square with a 115 foot wide vista towards the Queen's House.

King Charles II had wanted to live at Greenwich and the eastern half of the ❿ **King Charles Block**, the building nearest to the river towards Greenwich pier, is the only part of his planned 'King's House' to be realised. It was built in 1664-69 to the design of John Webb, pupil and son in law of Inigo Jones. Economic factors prevented further building and eventually the money ran out.

When Queen Mary rededicated the unfinished palace as a hospital Sir Christopher Wren was asked to devise a plan that would accommodate her wish to preserve the King's and Queen's Houses. This he did in his usual brilliant manner in what has been called 'the most stately procession of buildings possess' and after 1703 he was assisted in his work here by a series of outstanding architects including Sir John Vanbrugh and Nicholas Hawksmoor. Colen Campbell and James 'Athenian' Stuart also worked here.

After 125 years of residence in these splendid buildings the Royal Navy vacated the site in 1998 and they now house the University of Greenwich. There are two areas of the College open to the public and both are a treat to visit.

⓫ **The Painted Hall** completed to Wren's design in 1707 was decorated by Sir James Thornhill between 1708 and 1727. For 19 years he worked for a flat rate of pay, £3 per square yard of ceiling, £1 per square yard of wall. His subject matter ranged from the triumph of the reign of William and Mary, who are portrayed surrounded by the four cardinal virtues, to portraits of the great and good such as John Flamsteed, the first Astronomer Royal.

The other area available to visit is the ⓬ **Chapel in the Queen Mary block**, which is diagonally across the courtyard to the King Charles block. The original chapel interior was burnt out in 1779 and the present one is the work of James Stuart. The domed tower sits over the chapel entrance and a run of double

⑨ *Royal Naval College*

pillars is reminiscent of Perrault's colonnades at the Louvre in Paris. Light floods into the building from the three tiers of windows on the east wall.

The Thames Path, the 180 mile National footpath passes in front of these buildings. The path runs from the Thames Flood Barrier at Woolwich, just over four miles from here, to Kemble in Gloucestershire.

Standing on the Path, with your back to Wrens buildings you can gaze across the river to the wonders of **⑬ Canary Wharf.** During the 1980s financial boom Canary Wharf was conceived as a major new location to complete the golden triangle of world-class financial centres along with New York and Tokyo. It was felt that the buildings of London's traditional financial centre, the City, would not be able to cope with the rush of new technology that was going to be needed to compete in the new age money market.

Canary Wharf, built in 1880, had been one of the largest and busiest docks in Europe, but just 100 years later it lay abandoned. The area then became the focus of the government's Urban Development Corporation and the marriage of business and property developers was blessed. Originally conceived by the American developer G Ware Travelstead in the early 1980s the whole area still retains a flavour of Chicago and New York from an architectural point of view. Indeed American architects dominated the whole project.

"On Thames's bank in silent thought we stood:
Where Greenwich smiles upon the silver flood..."
Samuel Johnson, 1763

The first building to be completed at Canary Wharf was ⓮ **No1 Canada Square** by Caesar Pelli (1926-), an Argentine-born American, who had been responsible for the huge skyscraper and plaza at the World Financial Centre in New York. This steel-clad building is a true landmark, and is readily identifiable looking east from many parts of London by the flashing red light on its pyramidal top. The light is not for decoration but because the Wharf is under the flight path of aeroplanes using the City Airport. Pelli's obelisk like building sets the tone of what was to follow: tall, slim and with framed windows rather than strip glass.

Transport links, once the subject of much frustration, have almost been solved by the services of the Docklands Light Railway and the Jubilee Line extension, with its fabulous Canary Wharf station by Norman Foster. A shopping mall, a plethora of bars and restaurants, summer open air concerts and an impressive display of public art go some way to providing a quality environment for those who work, live and visit the area. If you have time, visit the Museum of London Docklands housed in a 19th century warehouse at West India Quay (see opposite for more info).

Again, with your back to Wren's building, turn to your right and walk along a little and you will see Greenwich Peninsular and the structure which is now called the ⓯ **O2 Arena** but commissioned to mark the beginning of the new Millennium. The Millennium Dome was intended as a celebratory structure offering a vast, flexible space for exhibitions, displays and events to which over six million people came during the year 2000.

Designed by eminent architect Richard Rogers the structure is 365m in diameter, with a circumference of 1km and a maximum height of 50m it providing 100,000m² of enclosed space (2.2 million cubic metres). The Dome is suspended from a series of 12 100m steel masts, held in place by more than 70km of high-strength steel cable which in turn support the Teflon-coated glass fibre roof.

In 2002 the 'Dome' became the 'O2 Arena', a 20,000 seat venue with some 25 restaurants, bars and cafés, and an exhibition centre, which has succeeded in attracting top acts thereby ensuring it's reputation as the British equivalent of New York's Madison Square Gardens.

You could, of course, walk along the Thames Path to visit the O2 Arena, where you will pass one of the last reminders of the rivers industrial past. Rusting silos, abandoned ship's berths and redundant gas holders are all that is left of the docks where hundreds of men once laboured in incongruously named Primrose Wharf, Piper's Wharf, Orchard Wharf and others. No doubt this area too will succumb to the building of riverside apartments.

If you are travelling from here to Central London you may like to consider taking the Riverbus from Greenwich pier close to where you are standing. The views from the boat are wonderful.

More Information:

Greenwich Foot Tunnel
Greenwich Pier, SE10
Isle of Dogs, E14
Transport: Island Gardens or
Cutty Sark DLR
Public access: Open all day,
lifts in operation daily 7am-7pm

The Cutty Sark
Tel: 020 8858 3445 for
enquiries
www.cuttysark.org.uk

St Alfege Church
Greenwich Church St, SE10
Tel: 020 8853 0687
www.st-alfege.org
Transport: Cutty Sark DLR,
Greenwich & Maze Hill Rail

Royal Observatory
Greenwich Park, SE10
Tel: 020 8858 4422
www.nmm.ac.uk
Transport: Cutty Sark DLR,
Greenwich & Maze Hill Rail

Flamsteed House
Greenwich Park, SE10
Tel: 020 8858 4422
www.nmm.ac.uk
Transport: Cutty Sark DLR,
Greenwich & Maze Hill Rail

Queen's House
Tel: 020 8858 4422
www.nmm.ac.uk
Transport: Cutty Sark DLR,
Greenwich & Maze Hill Rail
Admission free

National Maritime Museum
Romney Road, SE10
Tel: 020 8858 4422
www.nmm.ac.uk
Transport: Cutty Sark DLR,
Greenwich & Maze Hill Rail
Admission free

Painted Hall & Chapel of the former Royal Naval College
King William Walk, SE10
Tel: 020 8858 2608
www.oldroyalnavalcollege.org
Transport: Cutty Sark DLR,
Greenwich & Maze Hill Rail
Admission free

Ranger's House
Chesterfield Walk, SE10
Tel: 020 8853 0035
www.english-heritage.org.uk
Wheelchair access

Canary Wharf
Isle of Dogs, E14
Nearest transport Canary
Wharf LU & DLR
For information about events
see www.mycanarywharf.com

Museum of London Docklands
West India Quay,
Canary Wharf, E14 4AL
Tel: 020 7001 9844
www.museumoflondon.org.uk

02 Arena
Peninsula Square,
SE10 0DX
www.theo2.co.uk
Tel: 0844 856 0202

John Nash and the Via Triumphalis –
from Regent's Park to Buckingham Palace

1. **Gloucester Lodge & Gloucester Gate**
2. **Cumberland Terrace**
3. **Chester Terrace**
4. **Chester Gate**
5. **London Central Mosque**
6. **Hanover Gate**
7. **Hanover Terrace**
8. **Sussex Place**

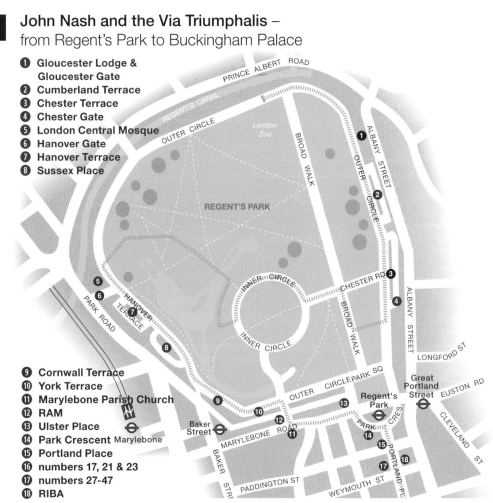

9. **Cornwall Terrace**
10. **York Terrace**
11. **Marylebone Parish Church**
12. **RAM**
13. **Ulster Place**
14. **Park Crescent**
15. **Portland Place**
16. **numbers 17, 21 & 23**
17. **numbers 27-47**
18. **RIBA**

19 Langham Hotel
20 BBC Broadcasting House
21 All Souls Church
22 Piccadilly Circus
23 Waterloo Place
24 The Institute of Directors building
25 Athenaeum
26 Carlton House Terrace
27 Duke of York's Column
28 Buckingham Palace
29 Buckingham Palace Ticket Office

2

This route takes you from the edge of Regent's Park down through the heart of the West End to the monarch's London residence, Buckingham Palace. The time taken to cover will depend very much on the temptations the walker gives into en route such as the Royal Institute of British Architects' bookshop, fashion stores, cafés and restaurants.

The 550 acres of Regent's Park at one time formed a small part of a huge forest and was the property of the Abbess of Barking until the dissolution of the monasteries in the 16th century when the land was appropriated by the Crown and used as a hunting ground; Elizabeth I entertained the Duke of Anjou here

in 1582. Following the execution of Charles I in 1649 the land was sold; only to be handed back to the Crown at the Restoration in 1660. Gradually most of the 16,000 trees were felled to make way for the farms that would flourish here for the next 200 or so years. This bucolic scene lasted until 1811 when the farm leases became due for renewal and it was seen that the land could be developed for prestigious housing, enhancing the area and adding to the royal coffers.

Architect John Nash (1752-1835), already a favourite of the Prince Regent, oversaw the whole project. However the grand scheme, the only one London has ever had, was not fully realised as money and effort were diverted into the enlargement of Buckingham Palace when the Regent became monarch in 1820.

Before Nash suggested a change of name to honour the Prince Regent, the area had been called Marylebone Park, that is 'place by St Mary's stream' ('bone' being a corruption of 'burna' meaning stream or water). At the top of the park, on the north edge, is the world famous Zoological Gardens (Regent's Park Zoo).

We start this walk at ❶ **Gloucester Lodge and Gloucester Gate** on the Outer Circle, our first encounter with the architecture of John Nash. The Lodge is a pleasingly symmetrical house with a large portico and fluted Ionic half columns. Gloucester Gate, the most northerly of Nash's 11 terraces, sports huge Ionic pilasters (these are the flat representations of a

Cumberland Terrace

Park Crescent

classical column usually placed against a wall). Both buildings date from 1827.

From the outset we can see that Nash was only building for the upper echelons of society, his scheme envisaged 'a boundary and complete separation between Streets and Squares occupied by the Nobility and Gentry, and the narrow Streets and meaner houses occupied by mechanics and the trading part of the community'

We now come to perhaps the grandest and the most flamboyant of all Nash's terraces, **②** **Cumberland Terrace**. Built 1826-27 it is 800 feet long, an essay in symmetry with the centre portion projecting forward and having ten great Ionic columns and an enormous pediment adorned with sculptured figures by J G Bubb. Indeed the central pediment was much noted at the time as being the second largest in England after that on St Paul's Cathedral. Cumberland Terrace looks every inch a palace rather than a set of apartments. If you only have time to look at one of Nash's buildings, this is probably the best example.

Further on is **③** **Chester Terrace**, again by Nash, dating from 1825. This building has the longest unbroken terrace of all, with 99 bays in a complicated but symmetrical system of division around a central section of seven bays and with a similar number of bays at each end (interspersed with the odd huge Corinthian column for decoration). Contemporary complaints were that Nash's workmanship was shoddy and rumours of rubble behind the stucco and other slapdash practices prevailed. Indeed this building was in such a bad state of repair that demolition was seriously contemplated after World War II. ❹ **Chester Gate** is the two storey building here, again by Nash and with Doric detailing.

We are now going to cross this lower portion of the park to view more Nash's terraces (*if you wish to miss these out make your way to* Park Crescent *(see map) which is fairly close by to continue the walk*).

From Chester Gate follow any of the footpaths to the Inner Circle and Queen Mary's Garden. Keeping to the south of the gardens look for sign posts to the Long Bridge where we cross the lake. Keeping the lake to your left we cross the Hanover Bridge and ahead you will see the unmistakable outline of the ❺ **London Central Mosque and Islamic Cultural Centre**. Designed by Sir Frederick Gibberd and Partners, 1972-78, this building is an exciting one, if only because it lends a certain exoticism to the Nash terraces with its gleaming copper dome and minaret. The main hall of the mosque is designed to accommodate 1,800 people (for more information see p.297).

In the shadow of the Mosque sits ❻ **Hanover Gate**, a small octagonal lodge house with a pitched roof and a sweet central chimney stack, forming a traffic island and marking the western entrance to the park. Designed by Nash 1822-23 it had additions made by Lutyens in 1909

Slightly further south is ❼ **Hanover Terrace**. Again by Nash and built 1822-23, the Terrace is 460 feet in length with four Doric columns at each end and six at the centre. The central pediment has a group of 13 white allegorical figures with a painted blue background reminiscent of a Wedgwood design.

Further south is ❽ **Sussex Place** and here Nash adds to a grand terrace of some 650 feet in length, steep-sided octagonal domes – which, Pevsner notes, are most 'unclassical'.

The next terrace we come to is ❾ **Cornwall Terrace**, the first, in fact, to be built in 1821. Although attributed to Nash and Decimus Burton, the design was probably more the latter's work.

After Cornwall Terrace we follow the Outer Circle round to ❿ **York Terrace**, designed by Nash and built 1824-26. It is a very long pair of terraces, providing a vista between them of Marylebone Parish Church, which had been built only a couple of years earlier. York Terrace has a Doric colonnade, giant Ionic columns at the ends and a central portico without any decorative sculpture.

Make your way down York Gate, towards ⓫ **Marylebone Parish Church**. The Church was built 1813-17 and designed by Thomas Hardwick on land donated by the Duke of Portland.

On the corner of York Gate and the busy Marylebone Road is the **12 Royal Academy of Music Museum**, known as the York Gate Collection, which is housed in a John Nash building. Visitors are welcome to view the rare musical instruments, original manuscripts, archives, images and other artefacts. It is also a wonderful opportunity to see the inside of the Grade I listed Nash building. The main RAM building dates from 1911 and was designed by Sir Ernest George Yates in brick with stone decorative trimmings. Within the courtyard between RAM and York Gate is a bold barrel-vaulted concert hall and recording studios inserted in 2001, and connecting to both buildings.

Making our way along Marylebone Road to the **13 Ulster Place** exit of Regent's Park, this terrace, named for George IV's younger brother, Frederick, Earl of Ulster and Duke of York, is an unusual Nash design in that it is devoid of columns and pilasters. However each of the two end bays has bay windows for emphasis.

Cross the Marylebone Road and we arrive at **14 Park Crescent** – Nash designed this to be a circus, which would have made it the largest in Europe, but only the southern half was realised. Nevertheless the crescent makes an impressive statement and it is probably more recognisably 'Nash' than any of the Outer Circle terraces. A single storey colonnade runs the length of each of these curving terraces which makes for simply elegant architecture. The generally pristine exterior decoration and

stucco work are the result of a total renovation in the early 1960's when many of the somewhat shabby houses were turned into offices.

Between the two terraces of Park Crescent is the start of **15 Portland Place**. Originally laid out by the Adam brothers in 1773 as a speculative building venture, the street was the widest in London at the time and the scheme was intended for grand, detached mansions. However the financial crises bought about by the American War of Independence resulted in houses of rather less ambition.

Nash did not need to make any changes to this arrangement as it suited his Via Triumphalis project beautifully. However within a relatively short time one of the finest Adam houses in London, Foley House, built in 1758, was demolished in 1864 to make way for the huge Langham Hotel and was the beginning of the end for little evidence now remains of Adam's work in Portland Place. However what has survived can be seen on the exteriors of **16 numbers 17, 21** (with Ionic pilasters and pediment), **number 23** and, best of all, **17 numbers 27-47** (the centre of which was unfortunately lost to World War II enemy bombing). **Number 48**, thought to have been designed solely by James Adam has an interesting double-door. Most of these buildings are now in commercial use rather than residential.

On the east side of Portland Place, at the corner with Weymouth Street, is the

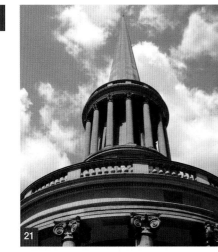

18 **Royal Institute of British Architects**, built 1932-34 by Grey Wornum. Designed in total sympathy with the Adam remains, it is no taller than any of the 18th-century houses yet it is instantly recognisable as a very modern piece of architecture. Made from Portland stone, everything about the outside of this building is crisply cut with square or rectangular windows and the huge bronze entrance doors flat roof and corner plot exaggerate this. There are also interesting bas-relief sculptures by Edward Bainbridge Copnall (1903-73); the figure above the main door is entitled 'Architectural Inspiration'.

At the end Portland Place, ahead of you, is the huge aforementioned 19 **Langham**

Hotel. Built in the 1860's by architects Giles and Murray, at a time when the railways and colonialism had brought greater mobility, the Langham was an outstanding example of the rash of hotels under construction at the time.

Across Portland Place, on the east side is 20 **BBC Broadcasting House**. This is one of those buildings which provokes strong feelings – people either love it or loathe it. Likened to a huge ship, the Tower of Babel and hated by the doyen of architectural writers Nicholas Pevsner, Broadcasting House was designed by G Val Myers and completed in 1931. The site is an extremely awkward one and the technical requirements of broadcasting made this an unenviable project. The superb sculptures on the exterior of the building are by Eric Gill; of particular note is 'Prospero and Ariel' placed above the main entrance. The demolition of some earlier extensions to make way for a new headquarters complex which, at 80,000 square metres (860,000 square feet), makes it one of the world's largest and most technically advanced broadcasting facilities. This new building wraps itself behind the heavy mass of Broadcasting House and provides an outdoor performance space close to All Souls Church. However, the saga of this scheme has been rather a bitter and protracted one with the original architect, Sir Richard MacCormac leaving the project at an early stage.

John Nash very cleverly placed the church of All Souls in Langham Place at a point were his Via Triumphalis needed to change direction at the top of Regent Street from Portland Place. He did this at the other end of Regent Street too, by gently taking one's gaze onto another vista. Nash, being the first architect to apply 'town-planning' on such a massive scale in London, is often compared with Haussmann, the man who re-organised so much of Paris in the late 1840's. Nash however was able to create his little tricks on the eye with twists and turns accommodating any awkwardness in the lay of the land, unlike Haussmann, who had to build in straight lines for purposes of security in post-Revolution Paris.

Nash designed **㉑ All Souls Church** in 1822-24 with a large, circular portico and pillars of the Ionic order with the roundness softening the corner into Langham Place. Atop the portico is a rather curious smaller version of itself from which rises a pointed spire. The inside is light and airy with galleries carried on Corinthian columns. The church is often used for services and concerts broadcast by the BBC. There are, additionally, occasional free lunchtime concerts (for more details see p.297). All Souls Church is the only Nash-building intact on this route, although it received extensive damage from enemy bombing during World War II.

Walking from Langham Place, down Regent's Street towards Oxford Circus, we come to the junction of two of the busiest shopping streets in the world – Oxford Street and Regent Street.

Oxford Circus has been subject to a two-year project, completed at the end of 2009 at a

Above: Bust of John Nash by Cecil Thomas in portico of All Souls Church. For more information on Nash see p.116.

cost of over £5 million, to relieve some of the serious traffic congestion in the area. A new pedestrian crossing modelled on the famously frantic junction adjoining Shibuya station in central Tokyo was installed and the jumble of street signs and railings have been swept away to make negotiating the area a much more pleasant experience.

Cross Oxford Circus and carry on walking down Regent Street.

Although we are still following the route of the Via Triumphalis, there is nothing left of Nash's much acclaimed sweeping architecture of Regent Street that had been completed by 1825. The buildings were similar to those we saw at Park Crescent and almost immediately became the focus of the London social scene for those of fashion. However in 1848 the distinctive colonnades were removed; it was rumoured they harboured prostitutes and other unsavoury characters and by the end of the century these premises were deemed too small for the purpose of retailing.

Regent Street now hosts many 'flagship' shops such as the Apple Store at number 235 (on your right, just after Oxford Circus).

We arrive now at ❷ **Piccadilly Circus**, formed when Nash needed to curve his Via Triumphalis into Piccadilly from Regent's Street. It is quite difficult to imagine – standing in the hubbub of people, traffic, and flashing advertisement hoardings – that this was once an elegant oasis of calm! Nash had placed a circle of stuccoed buildings here, not unlike Park Crescent. Unfortunately in the 1880s this arrangement was spoilt by the demolition of the north east quarter of the circle to accommodate the formation of Shaftesbury Avenue. By 1910 the trend for bright, electrically lit advertisements had been started by Bovril and Schweppes and a decade later even larger ones were in place and had become a successful tourist attraction.

The last stretch of Regent Street culminates in ❷ **Waterloo Place**, named after the then

recent battle against Napoleon. This is where Nash's Via Triumphalis was to terminate, at the entrance of Carlton House, the home of the Prince Regent. It was mooted that the most appropriate buildings for this area should be gentlemen's clubs and that their façades should be identical; however, this latter stipulation was unpopular and not enforced. For The United Services Club of 1826-28, on the east side of Waterloo Place, south of Pall Mall, now ❷ **The Institute of Directors building**, John Nash designed a masculine building with just more than a hint of Rome, with a broad two-storey portico consisting of double Doric columns at the lower level and Corinthian columns above.

However attractive this building is, it really does not compare with Decimus Burton's ❷ **Athenaeum**, also in Waterloo Place, on the west side, and also south of Pall Mall. Built in 1827-30 it is much more of a coherent whole with a very fine Doric frieze running on three sides, carved by John Henning junior. Above the entrance is a large gilt copy of the Pallas Athene of Velletri by E H Baily.

Heading straight on to Carlton House Terrace, we come to the beginning, or end, depending on which way the Prince was travelling, of Nash's 'Triumphant Route'. This street is named for the very large house that once stood on the spot, built originally in 1709, which then became the residence of Henry Boyle, the first Lord Carleton. Remodelled by Sir William Chambers, the house became the residence of the Prince of Wales, the future Prince Regent in 1772.

The Prince was noted for his extreme extravagance in all matters so it is perhaps no surprise that he engaged the eminent architect Henry Holland to turn Carlton House into a sort of 'Golden House of Nero'. The Prince also employed an army of French decorators and his painted rooms were the talk of the town, as was the debt he was running up a cool £640,000 by 1795. Even so, the Prince was unstoppable, adding a Gothic conservatory with cast iron fan vaults. The employment of the services of John Nash in 1813, initially to design a Gothic dining room for the Prince, was the beginning of a very long association and friendship.

By 1820 the Prince of Wales had become King George IV, and having no further use for Carlton House ordered its demolition.

㉖ Carlton House Terrace was designed by John Nash 1827-33 and the whole is pleasing on the eye – giving its best side perhaps to the view from St James's Park. The two long ranges, nine houses in each, are reminiscent of his work around Regent's Park and were the last of Nash's grand designs as he was to die not long after their completion in 1835. Although built as terraces each individual house is different and Nash was perfectly happy to allow other architects to embellish his basic work here. Numbers 7-9, until World War II, made up the German Embassy with

the interior having been remodelled by Albert Speer, Hitler's favourite architect. This is the only example of Speer's work in London (this building is not open to the public).

At number ten is the British Academy, an organisation that champions and supports the humanities and social sciences and the building is often open for small exhibitions. Next door is the Institute of Contemporary Arts (ICA); a dedicated space for new, experimental and independent arts practice and ideas. On site are two galleries, two cinemas, a theatre, a reading room, bookshop and a super café/bar.

The terraces form a rather good frame for the **㉗ Duke of York's Column** and the powerful granite flight of steps down to St James's Park. The Column is in honour of Prince Frederick Augustus, Duke of York and Albany (1763-1827), the second son of King George III and the Prince Regent's brother. The Column was erected 1831-34 and is loosely modelled on Trajan's Column in Rome. The drum and dome at the top are based on Hooke/Wren's Monument in the City. Designed by B D Wyatt the whole column stands at 137 feet tall, including the bronze statue of the Duke dressed in his Garter robes.

Although Nash's Via Triumphalis finished at the Duke of York's Column we can take in one more London gem, **㉘ Buckingham Palace**, a project in which John Nash became heavily involved. Go down the steps into The Mall, turn right and walk along to the Palace. There has been a house on the site since at least the mid 17th century, and it was John Sheffield, 1st Duke of Buckingham and Normanby who built his country house here in 1702-05 partly on land owned by himself and partly on Crown land. In 1762 George III purchased the house. The official residence of the monarch was St James's but the young King found the rambling and ramshackle apartments unsuitable for his new wife. Indeed the Royal couple, who had 15 children, were very content with Buckingham House. It was still, however, very much a house and not yet a palace.

It was on the succession of George IV that things changed dramatically. Against advice, he employed his trusted architect friend John Nash and between them they spent colossal amounts of money remodelling the building. Within three years, 1825-28, the exterior alterations had been completed.

When the King died suddenly in 1830, Nash was immediately sacked from his post. The thrifty, reliable architect Edward Blore was given the task of completing the work which was to take many years yet. Indeed George IV's successor, his brother William IV, died in 1837 without ever living at the Palace. The first reigning monarch to do so was Queen Victoria where she was said to have been 'most happy' and it has been the London residence of the royal family ever since.

The last major alteration to the building took place in 1913 when Sir Aston Webb added the east wing façade. This is the 'side' of the Palace which is most familiar, made from Portland stone in a neo-classic style but which has received much criticism, most usually because the façade is seen as 'predictable' and 'boring'.

During the summer months of August and September, when the royal family are on holiday elsewhere, the state rooms of the Palace are open to the public; a scheme that was started in the early 1990's to help raise funds to repair fire damage at Windsor Castle. Eighteen state rooms are usually available for viewing during the period of opening. Visitors enter through the Ambassador's Court and take the very grand staircase to the set of rooms created by Nash, which, despite all the past controversy, are the highlight of most people's visit.

㉙ The Ticket Office itself is a little gem designed by Michael Hopkins and Partners. The small timber cabin has a tensile fabric canopy which covers the whole structure and which is erected at the beginning of the tourist season and taken down at the end of it.

Cumberland Terrace

More Information:

**London Central Mosque
& Islamic Cultural Centre**
146 Park Road, NW8
Tel: 020 7724 3363
www.iccuk.org
Transport: Baker Street LU
See website for details
*Note: All visitors must remove
their shoes before entering
the building and women must
cover their heads*

**Royal Academy
of Music Museum**
Marylebone Road, NW1
Tel: 020 7873 7373
www.ram.ac.uk/museum

**Royal Institute of British
Architects (RIBA)**
66 Portland Place, W1
Tel: 020 7580 5533
www.architecture.com
*Transport: Regent's Park or
Great Portland Street LU*

All Souls Church
Langham Place, W1B 3DA
Tel: 020 7580 3522
www.allsouls.org
Transport: Oxford Circus LU

Buckingham Palace
The Mall, SW1A 1AA
*Tel: 020 7799 2331www.the-
royal-collection.org.uk*
Transport: St James's Park LU
*See website for opening times
& entrance charges*

South Bank Walk

- ① Tower Bridge
- ② City Hall
- ③ The Scoop
- ④ HMS Belfast
- ⑤ Hay's Wharf /Galleria
- ⑥ Cottons Centre
- ⑦ St Olaf House
- ⑧ No.1 London Bridge
- ⑨ London Bridge
- ⑩ Southwark Cathedral
- ⑪ Borough Market
- ⑫ George Inn
- ⑬ Golden Hinde

- ⑭ Winchester House
- ⑮ The Market Porter
- ⑯ Clink Museum
- ⑰ The Anchor
- ⑱ Southwark Bridge
- ⑲ Globe theatre
- ⑳ Millennium Bridge
- ㉑ Tate Modern
- ㉒ Bankside Lofts
- ㉓ Blackfriars (road) Bridge
- ㉔ Oxo Tower
- ㉕ Gabriel's Wharf
- ㉖ National Theatre

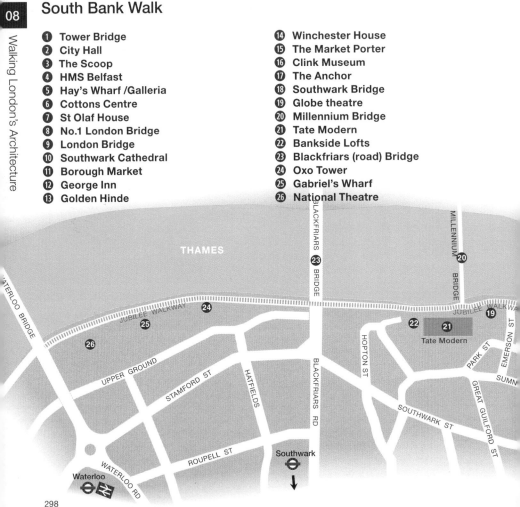

W alking along the south bank of the River Thames and taking in the variety of architecture and stunning views of the City over the water is one of the most pleasurable things to do in London today. However, this area hasn't always been so pleasant for Bankside was once notorious for its lowlife which included 'stews', a sort of combined bathhouse and brothel, bear baiting, unsavoury taverns and stinking prisons. These coexisted with lively theatres showing plays by Shakespeare and his contemporaries; indeed we shall encounter the Bard in a few of the

buildings on this walk. During the 18th century much of the area was given over to docks and industrial use and it has been only in the last 20 or so years that the south bank has become a place of leisure and pleasure again.

It is perfectly possible to do this walk at any time of the day or evening, depending if you specifically want to see the interior of any of the buildings en route. Please refer to the list at the end of the walk for details of the individual places of interest, p.311. There are plenty of places to stop for a drink or a meal throughout the walk.

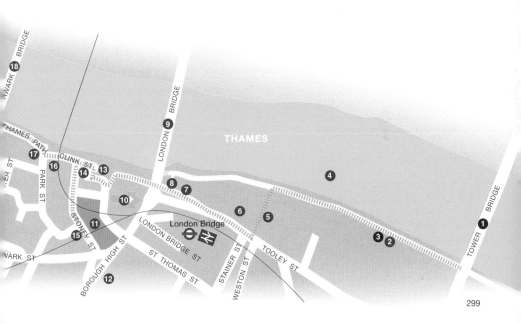

inclines so that each floor shades the offices below. There is a visitor centre and a flexible exhibition and function space at the higher levels with a public viewing gallery at the top, all which are open during the week and sometimes at the weekend, see p.236 for more details. The assembly chamber is definitely worth seeing; a transparent and open space looking out over the river to the City and reminiscent of Foster's Reichstag project in Berlin.

As we walk on along the Thames we pass ❸ **The Scoop**, to the right of City Hall, an 800 seat sunken amphitheatre which hosts free events throughout the summer months. City Hall and the Scoop are part of More London, a 13 acre development that stretches from Tower Bridge almost to London Bridge. The development includes a hotel, shops, cafés and office space for almost 20,000 people within a pedestrian area incorporating some interesting public sculpture and water features. Norman Foster and Partners were responsible for the master plan of the project.

Continuing west one comes to ❹ **HMS Belfast** a 11,500 ton battlecruiser launched in 1938 and which could apparently accommodate 950 men if needed. It has been a floating museum since 1971. Details of visiting times can be found below.

Walking on we arrive at ❺ **Hay's Wharf** originally built in 1651 and London's oldest and largest dock. The present warehouse was designed by Thomas Cubitt in 1856 and was

We are going to start this walk at the south end of ❶ **Tower Bridge,** details of which can be found on page 367 of this book. The Bridge is always worth viewing at close-quarters, even if you think you know the structure well and it offers one of the best views in London.

Walking west along the Thames path, with the river to your right, we arrive at the distinctive form of ❷ **City Hall**, which is described on page 236. In conventional terms, the building has no front or back. Its elegant shape is derived from a geometrically modified sphere, designed to minimize the surface area exposed to direct sunlight. The north facade, which will receive minimal direct solar heat gain, has un-shaded glazing whereas the south facade used for storing the vast amounts of butter and cheese imported from New Zealand so the building was nicknamed 'London's Larder'. In 1988 the building was restored and given a glazed roof, modelled on Milan's Galleria Vittorio Emanuele and is now a mix of offices, shops, bars and cafés, and home to a huge sculpture by David Kemp titled 'The Navigators'. Constructed in 1987 it pays homage to the areas shipping heritage. Hay's Wharf is certainly worth having a walk through, as too is its neighbour the ❻ **Cottons Centre**. The Cottons Centre is an office complex with an impressive landscaped atrium housing a number of works of sculpture and where there is often an interesting art exhibition to view. Designed by the London-based architectural practice of Twigg Brown, much thought has been given to the river-side exterior landscaping with a welcoming seating area.

There are good information boards along this stretch of the walk illustrating the history of the 'Pool of London', as the river between Tower Bridge and London Bridge is known, which constituted the farthest reach that could be navigated by a tall-masted vessel. The banks of the river were crammed with wharfs and ships vied with each other for space as goods, especially coal, was brought to the capital to sustain its ever-growing population. It is said that by the late 18th century the Pool was so congested with ships it was possible to walk from one side of the river to the other just by stepping from one vessel to another. The abrupt collapse of commercial traffic in the

Thames due to the introduction of shipping containers and coastal deep-water ports, such as Harwich, in the 1960s emptied the Pool and led to all of the wharves being closed down, and many being demolished. The area was extensively redeveloped in the 1980s and 1990s to create the new residential and commercial neighbourhoods we see today.

Walking towards London Bridge we walk past London Bridge Hospital (originally built as a warehouse in the 1860's) and pause at the next building along, ❼ **St Olaf House.** Built in 1931 as the offices for Hay's Wharf it now serves as an administration block for the hospital next door. This riverside frontage is adorned with Doulton faience panels by Frank Dobson (1886-1963), showing dock life and the unloading of goods titled 'Capital, Labour and Commerce'. It is well worth taking a short diversion into St Olaf Stairs, a passageway between St Olaf House and the pink granite building next door, in order to have a look at the front of the building. You will find further notes on this building on page 195 of this book.

The site of St Olaf House had been occupied for many centuries by St Olave's Church, which was the parish church for the area and which remained through all the changes to the district right up to the late 1920's. The church tower had always been a landmark in the area through medieval times.

Heading towards London Bridge, passing the cool presence of ❽ **No 1 London Bridge,**

which consists of two office blocks, one thirteen-storey, one ten-storey and both clad in soft pink granite and linked by a glass atrium. The eastern block, nearest to the bridge, has a dramatic overhang supported by a column clad in polished stainless steel; the window frames of the building are of the same material. Designed by the John S Bonnington Partnership this building really catches the light on all areas and must surely cheer the throng of workers as they stream over London Bridge between the railway station and the City.

There has been some sort of bridge over this part of the Thames since Roman times, indeed being able to cross the river here with relative ease is the very reason settlers stopped here and what we now call 'London' was born. A succession of bridges has served this area throughout history – the medieval bridge was lined with houses and shops although these were removed when it was widened in the middle of the 18th century. In 1824 a new stone bridge was built consisting of five arches, designed by the eminent engineer John Rennie. In 1924 it was found that not only was the unprecedented increase in traffic a problem but also one side of the bridge was sinking, albeit very slowly, and so the new present bridge was commissioned.

Imagine the surprise of the City of London authorities when an American developer, Robert P McCulloch, on hearing of the imminent disposal of Rennie's bridge, offered to buy it from them. Apparently it was just

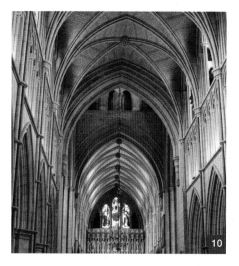

what he wanted for his leisure park being built near Havasu City, Arizona and so the 10,000 or so pieces of the bridge were dismantled and numbered before being shipped to the United States for rebuilding on dry land before water was diverted under it. What replaced it in London is a somewhat utilitarian prestressed concrete bridge by Mott, Hay and Anderson engineers with architect Lord William Holford.

Passing under **9 London Bridge**, past the Mudlark pub, a 'mudlark' being someone who made a living scavenging in the river mud, looking for items of value, and after a few more steps we have **10 Southwark Cathedral** on our left side, see p.32 of this book for brief description.

There is much to look at inside the Cathedral, especially the Shakespeare Monument and Window; the Harvard Chapel in celebration of John Harvard, the founder of the American university who was baptised here, and within that chapel the splendid, tall gilded tabernacle designed by A W N Pugin.

Once you have completed your visit to the Cathedral there is an opportunity for a digression or two. Almost next to Southwark Cathedral is the ⑪ **Borough Market**, a 'foodies' paradise, but only open for trade on certain days of the week. There has been, more or less, a market on this spot since the 13th century, if not earlier.

If it is liquid you require at this point, rather than food, then there are plenty of options in this area. One of the best, The George Inn, is about five minutes walk away, but is worth the diversion, being one of the most interesting pubs in London. To get there walk along the street between Southwark Cathedral and Borough Market, away from the river; this is 'Cathedral Street', but it becomes 'Bedales Street'. This will bring you to the very busy Borough High Street, cross at the traffic lights and carry on walking on under a grey bridge until you arrive at The George Inn at number 77. ⑫ **The George Inn** is London's only surviving galleried coaching inn and more details can be found on page 335 of this book. When you have finished retrace your steps back to the Cathedral and Market.

Walk towards the river down Cathedral Street, with a new-build office block to your right and Pickford's Wharf, an early 19th-century storage building to your left but which is now rather smart apartments with retail space at its ground floor. Here we see a full scale replica of ⑬ **The Golden Hinde**, the Tudor warship in which Sir Frances Drake circumnavigated the globe between 1577 and 1580. Tours can be made of the vessel and it can be hired for parties, see p.311 for more details.

Take the narrow street at the north of Picksford's Wharf building, the side away from the river. This is Clink Street and here we find the remains of ⑭ **Winchester House**, the London residence of the Bishops of Winchester from the 12th to the 17th century and which would have been not too dissimilar to Lambeth Palace further along the Thames. The grounds of the House would have extended down to the river where the successive bishops came and went by barge. Nothing is left of the original 12th-century building but what remain dates from the early 14th century; just part of two walls of the Great Hall with a few doorways. However, perhaps of greatest interest is the remains of a rose window which was restored in 1972. Seeing it in its skeletal form one wonders if it could have looked any more beautiful with coloured glass. The site is a 'Scheduled Ancient Monument' and enjoys the same protection as Stonehenge. In recent years Edward Cullinan Architects have sensitively incorporated these remains with restaurants and retail areas at ground level with residential and offices above.

If you are fond of diversions, particularly to public houses, here is another one for you. As you pass the building which incorporates the remains of Winchester House, turn left into Stoney Street and keep walking past the old warehouse buildings and shops, with Borough Market now on your left, until you come to a pub on the corner with Park Street. This is the ⑮ **Market Porter** bar and restaurant and a good example of the once ubiquitous Victorian corner public house with its warm, inviting interior. The building was transformed into the 'Third Hand Book Emporium' in the film 'Harry Potter and the Prisoner of Azkaban', and was situated next to 'The Leaky Cauldron'!

Retrace your steps back along Stoney Street to Clink Street. It is from the tall, gloomy building standing proud of its neighbours on your left which gives the street its name, for this is the site of The Clink, a notorious prison which functioned from the twelfth century until it was burnt-down in 1780 and was originally owned by the Bishop of Winchester. The ⑯ **Clink Prison Museum** is housed in the basement of the warehouse that was built over the site, details of which are below.

At the end of Clink Street, turning right into Bankside where we will find another historic pub ⑰ **The Anchor** which has at its core a mid-17th century building and is certainly a pleasant place to stop and contemplate the fantastic view across the river. It is said that it was from here that Samuel Pepys watched the destruction of the City in the Great Fire of 1666. Samuel Johnson, lexicographer and writer, frequently drank here and a copy of his wonderful dictionary of 1755 is on display here.

With the river to our right we carry on walking along Bankside, past the blocks of flats and the shiny black glass head office of the Financial Times, through the pedestrian underpass of ⑱ **Southwark Bridge**. This underpass is rather a joy with the relatively recent addition of five Westmorland green slate panels engraved by London artist Richard Kindersley depicting scenes from Frost Fairs that were held whenever the Thames froze over. The Fairs were held on the tideway on the Thames during the 15th to the 19th century when the British winter was more severe than now, and the river was wider and slower. The bridge itself is the second to have been constructed at this point on the Thames. The first was opened in 1819 to a design by John Rennie, a beautifully simple iron bridge of only three spans, a considerable feat of contemporary engineering, built to relieve the terrible traffic congestion that choked London Bridge. However Rennie's bridge was deemed too narrow to be useful and a new one was commissioned in 1912, but not completed until 1921 having suffered delays in building during the 1914/18 war. The Southwark Bridge, under which you pass, was designed by architect Sir Ernest George and Mott and Hay engineers in granite-faced steel with rather strange light coloured stone pier-headings with little 'windows'.

⑱ *Southwark Bridge*

Out of the bridge tunnel and with the river and the Bankside Jetty on our right, where one gets a great view of the City, just ahead of us is one of the most exciting additions to London in recent years the **⑲** **Globe Theatre**. Built just metres away from the original theatre that Shakespeare was familiar with, this new Globe was the brainchild of American actor and director Sam Wanamaker who founded what was to become the Shakespeare's Globe Trust in 1970 and some 20 years later work on the theatre was underway.

It is uncertain what the original theatre actually looked like but with the aid of modern scholarship and an adherence to accurate Elizabethan building methods a wonderful building has been constructed. Architect

Theo Crosby who gave Wanamaker's dream architectural expression, insisted only on natural materials and high-quality craftsmanship. Mass-produced materials were banned from the site. Handmade Tudor-sized bricks, 36,000 of them, were fashioned especially for the project and these required 90 tons of lime putty. Green oak laths and staves were used for both sides of the walls and 180 tons of lime plaster was required to cover the outer walls, beautifully crafted by Peter McCurdy and his company. The roof is made from 6,000 bundles of water reed from Norfolk and the Globe was the first building since the Great Fire of London in 1666 to be granted permission for a thatched roof.

Plays are performed regularly throughout the summer season and tours of the building are available, please see p.311 for details.

Walking on along Bankside we see on our left a cluster of houses. Number 49 is a three-storey early 18th-century building, numbers 50-52 Bankside are a century older and is the Provost's Lodging for the Dean of Southwark Cathedral. In between the houses is Cardinal Cap Alley which once led to a tavern, drinking house or brothel called the Cardinal's Hat.

Now it is difficult on what to focus first, the gloriously large expanse that is Tate Modern or the exquisite ⑳ **Millennium Bridge**. Bridge first then. Unfortunately, this will always be known as the 'wobbly bridge' since its unfortunate swaying episodes at its opening. Problems were pondered and solved, and the bridge is now perfectly stable. This wonderful bridge, also known as 'the blade of light' is the result of collaboration between architect Norman Foster, Arup engineers and sculptor Anthony Caro, providing a useful link between Bankside and St Paul's Cathedral and the City beyond. There is a wonderful view up and down the river from the centre of the bridge.

㉑ **Tate Modern** started life as the Bankside Power Station, generating electricity for London from 1952 to 1981 and was designed by Giles Gilbert Scott, designer of, amongst other things, the red K2 telephone box. The redundant building was threatened with demolition until in 1994 the Tate Gallery came

up with the genius idea of turning it into a space for displaying international modern art. After a £135 million conversion by Jacques Herzog and Pierre de Meuron, who fashioned galleries from iron industrial architecture, on May 12th, 2000 Tate Modern was opened. In its first decade an estimated 45 million visitors have been awed by this fabulous building, some may even have come to look at the pictures!

If you exit Tate Modern from the Turbine Hall you will see ahead of you a tall, yellow building which is part of the ㉒ **Bankside Lofts** development, a combination of converted and new buildings set around a new raised garden. A red-brick Italianate ex-cocoa mill is at the centre of the group. To its north is a 1950s building of similar height curving round the street line which has been extended upwards and sideways to form a snail plan spiral tower of stepping terraces with large steel windows in an orange/yellow rendered frame. Both buildings have enviable single and double height lofts on upper floors with commercial floors at ground and basement. To the south are Nell Gwynne's House (number 67 Hopton Street), a restored 17th-century cottage, which at one time was the home of the cocoa mill, and a five-storey brick new-build office building which also has a stepped section. To its east, and south of the garden, is the final element, a newly built loft building which is angled to gain good views of the City across the river. This project was designed by CZWG Architects for the Manhattan Loft Corporation and was completed in 1998. There is no public access to the site.

Walking on, again with the river to our right, first we pass under the Blackfriars Railway Bridge, rather grim at this level, then into the pedestrian underpass of ㉓ **Blackfriars (road) Bridge**. Dating from the 1860's and designed by Joseph Cubitt, Blackfriars Bridge is a wide, noisy thoroughfare for traffic and is named for the abbey on the other side of the river, which housed an order of Dominican monks who wore black robes. For our delight, the pedestrian underpass has within its tiled walls illustrations of the construction of the bridge.

Passing the Doggetts Coat and Badge public house and blocks of offices on our left and with the river still to our right, the path takes a very small left kink and here we have the ㉔ **Oxo Tower,** which has been a riverside landmark since it was built in 1928 as an Art Deco addition to a meat manufacturer's London base. At that time there was a ban on any form of neon-lit advertising in the area, however someone hit upon the idea of picking out the name OXO in coloured glass windows at the top of the tower and placing a strong light behind it and the name shone out into the London night. However, by the 1970s it had fallen into disrepair and was largely derelict.

In the 1980's the Tower was taken under the wing of the Coin Street Community Builders (CSCB), a social enterprise and development trust which seeks to make London's South Bank a better place in which to live, to work and to visit. They have transformed a largely derelict 13 acre site into a thriving mixed use neighbourhood by creating new cooperative 'affordable' homes, a park, the riverside walkway, sports facilities, cafés, bars, restaurants, galleries and shops. They also organise festivals and events and make this area of London a lively and diverse place. On the eighth floor of the Oxo Tower is a viewing platform, which can be accessed by the lift.

Walking on we pass ㉕ **Gabriel's Wharf**, its name hinting at its working past. This area was a derelict wasteland for a number of years until the 1980's when old garages on the site were given shop frontages and became the focus of craft workshops, boutiques and cafés and a lovely place to stroll around.

Passing more office blocks we come to the ㉖ **National Theatre** building designed by Sir Denys Lasdun, who was also responsible for the IBM office block, almost adjacent to the theatre that we have just passed. More properly named the Royal National Theatre, this building, a permanent home for the company formed in the early 1960's, was a long time coming, and its doors finally opened here on the South Bank in 1976.

The building actually contains three theatres – the largest is the Olivier, named for the great actor and the National's first artistic director Laurence Olivier, who did so much to make sure the dream of such an establishment became a reality. The Olivier has an open stage, audience seating for 1,160 and fans out in two tiers. The two other theatres are

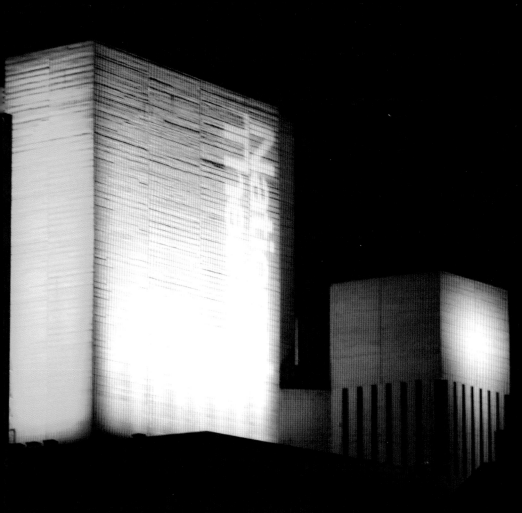

the Lyttleton, named for the National's first chairman of the Board of Governors, with a capacity to seat almost 900 patrons and has a more conventional proscenium-arch stage; the smallest theatre is the Cottesloe, a flexible studio space that can seat up to 300, depending on the production. Dressing rooms, rehearsal studios and offices are contained within the core of the building and there are bars, restaurants, cafés, ticket offices and retail spaces in the foyer areas at each of the individual theatres. The building is wrapped by interlocking terraces accommodating outdoor seating and viewing areas overlooking the Thames, with splendid views up and down the river.

The National Theatre building still courts controversy thirty-odd years after it's opening because of Lasdun's use of raw concrete left rough and 'unfinished' both inside and outside of the building, a method of construction sometimes called *breton brut*. In 1988, Prince Charles described the building as 'a clever way of building a nuclear power station in the middle of London without anyone objecting', but nevertheless it is Grade II listed building and is beloved, at least, by the thousands of theatregoers who patronise the place.

A ticket to see a play is not necessary to enjoy the building, which is open for most of the day and evening, and usually hosts interesting exhibitions and with free foyer music available most evenings. Indeed this is a splendid place to finish this South Bank walk. Buses are

available from Waterloo Bridge, details of this can be found in the 'Architecture with a View' section of this book, and underground trains are available from Waterloo Station nearby.

If you are still in the mood for some more architecture you could carry on walking in the same direction from whence you came, going under Waterloo Bridge, where you will find the South Bank complex which includes the Royal Festival Hall (see p.205). Further along and you will arrive at the 'London Eye', see 'Architecture with a View', and the former County Hall (see p.182). Crossing Waterloo Bridge which will take you to Parliament Square. Alternatively, make your way up to Waterloo Bridge, cross to the other side of the Thames, turn left and follow the 'Strand Walk' or turn right and do the 'Fleet Street and Beyond Walk' in reverse.

More information:

Greater London Authority
City Hall,
The Queen's Walk, SE1
Tel: 020 7983 4000
www.london.gov.uk
Transport: London Bridge LU/Rail

HMS Belfast
Tooley St, SE1
Tel: 020 7940 6300
www.hmsbelfast.iwm.org.uk
Transport: London Bridge LU/Rail

Hay's Galleria
Battle Bridge Lane, SE1
Tel: 020 7940 7770
www.haysgalleria.co.uk
Transport: London Bridge LU/Rail

Southwark Cathedral
London Bridge, SE1
Tel: 020 7367 6700
www.southwarkcathedral.org.uk
Transport: London Bridge LU/Rail

Borough Market
8 Southwark Street, SE1
Tel: 020 7407 1002
www.boroughmarket.org.uk
Transport: London Bridge LU/Rail
Usually open for trading Thurs,
Fri & Sat, please check website
for details

George Inn
The George Inn Yard, 77
Borough High Street, SE1
Tel: 020 7407 2056
www.nationaltrust.org.uk
Transport: London Bridge LU/Rail

Golden Hinde
Pickfords Wharf,
Clink Street, SE1
Tel: 020 7403 0123
www.goldenhinde.com
Transport: London Bridge LU/Rail

The Market Porter
The Market Porter,
9 Stoney Street, SE1
Tel: 020 7407 2495
www.markettaverns.co.uk
Transport: London Bridge LU/Rail

Clink Prison Museum
Clink Street, Southwark, SE1
Tel: 020 7403 0900
www.clink.co.uk
Transport: London Bridge LU/Rail

The Anchor Public House
34 Park Street, SE1
Tel: 020 7407 1577
Transport: London Bridge LU/Rail

Globe Theatre
21 New Globe Walk, SE1
Tel: 020 7902 1400
www.shakespeares-globe.org
Transport: Southwark LU
See website for details of tours
& theatre tickets

Tate Modern
53 Bankside, SE1
Tel: 020 7887 8752
www.tate.org.uk
Transport: Southwark LU
Admission free (except for
major exhibitions)

Oxo Tower
& Gabriel's Wharf
South Bank, SE1
Tel: 020 7021 1600
www.coinstreet.org
Transport: Southwark LU

National Theatre
South Bank, SE1
Tel: 020 7452 3000
www.nationaltheatre.org.uk
Transport: Waterloo LU/Rail

Strand Walk

1. **Royal Courts of Justice**
2. **St Clement Danes**
3. **'Roman Bath'**
4. **St Mary-le-Strand**
5. **Somerset House**
   Courtauld Institute of Art
   Courtauld Institute Gallery
   Gilbert Collection
6. **King's College London**
7. **Australia House**
8. **Bush House**
9. **India House**
10. **Savoy Chapel**
11. **6-10 Adam St**
12. **Royal Society of Arts**

This is a particularly good walk on a wet day as there are plenty of buildings to disappear into. We start this walk where the Fleet Street Walk finished, at the Temple Bar. We are now out of the City of London and Fleet Street has become the Strand. The street is named so because until the 19th century and the embankment of the river Thames, the Strand was very close to the river. The first building we stop at is the ❶ **Royal Courts of Justice** on the north side of the road (stand with your back to the Temple Bar – the monument with the griffin on the top – and the building will be on your right).

The Royal Courts of Justice, often referred to as the 'Law Courts', stand on a seven acre site which was cleared of its festering slum-dwellings in the mid 19th century to make way for a new Court of Justice. The Courts deal with civil cases, criminal cases are heard at the Old Bailey (see p.178).

The Royal Courts were conceived in the wake of the success of the Parliament building in Westminster, with the consequence that every submitting architect put forward plans in the Gothic Revival style. The design of George Edward Street (1824-81) was chosen and work began in 1871. Street had previously built many churches and looking at the Royal Courts of Justice one could be forgiven for thinking the building was actually a cathedral! By the time the construction was underway Gothic Revival was going out of fashion and, on its completion, the reception the building received

was cool to say the least. This is particularly sad given that the architect died the year before it was finished – the stress of the project being said to have been a large contributory factor in Street's relatively early death.

The façade, so familiar as the background to reports from the Courts on television news programmes, is complicated: bay after bay of free design with pinnacles and towers stretching up and a rose window over the main entrance. The whole is brick built, an estimated 35 million were used, faced in Portland stone, and contains 1,000 separate rooms, 88 of them court rooms, served by an estimated 3.5 miles of corridors. Immense care was taken over detailing, such as the metal work on the exterior, and this attention to detail extends to the interior.

The public is allowed into the court rooms to watch proceedings, and there is a small exhibition of legal dress. A good diversion from the walk is just to wander in and admire the splendour of Street's work (see p.319 for more details).

We now walk on to the church whose rear can be seen as we leave the Court. This is ❷ **St Clement Danes**, one of the two small churches which sit on islands in the middle of the Strand's heavy traffic, and whose name derives from the Danish settlers who came to the area in the 9th century.

The present church was built by Sir Christopher Wren in 1680-82, with additions to the tower and the provision of a spire by James Gibbs in 1719 but extensive restoration work was carried out in 1955 by Anthony Lloyd, who faithfully reproduced Wren's beautiful interior.

If the church is open and you have time, do go in and look at the plasterwork, particularly that on the barrel-vaulted ceiling and at the east end of the church. There is also a very good dark stained wooden gallery. This is the place to contemplate the immense task of the renovator, Anthony Lloyd, who studied photographs and drawings to re-create Wren's church and his work here is considered to be his most successful.

In 1958 the church was adopted by the Royal Air Force, hence the proliferation of RAF badges and rolls of honour.

On leaving St Clement Danes cross to the south side of the Strand and proceed west. Make your way to Surrey Street, just off the Strand, and look for the entrance to the ❸ **Roman Bath**, which will have a National Trust sign pointing you in the right direction.

Whilst known as a 'Roman Bath', there is certainly nothing to suggest that it is anything of the sort; the bricks are not Roman and there is no evidence of Roman settlement in the area. However, this was the site of a grand house owned by Thomas Howard, Lord Arundel (1586-1646). He had a passion for paintings, antiquities and travel and had been in Rome during the excavation of the Forum, so it is quite feasible that he would have returned with the idea of a Roman bath, perhaps with genuine decorations. The surrounding street names, Arundel and Surrey (he was also Earl of Surrey) commemorate the site's history. Dickens mentions this bath in his novel 'David Copperfield'. The 'Roman Bath' can be viewed through the window from the pathway at any time.

Back to the Strand and we can now cross the road to the other church that sits in the middle of the road. This is the church of ❹ **St Mary-le-Strand**, details of which can be found on p.102.

Return once more to the south side of the Strand to ❺ **Somerset House**. This was the site of a palace built 1547-52 by Edward Seymour, Duke of Somerset who foolishly fell out with his monarch Henry VIII, was duly executed in 1552 and the building passed into royal hands. The palace was the domain of the monarch's consort until the reign of George III and Queen Charlotte, who preferred Buckingham House. The buildings were demolished in 1775 and the architect William Chambers set about designing one of the first purpose-built office blocks in Europe. The offices were used for the Navy Board, the newly-formed Royal Academy of Arts and the Society of Antiquaries. Over the intervening years the buildings also housed the Registry of Births, Marriages and Deaths and the head office of the Inland Revenue.

Completed first were the buildings we come to first, those that face the Strand. As you pass through the entrance arch the building to your left is the Courtauld Institute of Art and, apart from those attending lectures or wishing to use one of the two art libraries, is not open to the public. The building to your right is the Courtauld Institute Gallery.

The Courtauld Gallery moved to Somerset House in 1990 and occupies rooms which were once home to the Royal Academy of Arts. Here is one of the best collections of art anywhere in Europe, particularly strong in major works by the Impressionists and Post-Impressionists – Degas, Cézanne, Manet, Renoir, Gauguin, Van Gogh and more. Other periods are well represented in the collection, particularly early Flemish and Italian painting (for more details see p.319).

After the Gallery continue further into the courtyard of Somerset House – looking to your left through a gap in the buildings you will see the rear of ❻ **King's College London** and the building designed by Robert Smirke in 1829. So much better than the unfortunate 1960's front of the College which faces the Strand.

The courtyard of Somerset House used to be a car park for the Inland Revenue but has been transformed into a new space for cultural events. Now known as Fountain Court, its new name is not misleading as there is indeed a charming group of fountains which magically turn into a skating rink during the winter months.

Somerset House holds a programme of temporary exhibitions in the Embankment Galleries which focus on contemporary fashion, architecture, photography and design. It is possible to walk through the south buildings of Somerset House and out onto the River Terrace, where you can take coffee, lunch, afternoon tea or supper during the summer months. A steel and glass walkway connects to Waterloo Bridge here.

It is interesting to remember that until the 19th century and the embankment of the Thames, the river lapped against the terrace immediately below the building. Can you see where boats would have sailed into the basement of Somerset House? This is still called the Water Gate.

After looking around William Chamber's magnificent neo-classical complex, we rejoin the Strand. Next stop on our walk are three of the buildings that languish between the Strand and Aldwych and are so often passed by when travelling by car or bus. All three buildings are of the early 20th century and were built as part of a town-planning scheme by the London County Council, rather in the mood of Nash and his Regent Street plan, but not nearly so ambitious. Slum dwellings were cleared and the tenants re-housed in blocks of flats on Drury Lane. Aldwych was to be the culmination of the widening and re-building of Kingsway and the architecture had to be fairly monumental. Unfortunately, as a group, the buildings look rather over-the-top, some might even say vulgar. It is most likely you will not be able to enter the buildings for security reasons, but the exteriors of Australia House and Bush House are worth looking at and are best viewed from the north side.

The first building of the group is ❼ **Australia House** and is on the extreme right of the group when you are looking at them with your back to Somerset House. Australia House is the oldest of the trio, built 1913-18 and designed by Marshall Mackenzie and was the first in a series of large buildings in London associated with Commonwealth countries, such as India House nearby and South Africa House in Trafalgar Square (see Whitehall Walk p.325).

Fittingly for a High Commission the building is very grand in a Beaux Arts design.

Some excellent sculpture is incorporated within, as with all the buildings in this group. To the left and right of the main entrance are the monumentally-sized 'Awakening of Australia' and 'Prosperity of Australia' by Harold Parker, a British born, Australian trained sculptor of note. Above and central to the entrance is a sculpture in a heroic vein, a bronze male nude wearing just a cloak and crown with four horses entitled 'Phoebus Driving the Horses of the Sun' by Australian-born Bertram Mackennal. All the sculpture dates from the early 20th century.

The centre building, ❽ **Bush House**, designed by the New York architects Helme and Corbett in 1920-23, was named for its first owner Irving T Bush, an American. His vision was that the building would be a large, grand showcase for manufactured goods and the interior decoration reflects this, with ample application of marble. Alas the economic climate changed and the luxury goods market on which Bush had set his sights faltered, so the building was bought by the Church of Wales. They in turn sold it to the Post Office Pensions fund who lease it to the British Broadcasting Corporation and since 1940 has been the home of the BBC's World Service.

The building is big and bold with two huge columns and two male figures, both twelve feet tall representing England and America, each with an outstretched hand holding a torch between them in the arched area above. Bush House looks very impressive from Kingsway during the evening when the façade is illuminated.

⑨ India House, by Sir Herbert Baker and Alexander Scott, was built in 1928-30 and its rather forgettable exterior belies its wonderful interior, mainly executed by Indian artists. If you are ever fortunate enough to be invited to tea by the Indian High Commissioner, do accept and take in the lovely carved jali-type open work decoration.

Cross back over the road to the south (Somerset House) side and negotiate the traffic at Lancaster Place to continue along the Strand. On your right you will find Savoy Street and from there you will find Savoy Hill which is the location of the **⑩ Savoy Chapel**, or to give the building its full title, The Queen's Chapel of the Savoy.

This very simple chapel dates back to the Savoy Palace of John of Gaunt, who was the younger son of Henry III and born in Ghent (hence 'Gaunt'). The palace was razed to the ground during the Peasants' Revolt of 1381.

The present building dates back to the early 16th century but a fire in the 18th century destroyed much of the original decoration, which has since been reconstructed. Note the nice heraldic details. In 1936 this became the chapel of the Royal Victorian Order and is

now a private chapel of the present Queen. However visitors are most welcome to this relatively unknown little gem.

Further west along the Strand you will come across Adam Street which has several excellent examples of Robert Adam's work at **⑪ numbers 6-10**. Another good example of his work is to be found just around the corner at the **⑫ Royal Society of Arts** in John Adam Street (see p.114 for further details).

Walking on along to the end of John Adam Street, which runs parallel with The Strand, you will see before you an excellent example of Post-Modern architecture in Terry Farrell's Embankment Place, details of which can be found on page 225. Turn right into Villiers Street and walk on where you will rejoin The Strand.

This concludes our walk but if you would like to look at some more architecture, and you have the energy, you could continue west along the Strand to Trafalgar Square which is easy to find with Nelson's Column at its centre. Now you are ready to start the 'Whitehall Walk' (see p.320).

⑤ Somerset House

More Information:

Royal Courts of Justice
Strand, WC2
Tel: 020 7947 6000
www.hmcourts-service.gov.uk
Transport: Temple LU
See website for opening times

St Clement Danes
Strand, WC2
Tel: 020 7242 8282
www.raf.mod.uk/
stclementdanes
Transport: Temple LU
See website for tours,
opening times & events

St Mary-le-Strand
Strand, WC2R
0207 836 3126
www.stmarylestrand.org
Transport: Temple LU
See website for opening times

Somerset House
Somerset House, Strand, WC2
Tel: 020 7845 4600
www.somersethouse.org.uk
Transport: Temple or Covent
Garden LU

The Courtauld Gallery
Somerset House, Strand, WC2
Tel: 020 7872 0220
www.courtauld.ac.uk/gallery
Transport: Temple or Covent
Garden LU

The Savoy Chapel
Savoy Hill, Strand, WC2
Tel:020 7836 7221
Open daily except Monday

319

Whitehall Walk

1. Trafalgar Square
2. Nelson's Column
3. National Gallery
4. Canada House
5. St Martin-in-the-Fields
6. South Africa House
7. Admiralty Arch
8. Admiralty House
9. Admiralty Screen
10. DEFRA
11. Old War Office
12. Horse Guards & Horse Guards Parade Ground
13. Citadel
14. Whitehall Court
15. Ministry of Defence
16. Banqueting House
17. Downing Street
18. Privy Council Chambers
19. Foreign & Commonwealth Office
20. Cenotaph
21. National Monument to the Women of World War II
22. New Government Offices
23. Portcullis House
24. Houses of Parliament
25. Scotland Yard
26. Westminster Underground
27. Westminster Abbey
28. St Margaret's Church

This walk starts and finishes at two world famous landmarks, Nelson's Column and the Houses of Parliament respectively and takes in fine examples of work by some of the best architects that Britain has produced. If started early enough in the day, the walk could culminate in a visit to Westminster Abbey. Refreshments can be obtained at the café and restaurant in the National Gallery, the crypt café at St Martin-in-the-Fields and the café at the Methodist Central Hall (see p.340). Whitehall enjoys easy access to St James's Park where you will find 'Inn the Park' (see p.349) by entering the park through Horse Guards Parade.

The recent re-routing of traffic from the north side of ❶ **Trafalgar Square** has given London an impressive new public space with a new café and plenty of places to sit and contemplate the surrounding buildings. The most famous landmark at the heart of the square is ❷ **Nelson's Column** (see right) and this monument together with the naming of the square, commemorates the British naval victory over the French at the Battle of Trafalgar on 21 October 1805. However it was 40 years after the event before it was decided to build some sort of memorial to the occasion and the man.

The site on which Trafalgar Square now stands has a long history of use. From at least the early 13th century it had been the Royal Mews; mews being a corruption of the French verb 'muer' meaning to moult, being the place where royal hawks were confined

❷ Nelson's Column

3

6

whilst moulting their feathers. During the 14th century the area was part of a pleasure garden and from the time of Elizabeth I it was the home of the royal stables. William Kent (1685-1748), architect responsible for Horse Guards Parade, built the Crown Stables here in 1732. The plot became vacant when the stables were re-located to Buckingham Palace, since when it has been a public area.

The first square on this site had been designed and built by John Nash in the 1820s but this was remodelled in the 1840s by Charles Barry when it was decided to honour Nelson and his victory. The memorial to Nelson is probably better appreciated from a distance, being 185 feet in the air, but is nonetheless impressive from any angle. The statue of Nelson itself stands at 17 feet, weighs 18 tons, was designed by E H Baily and executed in Craigleith stone from Edinburgh. The fluted Corinthian column on which the statue stands is of Devonshire granite from Foggin Tor carved by William Railton and the bronze Corinthian capital was inspired by examples from the Temple of Ultor, Rome. The bronze lions who lie at the bottom of the column were designed by Sir Edwin Landseer, who was one of Queen Victoria's favourite artists. The whole project was completed in 1868.

To the north of the Square stands the ❸ **National Gallery** built by William Wilkins between 1832-38, and to which the newly pedestrianised north terrace provides direct access. Built to house the nation's blossoming collection of publicly-owned art, it now ranks alongside the Louvre, the Prado and the Uffizi as one of the world's great art collections. Much criticism has been levelled at Wilkins' design, whose brief was to produce a crowning effect for the square, in that the building was seen to lack impact. Wilkins favoured, whenever possible, keeping his design 'pure' in the classical sense and perhaps lacked the ability to assimilate and to synthesise. The architect's decision to place a dome over the portico, with its eight Ionic columns from King George IV's newly demolished Carlton House in Pall Mall and turrets over the outer wings, attracted much derision. One critic likened the effect to a clock and two vases on a mantelpiece – but of less use! Wilkins also designed University College, in Gower Street in a similar classical fashion.

As the gallery's collection grew so the building has been extended, three times during the 19th century, twice in the early 20th, and a further addition at the rear of the building added in the 1970s. However the latest extension is the very substantial 'Sainsbury Wing', designed by the architectural partnership of Venturi, Rauch and Scott Brown, built between 1987-91. The rather sober exterior, incorporates echoes of Wilkins' Corinthian orders but takes nothing away from the main building's façade. The rather restrained and muted galleries inside are the perfect foil for the highly coloured collection of Italian and Northern European early Renaissance paintings displayed here.

Standing in Trafalgar Square with your back to the National Gallery you will find to your right ❹ **Canada House**, built by Robert Smirke between 1822-25 (see also the entry for British Museum p.125). This building was originally shared between the Royal College of Physicians and the Union Club. Smirke was a dedicated Greek Revivalist and this style is reflected in the unified Grecian Ionic order of this building. In 1924 the interior and some of the exterior was remodelled for the Canadian High Commission.

Still with your back to the National Gallery, to your left is the unmistakable frontage of James Gibbs' church of ❺ **St Martin-in-the-Fields**. Unmistakable that is, unless you live in parts of Ireland or North America where this was the prototype for 18th and 19th-century church building. Constructed under the New Churches Act of 1711, Gibbs took the unusual step of placing a tower and steeple almost over the portico. The interior is really not to be missed – very Wrenesque with huge columns and a balcony to three sides. Its nave is noticeably wide but not overly tall and surmounted by an interesting barrel vaulted ceiling. The interior was renovated and altered in 1887 by Sir Arthur Blomfield.

One famous incumbent vicar of St Martin was Dick Sheppard, who later became Dean of Canterbury Cathedral. Whilst at St Martin he opened the crypt as a retreat for homeless soldiers returning from the 1914-18 war and thereafter for anyone homeless. In 1924 he

also conducted from here the first church service to be broadcast on the radio. Concerts are performed at St Martin on a regular basis and the crypt has a very good café and shop.

Still to your left, but further down from St Martin is ❻ **South Africa House** (1935) by Sir Herbert Baker. Designed to be in keeping with the National Gallery and St Martin – its porticoes have been placed at the same level as Gibbs' church.

Walk down through Trafalgar Square, taking in the wonderful view stretching away down Whitehall towards the Houses of Parliament as you do so, and on reaching Whitehall to your right you will see ❼ **Admiralty Arch** designed by the respected architect Sir Aston Webb in 1908-11. The arch is part of a memorial to Queen Victoria, the other being her statue outside Buckingham Palace. The building is in fact three archways, all of equal height, with offices on either side, and makes a pleasing entrance to the Mall.

Continue along on the right hand side of Whitehall and you will find yourself outside ❽ **Admiralty House** built 1786-88 by S P Cockerell. Two and a half storeys tall, its most redeeming feature is its interior – which is sadly not open to the public. The house has been home to the First Lord of the Admiralty of whom Earl Grey (1806) of tea fame and Winston Churchill (1911-15 and 1939-40) are but two. Built as an extension to the Admiralty (built 1722-6 by Thomas Ripley) next door, the

rear of this whole complex can be viewed from Horse Guards Parade slightly further down Whitehall. In front of these buildings, facing Whitehall, is Robert Adam's ❾ **Admiralty Screen** made in 1760-61 when Whitehall was subject to a road-widening scheme. This is the first work Adam completed in London on his return from an extensive trip to Rome. The row of ten Tuscan columns against a blank wall hides the rather dour buildings behind and give a glimpse of Adam's blossoming genius.

Staying on this side but looking across the street to the white building that stands between Great Scotland Yard and Whitehall Place is ❿ **Department for the Environment, Food and Rural Affairs** (DEFRA). The rather splendid 'front' onto Whitehall is actually the side of the building and was designed by J W Murray in 1906-9 in a Classical style in-keeping with its neighbours, especially the Banqueting House, see p.47. DEFRA's immediate neighbour the ⓫ **Old War Office**, designed by Scottish architect William Young in 1898, and completed by his son Clyde Young, is a typical example of Edwardian Baroque.

Walking a little further down Whitehall you will come to two finely – dressed mounted guards, members of the Household Cavalry who are usually surrounded by picture-snapping tourists. You have arrived at ⓬ **Horse Guards Parade**. This was at one time the site of the tiltyard of Whitehall Palace, where in 1540 Henry VIII presided over a huge tournament with knights journeying from all parts of Europe to attend. In 1650 a guardhouse was erected but after much enlargement and re-building, finally fell into decay. It was decided the whole building needed re-designing and this was done by William Kent in 1748. Construction was undertaken after Kent's death and was finished in 1760.

The result is not only one of the best and most accessible buildings in Whitehall, but perhaps one of the finest examples of Georgian architecture in Britain. In contrast to Inigo Jones's flat-fronted Banqueting House (see later), Kent manages to create a quite dramatic Palladian-inspired building, using projection and recession and without a single column in sight. The building is surmounted by a cupola containing a clock, to which the 18th-century Londoner looked for the correct time. Note that there appears to be a black circle around the Roman numeral II (two o'clock) which is probably a reference to the time at which King Charles I was executed just across the street, outside the Banqueting House some 100 years earlier in 1649.

Walking through the arches of the building you will arrive at the Horse Guards parade ground, which leads on to the Mall and St James's Park. It is here in the parade ground that Trooping the Colour takes place every year in celebration of the Queen's official birthday on 10 June. The rather curious, creeper-clad building at the north-west corner of the parade ground is the ⓭ **Citadel**. Built in 1939 from blocks of compressed pebble and flint, it is the entrance to a series of deep underground shelters designed to house the country's political leaders during the air raids of the Second World War. It seems far too modern for its surroundings and yet it is a strangely attractive building and one of the few remaining examples of its type.

Return to Whitehall, and with your back to William Kent's magnificent building, almost directly opposite is Horse Guards Avenue. This short thoroughfare leads to ⓮ **Whitehall Court** which, built by Archer and Green and completed in 1887, is an eight-storey block of very superior flats, faced with Portland stone in an almost French Renaissance style.

Another interesting building in this Avenue is the massive ⓯ **Ministry of Defence** offices. Originally planned at the beginning of the 20th century, actual construction did not commence until 1938 with the project being delayed further by the outbreak of World War Two. Indeed the building took another 20 years to be completed. Designed by Vincent Harris, who had been responsible for several large public buildings such as Sheffield City Hall, Leeds Civic Hall and Manchester Central Library, this huge building is entirely faced in Portland Stone and has sculptures representing 'Earth' and 'Water' by Sir Charles Wheeler over the entrance. Perhaps the most exciting feature of this building, hidden within its basement and unable to be seen by the general public, is the preserved remains of the wine cellar of the former Whitehall Palace, which used to occupy the space, and a fine example of a Tudor brick-vaulted roof some 70 feet long and 30 feet wide. The area now serves as the focus for Ministerial social gatherings.

Back on Whitehall stands the magnificent **16 Banqueting House**. This building formed just a small part of the former Whitehall Palace, from which the road and indeed the whole area, takes its name. The story of Whitehall starts in 1514 when Cardinal Wolsey, then Archbishop of York, rebuilt the existing London house of the Archbishopric known as York Place. He built York Place in the grandest manner and in the latest fashion, but later fell foul of Henry VIII being dismissed in 1529. Henry lost no time in occupying York Place. The building was renamed Whitehall Palace and became the monarch's principal London residence until William III (1650-1702). Henry acquired the land round about (what is now Horse Guards Parade) and had a tiltyard, four tennis courts and a cockpit built – truly a 16th-century leisure complex!

Banqueting House, Inigo Jones's addition to Whitehall Palace, was finished in 1622 in the reign of James I and may have been the intended start of an improvement plan for the whole site, but nothing further was built. Whatever architectural merit the building exudes (see p.47 for further details), its popular fame rests on its association with the execution of Charles I.

On the morning of Saturday 27th January 1649 in Westminster Hall, the clerk of the court read to the King his fate that 'this court doth adjudge that he the said Charles Stuart…shall be put to death by severing his head from his body'. The King was not allowed to speak but taken back to Whitehall and later the same day transferred to St James's Palace. Over the next two days workmen were busy setting up the scaffold against the walls of the north side of the Banqueting House facing Whitehall, and the building which epitomised the spirit of the Stuarts, with flamboyant masques and sumptuously painted ceiling, was now to be the backdrop for the dynasty's darkest hour.

The King was executed at two o'clock on January 30th, having been led from the private chambers through the hall of the Banqueting House and on to the scaffold via one of the large windows, which had been removed for the purpose. Charles won sympathy by his display of dignity at his trial and execution.

On 5th January 1698 Whitehall succumbed to a terrible fire which destroyed practically all of the Palace, although the Banqueting Hall miraculously escaped. The Court moved to St James's (see p.42) and Whitehall was never re-built.

Proceed south along Whitehall and on the same side of the road as Horse Guards Parade we arrive at the security gates that prevent entry to **17 Downing Street**, the official London residence and office of the Prime

Minister (Number 10) and of the Chancellor of the Exchequer (Number 11). If you are able to stop and peer through the gate note the modest Georgian façade of number 10 which is misleading as the original house now connects with a much larger and grander house looking onto the Horse Guards parade ground. Downing Street dates from the late 17th century when it was developed by Sir George Downing, a speculative builder, after whom the street was named. Between 1766 and 1774 many alterations were made, but the street's façade has changed little since then. Number 10 was gifted to the country's first Prime Minister Sir Robert Walpole, by King George II in 1732.

In Whitehall on either side of Downing Street are government offices dating from the 19th century. To the north, that is the side closest to Trafalgar Square, stand the **18 Privy Council Chambers** designed by Sir Charles Barry and built between 1844-5. On the south of Downing Street is the **19 Foreign and Commonwealth Office**, designed by Sir George Gilbert Scott and constructed between 1862-75. The conception and birth of this building is steeped in controversy, an episode in the history of London architecture known as 'the Battle of the Styles'. Changes in government during the planning meant Gilbert Scott had to modify his plans for a Gothic construction to something more Italian. The final result, as we can see, is every inch a neo-Renaissance palace that would not look out of place in Florence.

The Foreign and Commonwealth Office is a huge complex; in reality four separately functioning blocks, each arranged around its own courtyard and linked by a large quadrangle at the centre. The India Office and the Foreign Office are at the rear, overlooking St James's Park and The Home Office and the Colonial Office face Whitehall. The interior of this whole building is particularly sumptuous, with grand reception rooms, dining rooms, suites of conference rooms and a domed State Staircase of marble, mosaic and gilding. This building is usually open to the public during 'Open House' weekend in September, see p.377 for further details.

In the centre of the busy Whitehall roadway there are statues and memorials, two of particular note being in the immediate vicinity. The first is the **20 Cenotaph**, a word that means 'empty tomb'. This is the national memorial to those who lost their lives in both World Wars and all conflicts involving Commonwealth armed forces. Originally a simple wooden affair used as the focus of the 1919 victory parade, the Portland stone Cenotaph we see now was designed by the architect Edwin Lutyens and was in place by 1920. Slightly further back along the road is the **21 National Monument to the Women of World War II**. The sculpture stands 22 feet high, 16 feet long and 6 feet wide and the lettering on the side replicates the typeface used on war time ration books. There are 17 individual sets of clothing and uniforms around the sides, symbolising the hundreds of different jobs women undertook in World War Two and then relinquished to the homecoming men at the end of the war. Designed by sculptor John Mills, it was unveiled by The Queen in July 2005.

Continuing towards Parliament Square, the very last building on this side of Whitehall is the **㉒ New Government Offices**, which primarily house HM Treasury. Designed in 1898 by J M Brydon in a Neo-Baroque style these were finally completed in 1915. The basement of this building contains the Cabinet War Rooms used by Winston Churchill during the 1939-45 war. These once top secret rooms have been preserved in their original state since 1948 and are now open to the public (for more details see p.331).

In our journey down Whitehall we have arrived at Bridge Street and if you look to your left you will see **㉓ Portcullis House**. Completed in 2001 this building is the outcome of a very long, drawn-out process to consider development of the area. Michael Hopkins and Partners were commissioned to design office and committee room accommodation for Parliament in 1989, the same year it was mooted that an extension of the Jubilee line of the London Underground should be routed to include a station at Westminster. The need for total security of the Houses of Parliament ruled out the station being placed below Parliament, so it was incorporated into Michael Hopkins and Partners brief for the office site; work on which started in early 1994. Portcullis House

㉔ *Houses of Parliament*

27

The building is highly efficient and uses only approximately one third of the fuel of conventionally air-conditioned offices, being heated by recycled exhaust heat from the system and cooled by groundwater from deep bore holes. The cost of the building was a cool £231 million.

26 **Westminster Underground** station below Portcullis House is a modern miracle of engineering. Its design had to take into consideration the existing District and Circle lines, which had to remain open and fully operational during the building work; care had to be taken with regard to the foundations of the nearby Houses of Parliament and Westminster Bridge; provision had to be made for the six massive column foundations of Portcullis House above. The result is a bold statement which celebrates these engineering feats – a 130 feet deep, 72 feet wide space which contains a series of intersecting escalators capped with a glass roof. The decoration is subdued, granite grey and steel. A fantastic piece of architecture.

not only had to fit in with the Gothicised-Classicism of the **24** **Houses of Parliament** over the road (see p.141) but also Norman Shaw's much admired **25** **Scotland Yard** building next door. Indeed the new building strongly echoes the sloping roof and tall chimneys of Shaw's building.

Portcullis House, and Scotland Yard House, which is also used as Parliamentary offices, can accommodate 450 Members of Parliament and their administrative staff. Within the new building there are seven Select Committee rooms, two TV interview studios, a post office, café and eight meeting rooms arranged on seven floors around a central courtyard.

The walk can end here but if time permits the delights of **27** **Westminster Abbey** can be explored (p.25) passing **28** **St Margaret's Church** (see p.41) and the Houses of Parliament on the way. Note the bust of Charles I placed on the church wall, he gazes over towards the Houses of Parliament, with the statue of Oliver Cromwell in front – his head bowed.

More information

National Gallery
Trafalgar Square, WC2N
Tel: 020 7747 2885
www.nationalgallery.org.uk
Transport: Charing Cross LU/Rail
Admission free

St Martin-in-the-Fields
Trafalgar Square, WC2N
Tel: 020 7766 1100
www.stmartin-in-the-fields.org
Transport: Charing Cross LU/Rail

Household Cavalry Museum
Horse Guards, Whitehall, SW1A
Tel: 020 7930 3070
*www.householdcavalry
museum.co.uk*
*Transport: Charing Cross
LU/Rail, Westminster and
Embankment LU*

Banqueting House
Whitehall, SW1A
Tel: 0844 482 7777
www.hrp.org.uk
*Transport: Charing Cross
LU/Rail, Westminster and
Embankment LU*

Houses of Parliament
Houses of Parliament, SW1A
www.parliament.uk
*Transport: Charing Cross
LU/Rail, Westminster and
Embankment LU*
*See website for opening times
and entrance charges*

Westminster Abbey
20 Dean's Yard, SW1P
Tel: 020 7222 5152
www.westminster-abbey.org
*Transport: Westminster
and St James's Park LU*

Church of St Margaret
20 Dean's Yard, SW1P
Tel: 020 7222 5152
*www.westminster-abbey.org/
st-margarets*
*Transport: Westminster
and St James's Park LU*
Admission free

Cabinet War Rooms
*Clive Steps, King Charles
Street, SW1A 2AQ*
www.cwr.iwm.org.uk
*Transport: Charing Cross
LU/Rail, Westminster and
Embankment LU*

Inn the Park
*St James's Park
(west of Horse Guards
Parade), SW1A 2BJ*
Tel 020 7451 9999
www.innthepark.com
*Transport: Green Park and St
James's Park LU*
See p.349 for a full review

Skylon, see p.343

09

**EAT & DRINK
ARCHITECTURE**

No matter whether it is fine dining or just a cup of tea, the following offer an opportunity to take refreshment in some of London's most interesting buildings.

Café Below
C1087+

St Mary-le-Bow, Cheapside, EC2V 6AU;
Tel 020 7329 0789; www.cafebelow.co.uk;
Nearest transport St Paul's and Bank LU;
See website for opening times

The City offers many eye-wateringly expensive restaurants and ubiquitous high street chain cafés, however the Café Below not only offers delicious, wholesome food and drink from early breakfast to late(ish) supper, but also the chance to sit amongst and admire some exquisite Norman architecture.

Café Below operates in the crypt of Sir Christopher Wren's St Mary-le-Bow (see p.77 for a description of this church) constructed on the site of the church of circa 1087, but which was destroyed in the Great Fire of 1666. Wren chose to preserve the Norman columns, piers and vaulting, some of which were made from re-used Roman brick, as far as he could.

George Inn
C1676+

George Inn Yard, 77 Borough High Street, Southwark, SE1 1NH • Tel 020 7407 2056 • www.nationaltrust.org.uk • Nearest transport London Bridge LU & Rail • See website for opening times

Tucked away in a cobbled courtyard just off Borough High Street, the George Inn is a unique survivor – the last galleried inn left in London. Coaching inns were once commonplace and here the Old Bar was once the waiting room for coachmen and passengers. The coming of the railway to the area in 1899 resulted in the demolition of the north wing and centre of the original inn, so we are left with just one third of the original. Charles Dickens was a regular visitor and liked to frequent the Coffee Room, now the Middle Bar, and he mentions this inn in Little Dorrit (1857).

Inns have occupied this site since medieval times, this building dating from about 1676 and the wealth of oak beams and lattice windows make the building very atmospheric.

Bar and bar food available daily. An a la carte restaurant open Monday to Saturday. Please telephone for reservations. *Area Map p.8, B:1*

The Orangery
1704-05

The Orangery, Kensington Palace, W8 4PX • Tel 0844 482 7777 • www.hrp.org. uk/KensingtonPalace • Nearest transport Kensington High Street LU • See website for opening times

Designed by Hawksmoor and built in 1704-5. It was here the Queen would distribute gifts of specially minted coins to poor people on Maundy Thursday and where she would perform the ceremony known as 'Touching the King's Evil'. People from all walks of life would travel here to be physically touched by the Monarch in the belief they would be cured. In 1712 the infant Samuel Johnson was brought here from his Warwickshire home for just this reason. Queen Anne was the last Monarch to perform this service which had begun in the Middle Ages.

The exterior of the Orangery is of reddish brickwork and the interior is a confection of pure white. A short flight of stairs takes the visitor to the main front door which opens into a large rectangular room decorated with Corinthian columns. The carvings over the end arches are thought to be by Grinling Gibbons.

The Orangery is open to everyone, not just to Kensington Palace visitors and during the summer months tables and chairs are also available outside. Open most days from breakfast to afternoon tea.

St John's, Smith Square
Thomas Archer, 1713-28

The Footstool Restaurant, St John's, Smith Square, SW1 • Tel 020 7222 2779 • Nearest transport St James's Park LU

St John's is considered to be one of the finest examples of English Baroque architecture to be found anywhere. Built as part of the 'Fifty Churches' scheme (see p.87) during the reign of Queen Anne, to a Greek-cross plan, the north and south 'arms' of the building have enormous Doric columns and these mark the two entrances. The east and west ends each have a large Venetian window and Doric pilasters. However, on first seeing the church, one's eye is immediately drawn to the four corner towers – circular with short Doric columns set diagonally and each topped by a small pineapple ogee lantern.

The church was severely damaged by enemy bombing in 1941 and was restored by Marshall Sisson 1965-69 as a concert hall. With its excellent acoustics and varied programme of classical music, St John's is now a much-valued venue in the heart of Westminster.

However, one does not need to attend a concert to savour the delights of the interior of St John's for in the brick-vaulted crypt there is the superb Footstool restaurant. An à la carte British menu, light buffet, drinks and snacks are available weekday lunch times and from 5.30pm onwards on concert evenings. *Area Map p.6, B:1*

Rex Whistler Restaurant, Tate Britain
Sidney R J Smith et al, 1893+

Tate Britain, Millbank, SW1 • Tel 020 7887 8000 (reservations 020 7887 8825) • www.tate.org.uk • Nearest transport Pimlico or Westminster LU • See website for opening times

Although a visit to Tate Britain is always a treat, discovering new works of art and revisiting favourites, the architecture is of interest in itself. The main building was built with money donated by the sugar tycoon Sir Henry Tate on the boggy site of a miserable prison known as Millbank Penitentiary. A large projecting portico and fairly shallow dome give this building a classical air, but with a little Victorian over-enthusiasm.

The recent extension to the Tate, the Clore Gallery added in 1987, by the eminent architect the late Sir James Stirling, was built to house the Tate's wonderful collection of paintings by J M W Turner.

The restaurant at the Tate is a very grand affair, decorated with murals executed by a young Rex Whistler in 1926-27, after whom it has been named. Appropriately he took as his subject 'The Expedition in Pursuit of Rare Meats'. Open daily from breakfast to dinner, and booking ahead is almost essential.

The Black Friar
H Fuller Clark, c1905

The Black Friar, 174 Queen Victoria Street,
EC4 • Tel 020 7236 5650 • Nearest transport Blackfriars LU & Rail • Open daily
lunchtimes to mid evening (this is a City
pub so has shorter opening hours)

First built in 1873, this is a typical London-pub-on-the-corner wedge shaped building. Of
earlier pedigree than those of the 1890s pub
boom, the Black Friar was given a new ground
floor sometime at the turn of the last century.
The interior was completely redecorated by
Herbert Fuller Clark and his colleague artist
Henry Poole and what was accomplished
needs to be seen to be believed. The entire
bar area is decorated with red and green
marble depicting the activities of the monks
who lived on the site when the land belonged
to the Dominican, or Black Friars, monastery.
The whole work was executed in an Arts
and Crafts manner and it is a truly unique
experience to come and sip a beer in this pub.
Area Map p.8, A:2

*Right: The Black Friar Public House. Many wedge-shaped public houses were built in London during
the late 19th century*

Bibendum Oyster Bar & Restaurant
François Espinasse, 1909-11

Bibendum, Michelin House, 81 Fulham Road, SW3 • Tel 020 7581 5817 • www.bibendum.co.uk • Nearest transport South Kensington LU • See website for opening times

The style of this building hovers between Art Nouveau and Art Deco – with colourful decorations and motifs playing on the theme of wheels and tyres as befitting the former British Head Office of the Michelin Tyre Company. Built 1909-11, this is a very early example of what could be achieved with reinforced concrete. Michelin sold the building in 1985 to Terence Conran and Paul Hamlyn who began an extensive programme of renovation and reinvention. The result is a stylish café, restaurant and oyster bar, with a ground floor crustacean stall should you wish to buy something fresh to take home.

'Bibendum' is the name of the Michelin man, (who is surely Bertie Bassett's Gallic uncle), hence the name of this very fashionable establishment.

Left: Bibendum Oyster Bar & Restaurant

The Ritz
Charles Mewes, 1903-06

The Ritz, 55 Piccadilly, W1 • Tel 020 7493 8181 • www.theritzlondon.com • Nearest transport Green Park LU • See website for opening times

Whether taking tea, or propping up the bar, do take a closer look at the first steel-framed structure in London. This lovely building looks as though it strayed in from Paris and indeed the architect did design the Paris Ritz in 1899; very wisely repeating all the successful parts here.

If you are unable to venture in to the hotel, through lack of time or shortage of funds, stay outside and admire the ground floor arcade; again very French. The whole building is faced in Norwegian stone at the ground floor with Portland stone above.

Tea at the Palm Court of the Ritz costs in the region of £40 per person, but is truly a treat you will not forget in a hurry. You will need to book at least six weeks ahead.

Wesley's Café at the Methodist Central Hall
Lanchester & Rickards, 1905-11

Methodist Central Hall, Storey's Gate, SW1 • Tel 020 7222 8010 • www.c-h-w. com • Nearest transport St James's Park or Westminster LU • Open for morning coffee, light lunch & afternoon tea Mon-Sat 10am-4pm

The café in this splendid Edwardian baroque building is a bit of a secret in this almost café/ restaurant-free zone of Westminster. Tours of this splendid building are offered every day of the week – please enquire at reception. Please see p.180 for a description of this building.

Renaissance London, Chancery Court Hotel
Moncton & Newman, 1912-19

Renaissance London, Chancery Court Hotel, 252 High Holborn, WC1V • Tel 020 7829 7000 • www.mariott.co.uk • Nearest transport Holborn LU • See website for opening times

A rather slick, comfortable hotel, restaurant and bar in a lovely building that still oozes Edwardian grandeur. Built 1912-19 by Moncton and Newman and converted in 1998 by Bennett and Son. A baroque-style dome sits over the entrance – walk through to the Lobby Lounge to enjoy coffee or afternoon tea whilst you recline in the ample upholstery, or sip a champagne cocktail in the marble lined bar. All in the name of architectural interest, of course. *Area Map p.2-3, C:1*

Oxo Tower
Albert W Moore, 1928

Oxo Tower Wharf, Barge House Street, SE1 • Tel 020 7803 3888 • Nearest transport Blackfriars LU & Rail • www.harveynichols.com • See website for opening times

The Oxo Tower was built in 1928 as an Art Deco addition to a meat manufacturer's London base. At this time there was a ban on any form of neon lit advertising in the area, so one bright spark thought of picking out the name OXO in coloured glass windows at the top of the tower and placing a strong light behind it which shone out into the London night.

The Tower, which sits equidistant between Blackfriars Bridge and Waterloo Bridge and long abandoned by its originators, is now part of the Coin Street Housing Association. Shops, galleries and small workshops occupy the first three floors and the next five floors consist of affordable-housing, while the top floor is devoted to the restaurant, brasserie and bar.

Both the restaurant and brasserie are modern and spacious and lack any form of cosiness, but the views over the Thames are spectacular, especially in the evening.

Foyer Bar, Claridge's
Oswald Milne, 1931

Claridge's, 49 Brook Street, W1K 4HR •
Tel 020 7629 8860 • www.claridges.co.uk
• See website for opening times

The epitome of glamour and with a reputation
for impeccable, professional service, Claridge's
is one of London's most iconic hotels. In
business since the very early 19th century and
noted for its late 1920's Art Deco makeover by
architect Oswald Milne the hotel has not rested
on its considerable laurels.

In 1999 Claridge's embarked on the first major
designer restoration since the 1930s when
New York-based designer Thierry Despont
was brought in to revitalize the Foyer area.
He used archive photographs of the Ballroom
Extension of early 1930s as inspiration and the
space was completely made over in a modern
Art Deco style, with a magnificent silver-white
light sculpture by artist Dale Chihuly as its
centrepiece. Created from more than 800
individually hand-blown glass pieces, it hangs
from the Foyer's 18ft high ceiling.

The refurbishment of the Foyer was seen as
such a success that shortly after its completion
Thierry Despont was invited back to work on
the Gordon Ramsey restaurant at the hotel.

The Foyer is open every day from breakfast
through to the evening, with live music to
accompany the sumptuous afternoon teas.

Babylon Restaurant and Roof Garden, Kensington
Ralph Hancock, 1938

The Roof Garden & Babylon Restaurant,
99 Kensington High Street, W8 5SA (Access to the building is via Derry Street, off
Kensington High Street) • Tel 0207 368
3993 • www.roofgardens.virgin.com •
Nearest Transport LU Kensington High
Street LU • See website for opening times

One hundred feet above the busy Kensington
High Street, is one of the capital's best kept
secrets, a huge roof garden and restaurant
with wonderful views across London. Added
in the late 1930's to the fashionable Derry and
Toms store built 1929-31 in a vaguely Beaux-
Arts style. The Roof Garden was the dream of
Trevor Bowen, vice president of Barkers, who
owned Derry and Toms and had built a shop
next door, see 'Shopping and Architecture'
section of this book. Bowen employed Welsh-
born landscape architect Ralph Hancock to
realise his dream, having seen his gardens at
the Rockefeller Centre, New York.

In total the roof garden measures some 1.5
acres and has three themed areas – the
Spanish Garden, inspired by the Moorish
Alhambra in Granada, Spain; the Tudor
Garden, filled with evergreen shrubs and lilies,
roses, wisteria and lavender which perfume the
air during the summer months and the English
Woodland, which is a riot of colour in the

Left: English woodland garden, Babylon Restaurant

Skylon Restaurant, Grill & Bar
Hidalgo Moya and Philip Powell, 1951

Royal Festival Hall, Belvedere Rd, SE1 8XX
• Tel 020 7654 7800 • www.skylon-restaurant.co.uk • See website for opening times

The design of this Conran Restaurant won the prestigious Time Out Eating and Drinking award in 2007. This cool, contemporary venue sits well within the Modernist host building of the Royal Festival Hall. Clever lighting has, to a large degree, turned the cavernous space of this part of the Grade 1 listed building into intimate dining areas with wonderful views from the huge plate glass windows over the Thames to the centre of London.

springtime. With 70 full-sized trees and ponds teeming with wildlife, not to mention ducks and flamingos, this place is a delight to visit.

Amidst this paradise is the Babylon Restaurant with some of the best views across London serving lunch and dinner most days with an opportunity for alfresco dining during warmer weather. Please telephone or see their website for opening times, menus and booking information. The garden is occasionally open to non-diners, see the website for details.

Named in honour of the structure that stood at the heart of the 1951 Festival of Britain, on the site of what is now the Royal Festival Hall. Designed by two young architects Hidalgo Moya and Philip Powell in collaboration with structural engineer Felix Samuely, the Skylon stood 105 metres tall. The cigar-shaped steel construction captured the imagination of the nation, its futuristic form pointing to an optimistic period for a war-torn Britain. Despite its popularity, the Skylon, and the other exhibits was torn down by the incoming government of Winston Church later that year. However the Skylon lives on in the choice of name for this restaurant. For further details of the Royal Festival Hall please see p.205.

Vertigo, Tower 42
Seifert and Partners, 1970-81

Vertigo – Tower 42, 25 Old Broad Street, EC2N • Tel 0207 877 7842 • www.vertigo42.co.uk • Nearest transport Bank LU • See website for opening times

Champagne and seafood bar located 590 feet up the famous Tower 42 (formerly known as the NatWest Tower) in the heart of the City. Built 1970-81 by Seifert and Partners, the building has a stabilising concrete service core with floors cantilevered out from it, and the whole is enclosed in a glass sheath. For ten years this was the tallest building in London, indeed in Britain, until the towers of Canary Wharf sprang up.

The views from this bar are the best in London and the food and drink is outstanding too.
Area Map p.8, C:2

Blueprint Café at the Design Museum
Sir Terence Conran, 1988-89

Blueprint Café, The Design Museum, Shad Thames, SE1 • Tel 020 7378 7031 • www.blueprintcafe.co.uk • Nearest transport London Bridge LU & Rail • See website for opening times

Built on the site of a disused warehouse on the banks of the Thames in 1988-89, before the area became truly fashionable, one could be forgiven for thinking they had stumbled upon something that had strayed from the Bauhaus. However, on a particularly sunny day with the proximity of the water this building has something of a seaside promenade about it.

The building is of white painted and rendered brick and its primary purpose is to house a museum dedicated to all aspects of 20th-century design from kitchen appliances to chairs, from packaging to computers. The museum was founded by Terence Conran and Stephen Bayley to highlight the need for good design at every level.

The glazed balcony overlooking the Thames is a spectacular setting for the Blueprint Café, which serves good modern European fare.
Area Map p.8, C:1

Pizza Express, Alban Gate
Terry Farrell, 1988-92

Pizza Express, 125 London Wall, Alban Gate, EC2Y 5AJ • Tel 020 7600 8880 • www.pizzaexpress.com • Nearest transport Moorgate LU/Rail, St Paul's LU • See website for opening times

The Pizza Express chain has always, wherever possible, sited its restaurants in architecturally interesting places and this property provides an opportunity to eat lunch or supper inside a piece of very modern architecture. The Alban Gate complex spans the busy London Wall roadway at Wood Street and Terry Farrell, its architect, likens it to a gigantic gatehouse. Completed in 1992 Alban Gate provides 8.6 acres of office space in granite of differing colours and glass.

There are in fact two Pizza Express restaurants here, almost side by side and mirror images of each other. Although it's almost impossible to see out of the windows whilst dining, it is fun to contemplate the glass and steel and wonder what is holding it all up!

This restaurant is situated near the Museum of London and the delights of the City.
Area Map p.8, B:3

British Library Coffee Shop
Colin St John Wilson & Partners,1997

The British Library, 96 Euston Road, NW1 • Tel 020 7412 7332 • www.bl.uk • Nearest transport Euston LU & Rail and King's Cross/St Pancras LU & Rai• See website for opening times

The impetus to form the British Library came from the donation of his father's book collection by George IV to the British Museum. The library moved from the British Museum to new premises in 1999 and the King's Library is now attractively displayed in the Tower of Books which can be seen by all in the entrance hall, but which can be contemplated more closely from the comfort of the Coffee Shop.

Open to the public in general as well as library users and exhibition visitors, the self-service coffee shop offers coffee, pastries, light lunches and afternoon teas

Portrait Restaurant & Bar, National Portrait Gallery
Dixon and Jones, 1994-2000

National Portrait Gallery, St Martin's Place, WC2H 0HE • Tel 020 7312 2490 (Restaurant), 020 7306 0055 (Gallery) • www.npg.org.uk • Nearest transport Charing Cross LU/Rail or Embankment LU • Table reservations are essential for the restaurant • See website for opening times

The main body of the Gallery is the original 1896 building by Ewan Christian and was designed to blend with its neighbour the National Gallery – indeed perhaps a little too successfully as many people miss the National Portrait Gallery altogether believing it to be part of the huge gallery next door. Despite its excellent collection of portraits of the great, the good and the interesting the National Portrait Gallery was never particularly busy and rarely did visitors venture further than the first floor; if they entered at all. The site was cramped and there was little chance of expansion.

In 1994 the then director, Charles Saumarez, and the Gallery trustees appointed Jeremy Dixon (who also worked on the Covent Garden refurbishment) and Edward Jones to conjure up some space, seemingly from nowhere. Miraculously a three-storey atrium was gleaned from an old, narrow service yard and a long escalator now whisks visitors up to the top floor, where the earliest portraits are hung. The visitor can then percolate down through the collection enjoying a gallery that now feels spacious and light. However, the charming

front façade of the building is unchanged so the unsuspecting visitor gets quite a surprise on entering.

As with nearly every new building extension, provision was made for a public restaurant. At 92 feet above ground level on the fifth floor of this new Ondaatje Wing it has spectacular views over Nelson's Column down Whitehall and on to the Houses of Parliament. The 80 seat restaurant and 25 seat bar area is under the care of Searcy's catering, serving good British fare. *Area Map p.6, B:3*

Right: Ondaatje Wing, National Portrait Gallery

Tate Modern
Sir Giles Gilbert Scott, 1947-63
Herzog & de Meuron, 1994-2000

Tate Modern, Bankside, SE1 • Tel 020 7887
8888 • www.tate.org.uk • Nearest transport
Southwark LU (Jubilee line) • See website
for opening times

This building should be intimidating; after
all it is huge, new and displays modern art!
However it is one of the most successful
National Lottery funded projects. All sorts of
people come here and not necessarily those
who would frequent, say, the Royal Academy.
Part of this popularity is due to the building
itself – £134 million was lavished on to its
conversion from a disused power station to a
vibrant modern art venue. Its spaces, from the
vast Turbine Hall to user friendly galleries, have
proved to be a real hit.

The architects, Herzog and de Meuron, made
plenty of provision for dining within the building.
The top floor (level 7) restaurant is fun and has
good views – but only from a very few tables; it
is always busy but worth queuing for. However
the best treat is coffee, lunch or tea in the
Friends Room on level 6. This enjoys fabulous
views to the Thames side but equally interesting
views to the south of London from the rear
terrace. Not so many landmark buildings
maybe but a wonderful panorama nonetheless.

Inn the Park
Michael Hopkins, 2004

Inn the Park, St James's Park (west of Horse Guards Parade), SW1A 2BJ • Tel 020 7451 9999 • www.innthepark.com • Nearest transport Green Park and St James's Park LU

Made from Austrian Larch wood, which has been left untreated externally so that it gradually weathers over time, this café has been cleverly designed by Michael Hopkins to appear as part of the landscape. Even the surrounding grassy areas continue over the structure's roof and the glass frontage gives diners superb views of the nearby lake. Within its curved walls there is seating for over 100 diners and the same number again on the covered terrace outside.

Open everyday, from breakfast to dinner, this café/diner is managed by Oliver Peyton who has provided imaginative, delicious seasonal menus since its opening in 2004.
Area Map p.6, B:2

Left: Views across the Millennium Bridge (see p.369) to St Paul's Cathedral (see p.61) from Tate Modern (see p.230)

St Pancras Grand Champagne Bar, St Pancras Station
William Barlow,1868 / Martin Brudnizki Design Studio, 2008

St Pancras Station, Upper Concourse, Euston Road, N1C 4QL • Tel 020 7870 9900 • www.searcys.com • Nearest transport King's Cross & St Pancras LU & Rail • See website for opening times

The recent transformation of this railway station is truly astonishing. For a great many years it was a rather grim place where commuters and visitors would have been hard-pressed to buy a decent coffee or sandwich. Now St Pancras Station is itself a destination, not merely somewhere to pass through, thanks to the addition of shops, bars, cafés and restaurants, as part of the £800 million restoration and extension. Trains run not only to the north of England from here but also to the Continent via Eurostar and the high-speed link to the Channel Tunnel; the centre of Paris under three hours away.

The most glamorous of all the additions is the Champagne Bar, at 96 metres Europe's longest, situated below the magnificent Barlow Shed and allowing a full appreciation of the amazing architecture of the station. When the station first opened in 1868 William Barlow's train shed was an outstanding feat of Victorian engineering. The roof is 689ft long and 100ft high and with a span of 243ft it held the record for the worlds largest enclosed space for many years. During recent restoration work it has been completely reglazed and the paint work returned to its intended pale sky blue.

The Bar's main seating area consists of comfortable booths accommodating six people; each booth has its own adjustable fan heater and a black Art Deco-inspired lamp which dispenses a flattering pool of light. There are also tables for two and plenty of standing-room for larger groups. The Bar is open seven days a week for drink and food, including a most sumptuous afternoon tea. For further information about this wonderful building see p.154.

Rotunda Bar & Restaurant, King's Place
Dixon-Jones, 2008

Kings Place, 90 York Way, N1 9AG • Tel 020 7014 2840 • www.kingsplace.co.uk/food-drink/rotunda-bar-restaurant • Nearest Transport King's Cross & St Pancras LU/Rail • See website for opening times

Like its neighbour St Pancras Station, the King's Cross Station area was a frankly unappealing place; certainly not many would want to linger where the grubby, long-neglected buildings stood forlorn. Thankfully, the multi-million pound, 67 acre redevelopment of the area has brought benefits to residents and visitors alike.

King's Cross Station itself, designed by Lewis Cubitt and first opened in 1852, is receiving a major face-lift, as is the adjacent Great Northern Hotel of 1854 by the same architect. Office space to the tune of 4.9 million square feet has been created; 2,000 homes and serviced apartments will be available, in a mix of owner-occupied, rented and 'affordable' options. Even the remaining landmark gas holders built between 1879 and 1881 for the Gas, Light and Coke Company have been preserved and have been incorporated into the housing scheme.

The new University of the Arts, which incorporates the prestigious Central Saint

Martins School of Art and Design, attracting over 4,000 students, has been built on the site of the old Granary and Eastern Goods Yard, with 650 units of student accommodation provided. New theatres, exhibition spaces and community spaces, such as the Eureka! Children's Museum and The House of Illustration, occupy existing refurbished heritage buildings. Serious consideration has been given to open spaces and the Camley Street Natural Park, two acres of wild green space so close to the heart of the Capital, is an inspiration to all.

One of the most exciting new-builds of the scheme, designed by architects Dixon-Jones, is 'Kings Place' which brings together under one roof a dining venue, a conference and events centre, and office complex. Containing two public concert auditoriums, the larger, with a seating capacity of 450, has an oak veneer interior from the same 500-year old German oak tree. After felling, the wood was cut into 5m lengths and boiled at 80 oC for one week, then sliced. The tree has produced an acre of superb veneer, it covers the wall panels, columns, roof coffers, doors, the back of seats, and the musicians desks. The other, is a smaller, flexible 250-seat space, making this an attractive music venue and indeed is now the home of the world-renown Orchestra of the Age of the Enlightenment. There are also two major spaces designed specifically for the display of visual arts, Pangolin London and Kings Place Gallery.

The Kings Place building itself has an attractive frontage onto York Way with a three-layered undulating glass façade; a free-standing transparent surface made up of hundreds of very slightly curved sheets of glass, produced in a factory near Venice. Enter here and the visitor is lead to a magnificent atrium which gives views up to all seven levels as well as bringing light into the central core of the building.

Also visible to the rear is the Battlebridge Basin and one of the larger basins on the Regent's Canal, which opened from Paddington to Camden in 1816 and onward to the basin at Limehouse in 1820. The Basin was used for the trans-shipment of goods to and from the canals and was kept busy handling goods such as ice, imported from Norway and used for making such delicacies as ice cream. The former ice warehouse is now the London Canal Museum here in the Basin.

Some of the best views of the Basin can be obtained from the King's Place Rotunda Bar and Restaurant, where al fresco dining is available during the summer months. Customers can sit at the Bar for drinks and lighter meals, with a table service for lunch and dinner. Quality food takes pride of place, with much of the meat served here raised at the restaurants own farm in Northumberland. Both Bar and Restaurant are open seven days a week.

Chiswick House Café
Caruso St John Architects, 2010

Chiswick House Café, Chiswick House & Gardens, Burlington Lane, W4 2QN • Tel 0208 995 6356 • www.chiswickhousecafe.co.uk • Nearest Transport Turnham Green LU, Chiswick Rail • See website for opening times

This café building was constructed as part of the major landscaping project carried out between 2006 and 2010 at one of London's most exquisite properties, Chiswick House (see p.104 for further details) and was named RIBA London Building of the Year 2011.

Created by the ever innovative architectural practice of Caruso St John, this little building is no neo-Palladian pastiche, but rather its elevation recalls the arcaded facades of the stable wings of country villas in the Veneto, such as Palladio's Villa Angarano. This is particularly fitting as the café is built on the site of the old stables, to the east of the house. The smooth stone colonnade provides covered exterior seating around the main room of the café, from where visitors have a superb view south of the surrounding lawns and mature trees.

Open most days of the year, the café is available to visitors to the house as well as those using the park

Barkers, Kensington High St see p.363

10

SHOPPING & ARCHITECTURE

As if one needs
an excuse to go
shopping, here
is a short list of some of
the architectural gems in
London which just happen
to be retail outlets too.

Right: Leadenhall Market, designed by Sir Horace Jones 1880-81, see p.359

Burlington Arcade
Samuel Ware, 1819

Burlington Arcade, Piccadilly, W1 • www.
burlington-arcade.co.uk • Nearest transport Green Park and Piccadilly Circus LU

One of three shopping arcades off Piccadilly,
the other two being the Princes and the
Piccadilly, both of which are on the opposite,
south side of the road. Burlington Arcade
was built in 1819 by the architect Samuel
Ware (1781-1860) for Lord George Cavendish,
who owned Burlington House. The arcade
formed the western boundary to Cavendish's
property and it is said that the impetus behind
its construction was to stop passers-by
flinging rubbish into his Lordship's garden, not
because he wanted to make money from this
piece of speculative building!

The arcade consists of two rows of small, bow-
fronted, shops with rooms above, set in a narrow
passage, some 585 feet long, which becomes
wider and one-storey taller in three places. At
every fourth shop a cross arch rests on Ionic
pilasters, thereby adding variety and the whole
passage is top lit from windows in the roof.

The shops cater for the luxury end of the market;
cashmere, pure Irish linen, leather goods, pens,
and jewellery. Security is provided by the frock-
coated, top-hatted Beadles who are instructed
to eject anyone running, carrying large parcels,
whistling or generally causing a nuisance – you
have been warned. *Area Map p.6, A:2*

Royal Exchange
Sir William Tite, 1841-44

Royal Exchange, between Threadneedle Street and Cornhill, EC3 • www.theroyalex-change.com • Nearest transport Bank LU • Grand Café Tel 020 7618 2480 • See website for opening times

This building is often mistaken for the Bank of England, which is just over the road in Threadneedle Street. With its massive portico supported by huge Corinthian columns, the front of the building is much wider, at 175 feet, than the back 119 feet. This is the third Royal Exchange building on the site, the others having burned down in 1666 and 1838; the present building was declared open by Queen Victoria in 1844.

The 'Exchange' was established by Sir Thomas Gresham, a successful merchant and favoured courtier, in 1565. Prior to this City merchants and traders had carried out their business in a fairly informal way, gathering together in the street twice a day, but after visiting the Antwerp Bourse Gresham decided that a more formal setting was needed for business in London. The first building was opened in 1570 by Elizabeth I, who gave it its Royal title and it is from its steps that the new monarch is announced to the City.

The Royal Exchange ceased to be a business institution in 1939 and since then the building has been occupied by various organisations including the Guardian Royal Exchange Assurance until 1991. Disused and neglected after this time it was decided to breathe new life into the place by turning it into a retail and restaurant complex.

The interior of the Exchange forms a covered quadrangular surmounted by colonnades, with a statue of Queen Victoria by Thornycroft at the centre and a series of paintings around the walls of the courtyard by artists such as Lord Leighton, Frank Brangwyn, and Stanhope Forbes.

The shops within the Exchange are bordering on the luxury end of the market with Tod's, Agent Provocateur, and Jo Malone amongst them, and they are fun to browse. The restaurant at the centre of the building is the Grand Café and Bar, a Conran venture, which offers sustenance of the highest quality from breakfast to dinner. The Mezzanine Bar serves champagne wines, beers and cocktails and is a super place from which to take in the architecture. *Area Map p.8, B:2*

Leadenhall Market
Sir Horace Jones, 1880-81

Leadenhall Market, Gracechurch Street, EC3 • www.leadenhallmarket.co.uk • Nearest transport Bank and Monument LU

The name 'Leadenhall' comes from a large medieval house which once stood close by to this site, which apparently had a lead roof, with the market being established on adjoining land. The house, its estate and the market were sold to the City Corporation at the beginning of the 15th century. House and market both perished in the Great Fire of London but were quickly rebuilt on a plan around three courtyards.

The present market, designed by City architect Sir Horace Jones, in 1880-81, is a lovely structure built on the cross-plan of the old street configuration. The main entrance, off Gracechurch Street, has engaged, fluted columns in dark-red and cream paintwork with gilded capitals. These appear to support a stone pediment with carved decorations and a fairly small, simple clock.

The market still sells fresh meat and fish but is mainly given over to fashion, with shops such as Jigsaw and Hobbs doing a brisk trade during the City lunchtime. *Area Map p.8, C:2*

Harrods
Stevens and Munt, 1901-05

87-135 Brompton Road, Knightsbridge, SW1 • Tel 020 7730 1234 • www.harrods.com • Nearest transport Knightsbridge LU • See website for opening times

The store's motto is: 'omnia, omnibus, ubique' (everything for everyone, everywhere) and Harrods could indeed at one time brag that they could supply anything from a packet of pins to an elephant! Henry Charles Harrod began this retail legend as a tea merchant in the early 19th century at Eastcheap in the City, moving to Knightsbridge in 1849. It stayed a thriving, family-run shop until 1889 when it became a public limited company. Its present building was constructed between 1901-05, with additions made until the 1930's.

The building, with its famous terracotta façade, was designed by the architectural practice of Stevens and Munt and at its completion, was declared the largest department store in Europe, occupying a site of some 4.5 acres, with a total retail space of 13.5 acres over five floors. To see the tilework in the magnificent Food Hall on the ground floor is alone well worth the trip to Knightsbridge as is the Art Deco ladies' restroom on the first floor and the gentlemen's hairdressers in the basement.

The famously comprehensive Toy Department is where A A Milne purchased the original Pooh bear for his son Christopher.

Selfridges
David Burnham et al, 1906+

Selfridges, 400 Oxford Street, W1A •
Tel 0800 123 400 • www.selfridges.com •
Nearest transport Bond Street LU

Arguably London's most popular department
store since it was first opened in March 1909,
Selfridges was the brainchild of its owner,
American-born Henry Gordon Selfridge (1858-
1947), who learned the business of retail in
Chicago. He brought the art of browsing to the
London shopper who up until this point was
used to simply being shown items selected by
the shopkeeper – this was a radical departure.

Selfridge bought the huge plot in 1906 and
set about creating a building the likes of which
Londoners had not seen before. Massive shop
windows separated by short pillars dominate
the ground floor while gigantic Ionic columns
stretch up from the first floor to the exquisitely
carved attic floor balustrade. Over the central
entrance recess is an 11 feet figure named
'Queen of Time' as well as a huge clock, both
of which were installed in 1931. The whole
project took nearly 30 years to complete and a
number of architects were involved, the most
prominent being Daniel Burnham of Chicago.

Major refurbishment started in 1995 and has
given the interior a much lighter, more modern
feel with a huge atrium accommodating a
series of escalators from which all floors can
now be accessed. *Area Map p.4, B:1*

Fortnum and Mason
Wimperis, Simpson & Guthrie, 1926-29

Fortnum and Mason, 181 Piccadilly
Circus, W1 • Tel 020 7734 8040 • www.
fortnumandmason.com • Nearest transport Green Park and Piccadilly Circus LU

This enterprise was started in the 1770s by
Charles Fortnum – who, as a former footman
in the royal household of George III knew a
thing or two about service – and his friend
John Mason, who owned horses and a yard
close-by and who dealt with the deliveries.
They made their reputation by importing exotic
foods and supplying such to the gentlemen's
clubs of London.

In the late 19th century Fortnum and Mason
took the radical step of stocking Heinz canned
food, becoming one of the first stores in the
world to do so but is still most famous for
being the Queen's grocer.

Fortnum and Mason started their business
in premises close to their present shop in
Piccadilly, which was built in 1926-29 by
Wimperis, Simpson and Guthrie who, given
the shop's pedigree, chose a Georgian style.
The fussy automated clock by Eric Aumonier
was made in 1964, but appears to come from
an earlier era, and on the hour four foot high
mechanical replicas of the original Mr. Fortnum
and Mr. Mason emerge and bow to each other.

Waterstone's (formerly Simpsons of Piccadilly)
Joseph Emberton, 1935-36

Waterstone's, 203-206 Piccadilly, W1 • Tel 0843 290 8549 • www.waterstones.com • Nearest transport Piccadilly Circus LU • See website for opening times

It is easy to walk by this building and not realise its significance for 20th-century architecture. This was the first shop in Britain to have an uninterrupted curved-glass front made possible by arc-welding the wide-span steel-frame, rather than using bulky bolted joints. The method had been pioneered the year before at the renowned De La Warr Pavilion in Bexhill-on-Sea by Mendelsohn and Chermayeff, who were members of MARS (Modern Architecture Research) set up in 1933. Notable among the group were Walter Gropius, Marcel Breuer, Ove Arup, Hugh Casson, and John Betjeman.

The interior was designed to domestic proportions as a series of rooms with an open-well staircase (there is an apologetic notice explaining why the handrail appears to be a little short for today's customers); note also the original hanging light fitting.

The shop was originally commissioned by Alexander Simpson for his quality menswear store. The move to Piccadilly was prompted by success of the DAKS brand of trousers with their patented self-supporting waistband. During the very early 1970s the writer Jeremy Lloyd was employed as an assistant and it from his short spell at Simpsons that the idea of a television sitcom blossomed into 'Are you Being Served?' which in 1979 was turned into an American version called 'Beanes of Boston'.

In 1999 the shop was sold to Waterstone's and is now their flagship store, on the top floor of which is a bar conveniently located next to the 'Art and Architecture' section. From the comfort of the bar there is a wonderful view south, over the rooftops towards the Palace of Westminster. *Area Map p.6, A:2*

Peter Jones
W Crabtree et al, 1936-38

Peter Jones, Sloane Square, SW1W 8EL
• Tel 020 7730 3434 • www.peterjones.
co.uk • Nearest transport Sloane Square
LU • Wheelchair access • See website for
opening times

Peter Jones is part of the John Lewis
Partnership chain and one can purchase
almost anything in the way of household,
electrical, sports goods and fashion. This
was one of the first uses of the glass curtain
wall in Britain and was heavily influenced
by Mendelsohn's designs for the Schoken
department stores in Stuttgart and Chemnitz.
The concept of curtain walling in modern
buildings is a thin subordinate wall, usually
made of glass or metal, held between piers or
other structural members but which are not
load-bearing.

This fine building– which has something of
the ocean-going liner about it – has recently
been the subject of a £100 million renovation
programme adding air conditioning, new
restaurants, over 20% extra retail space and a
dramatic central atrium in which escalators to
all floors are sited.

Left and above left: Central atrium, Peter Jones
Right: Barkers

Barkers
Bernard George, 1937-38

Barkers, 63-97 Kensington High Street, W8 • Nearest transport Kensington High Street LU • Open daily, usual shop opening hours

It was during the heyday of the department store, that is the first 60 or so years of the 20th century, that Bernard George was given the brief to remodel the highly successful Barkers store. The building he was to re-vamp had originally been designed by the much respected architect Sir Reginald Blomfield in 1912-13.

Bernard George presented Kensington High Street with an outstanding example of Art Deco. The unmistakable outline of the building owes much to the twin glass towers which soar above neighbouring rooflines. The facade has some remarkable ornamental stonework and do note the exquisite murals celebrating the art of chic shopping.

Alas, unlike its rivals Harrods and Selfridges, Barkers succumbed to the economic downturn of recent decades and is no longer a department store closing for business in 2006. The building is now occupied by an upmarket organic food emporium.

It is interesting to contrast the splendour of Barkers with the nearby building which houses Marks and Spencer at Nos 99-121 Kensington High Street – this was also designed by Bernard George in a 'Moderne' style, and looks rather subdued compared with its neighbour.

This too was originally built as a department store in 1935 for Derry and Toms, another victim of changing economic fortunes. What is remarkable about this particular building is that unknown to most of the shoppers, the building has a truly spectacular one and a half acre roof garden, details of which can be found in the previous section of this book.

View from The London Eye, see p.371

11

**ARCHITECTURE
WITH A VIEW**

Many of the buildings already mentioned afford great views across London, particularly some of those in the 'Eat and Drink Architecture' section. Don't forget places such as the dome of St Paul's Cathedral (Golden Gallery) welcome visitors (see p.61).

Right: View from The Monument

The Monument
Sir Christopher Wren and Robert Hooke, 1671-76

Monument Street, EC3 • Tel 0207 626 2717 • www.themonument.info • Nearest transport Monument LU • See website for opening times and admission charges

This work is often attributed to Wren alone and yet it has all the hallmarks of a Robert Hooke project, particularly given that the basement was arranged so that he could carry out his experiments and observations with the aid of the column itself, which he used as a sort of telescope.

Erected as both a memorial to the devastated City of London after the Great Fire of 1666 and as a morale-booster to those who were struggling to put the City back together, the Monument stands at 202 feet, taller than Trajan's Column in Rome, and is still believed to be the tallest isolated stone structure in Europe. There are 311 steps to the observation gallery where a spectacular 360 degree view of the City and beyond awaits.

Made from Portland Stone, this fluted Roman Doric column is topped with a bronze urn with flames licking the sky. *Area Map p.8, B:2*

Tower Bridge
Sir Horace Jones, 1886-94

The Tower Bridge Exhibition, Tower Bridge, SE1 • Tel 020 7403 3761 • www.tower-bridge.org.uk • Nearest transport Tower Hill LU • See website for opening times and admission charges

Architect Sir Horace Jones collaborated with engineer Sir John Wolfe Barry to design this definitive London landmark. Victorian technological wizardry hides behind architecture which was designed to be in keeping with the Tower of London nearby; the architect referred to it as 'a steel skeleton clothed in stone'

At the time of its construction the Thames and the Pool of London was used intensively, with the bascules of the bridge being raised many times during a working day. A walkway was needed so that pedestrians were able to cross the river even when ships were passing underneath. This was done by means of a high walkway – which was not popular with those who suffered from vertigo! However, the whole walkway has now been glassed in and some of the best views in London can be taken in from here.

The Tower Bridge Exhibition, on the south bank of the Thames just by the bridge is a well thought out presentation of its history and engineering. *Area Map p.8, C:1*

Waterloo Bridge
Rendell, Palmer and Tritton, 1937-42

Waterloo Bridge, approached from Lancaster Place on the north bank or Waterloo Road on the south; Free access.

All those of a certain age will remember the song 'Waterloo Sunset' by the Kinks and think of Julie and Terry meeting here. Who could blame them, the views are splendid. The river frontage of Somerset House is particularly interesting; from here you can see the water gate that allowed boats into the complex although it's been land-locked since the embankment of the river.

The bridge was built in 1937-42, with Gilbert Scott acting in an advisory role to the architects. This bridge replaced the much-loved one of 1811 by Rennie, the foundations of which were considered unstable.

The artist Barbara Hepworth was asked to submit plans for sculptures which it was hoped would adorn the finished bridge, but the scheme did not materialise.

Millennium Bridge
Foster & Partners, 2000

Millennium Bridge, spans the Thames from St. Pauls Cathedral to the Tate Modern, Bankside, SE1 • Nearest transport Monument LU, Blackfriars LU/Rail and Southwark LU

Unfortunately, this will always be known as the 'wobbly bridge' since its unfortunate swaying episodes at its first opening. It's perfect now. The architect collaborated with the sculptor Anthony Caro to produce this 'blade of light'. Traffic–free bliss and the best view of St Paul's and the rest of London. Fantastic!
Area Map p.8, A:2

Left: Millenium Bridge. The 325 metre bridge was built to link St Paul's and the City with the South Bank. The 4m wide aluminium deck is flanked by stainless steel balustrades and is supported by cables to each side which dip below the deck enabling unimpeded views up and down the river

Right: The London Eye

The London Eye
Julia Barfield and David Marks, 1993-2000

Jubilee Gardens, Embankment, SW1 • Tel 0870 5000 600 (Booking line) • www.london-eye.com • Nearest transport Westminster LU and Waterloo LU/Rail • Booking is highly recommended but it is possible to purchase tickets at County Hall (next to the London Eye) but be prepared to queue • See website for opening times and admission charges

One of the most popular structural projects ever carried out anywhere was conceived at the kitchen table of architects Julia Barnfield and David Marks in 1993. This was the year that marked the centenary of the unveiling of the 'Big Wheel' at Chicago's World Columbian Exposition designed by George W Ferris. The Ferris Wheel became the main attraction of the fair – just as the London Eye was to become the 'hit' of millennium celebrations in London when it first took paying passengers in January 2000.

The wheel of the London Eye is the largest of its kind ever built at a height of 450 feet. The foundations consist of 44 concrete piles, 110 feet deep, sunk in by 2,200 tonnes of concrete. The holding backstay cables are held in place by 1,200 tonnes of concrete and about 1,700 tonnes of steel was used in the construction – the statistics are mind-boggling.

Each of the 32 capsules gently glide the visitor up into the air above the buildings of London and provide a panorama of up to 25 miles in all directions – with the whole trip taking 30 minutes. This is an experience not to be missed, even if you normally do not like 'heights,' and the ride feels as though you are

hardly moving. It is difficult to recommend the best time of day to enjoy the trip – but a particular favourite is dusk when the lights are coming on all over London; sheer magic. The whole of the capital city stretches out before you and the higher you rise the smaller and more model village-like it becomes – the perfect way to appreciate London's fabulous architecture. *Area Map p.6, C:2*

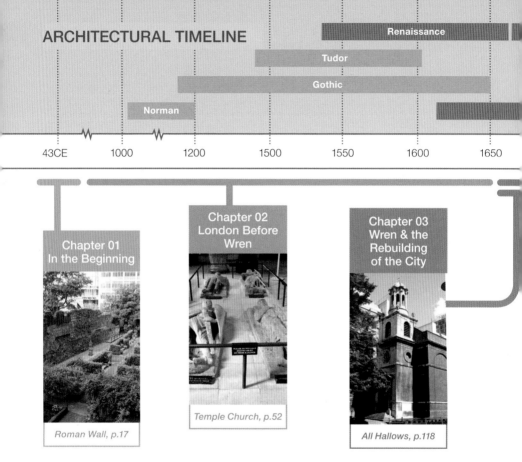

ARCHITECTURAL TIMELINE

Renaissance

Tudor

Gothic

Norman

| 43CE | 1000 | 1200 | 1500 | 1550 | 1600 | 1650 |

Chapter 02
London Before
Wren

Chapter 01
In the Beginning

Chapter 03
Wren & the
Rebuilding
of the City

Temple Church, p.52

Roman Wall, p.17

All Hallows, p.118

Above (in pink): Architectural Timeline – major periods and styles of British architecture set within their time periods.
Below: See the chapters set within the Architectural Timeline

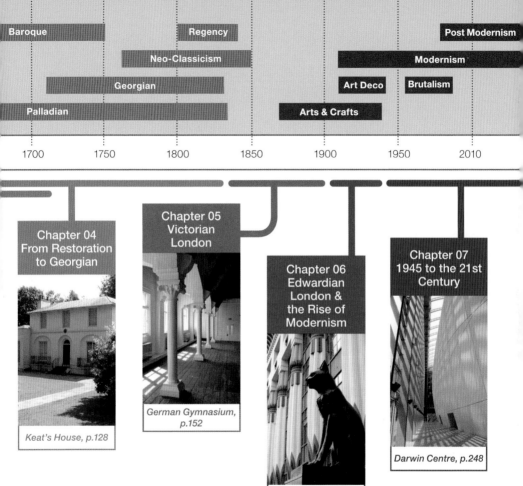

Baroque

Regency

Post Modernism

Neo-Classicism

Modernism

Georgian

Art Deco

Brutalism

Palladian

Arts & Crafts

1700   1750   1800   1850   1900   1950   2010

Chapter 04
From Restoration
to Georgian

Keat's House, p.128

Chapter 05
Victorian
London

*German Gymnasium,
p.152*

Chapter 06
Edwardian
London &
the Rise of
Modernism

*Carreras Cigarette
Factory, p.186*

Chapter 07
1945 to the 21st
Century

Darwin Centre, p.248

Glossary

Abacus: A flat slab (usually of stone or marble) forming the top of a capital.

Ambulatory: A passage (usually at the eastern end of a church) around the sanctuary.

Amphitheatre: An open-air theatre with tiered seating.

Apse: The semicircular end of a Roman basilica (a building used for administrative purposes). The apse was subsequently incorporated into church architecture.

Arcade: Series of arches supported by columns or piers. Also refers to a covered shopping street.

Ashlar: Stone blocks cut into a regular size.

Atrium: A covered court rising through all storeys of a building (especially Roman or 20th century).

Attached or Engaged Column: One that partly merges into the wall and is thus not freestanding.

Bay: Division of an elevation by regular verticals such as arches or windows.

Boss: An ornamented projection usually at the intersection of vault ribs.

Buttress: A wall built at right angles to the main wall to stabilise it or take the thrust of the arch or vault behind. A 'flying buttress' of the Gothic period transmits the thrust to a heavy abutment by means of an arch.

Capital: The head of a classical column.

Caryatids: Female figures supporting an entablature (as seen on the northern exterior of St Pancras New Church, Euston Road, London NW1)

Chancel: Sited towards the eastern end of a church, separated from the nave. Used by officiating clergy and choir.

Clerestory: The wall above the aisles of a church (especially Norman and Gothic) pierced by windows.

Coade Stone: Artificial stone manufactured in London circa 1769-1840.

Concrete: A mixture of cement (ie calcined lime and clay), aggregate (ie small stones or broken brick), sand and water. First used by the Romans but the knowledge of this material was lost at the end of the Roman Empire and only rediscovered during the 15th century. Reinforced concrete contains steel rods for additional support.

Crypt: Underground vaulted chamber, usually at the eastern end of a church, and which sometimes held specific chambers for relics.

Cupola: A dome, and more usually a small dome placed upon a larger one.

Curtain Wall: Non load-bearing external wall (20th-century building); also the wall connecting two towers of a castle or fort.

Dormer: A window projecting from the slope of a roof. 'Dormer' is French for 'to sleep' and often these windows let air and light into roof voids to allow the space to be used as a bedroom.

Eaves: The overhanging edge of a roof.

Entablature: The collective name for the three horizontal members (architrave, frieze and cornice) in classical architecture that is supported by the column.

Fenestration: The arrangement of windows in a building.

Gable: The triangular part of an end wall of a sloping roof.

Hammerbeam: Timber beam projecting from a wall, often elaborately carved.

Hypocaust: Underfloor heating system perfected by the Romans.

Keystone: The top central stone in an arch or vault.

Lancet Window: Long, slim, pointed window.

Lantern: Windowed turret, usually circular, upon a dome.

Lintel: Flat stone or beam above an opening in a wall.

Nave: The central, usually the largest, space in a church.

Pediment: The triangular part above the entablature.

Pilaster: Column, usually square or rectangular, or pillar slightly projecting from a wall.

Rendering: The plastering on the outside wall of a building.

Reredos: Screen, usually painted or carved, behind the altar in a church.

Rood Screen: A partition between the nave and choir of a church – usually carved.

Rotunda: A building or room circular in plan and often with a dome over it.

Rustication: Tooled surface of building stone made to look exaggeratedly rough.

Stucco: A mixture of lime plaster and sand applied to exterior walls – usually to hide inferior brickwork – and often marked to give the impression of stonework.

Vault: Arched stone or brick roof or ceiling.

Bibliography

A History of London, *Stephen Inwood* (Macmillan, 1998)

Dictionary of British Architects 1600-1840, *Howard Colvin* (Yale University Press, 1995)

English Architecture, *David Watkins* (Thames & Hudson, 1979)

In Search of London, *H V Morton* (Methuen, 1951)

Liquid History, *Stephen Croad* (Batsford, 2003)

London A-Z, Newer editions have the principal buildings marked (Geographers' A-Z Map Company)

London – Bread and Circuses, *Jonathan Glancey* (Verso, 2001)

London: A Social History, *Roy Porter* (Penguin, 1994)

London's Riverscape – Lost and Found (The London's Found Riverscape Partnership, 2000)

Museums & Galleries of London, *Abigail Willis* (Metro Publications, 2000)

Oxford Dictionary of Architecture, *James Stevens Curl* (Oxford, 1999)

Oxford Dictionary of London Place Names, *A D Mills* (Oxford, 2001)

Restoration London, *Lisa Picard* (Phoenix, 2003)
Lisa Picard has also written **Elizabeth's London** and **Dr Johnson's London** (Weidenfeld and Nicholson 2003 and 2000 respectively).

Style City London (Thames and Hudson, 2003)

The Buildings of England, *Nikolaus Pevsner* (Founding Editor) (see www.pevsner.co.uk)

The Great Stink of London, *Stephen Halliday* (Sutton Publishing, 1999)
Stephen Halliday has also written **Underground to Everywhere** (Sutton Publishing, 2001)

18 Folgate Street, *Dennis Severs* (Chatto and Windus, 2002)

Websites

www.londonopenhouse.org – The London Open House is a registered educational charity concerned with London and its architecture. Open House organises an annual weekend event when hundreds of buildings open their doors to the public – private houses, offices, medical schools, theatres, etc, most of which do not usually allow public access. This event usually takes place during the third weekend of September – consult the website for dates and venues.

www.architecturelink.org.uk – Provides useful information about architecture, especially buildings in London of the 20th and 21st century.

www.museumoflondon.org.uk – Invaluable information about the history and people of the capital.

www.architecture.com – The website of RIBA (Royal Institute of British Architects). News and details of exhibitions and projects as well as access to the extensive RIBA library. Also useful information if you are thinking of hiring an architect or becoming one yourself!

www.c20society.org.uk – Originally called the Thirties Society the society changed its name to the Twentieth Century Society when good post-war buildings became under threat.

www.london-city-churches.org.uk – A valuable site packed with information and illustrations of the fifty or so churches within the City of London.

www.artsline.org.uk – Information service for people with physical disabilities, a comprehensive guide on access to London's buildings.

www.lookingatbuildings.org.uk – Created by the Pevsner Architectural Guides this is a comprehensive website, with pages on building types, architectural styles and traditions, building materials and methods of construction. Research tools include a glossary, index of architects and their works, and a guide to further reading on all aspects of English architecture.

www.newlondonarchitecture.org – NLA is a focus for the debate and discussion of issues facing architecture, planning, development and construction in the capital. Find out about projects that are recently completed, currently under construction or planned to alter London's fabric over the coming years.

Index

1-3 Willow Road 171, **197**
6-10 Adam Street 7, 318
38 & 39 Cheyne Walk **177**
44, Berkeley Square **106**

A

Adam, Robert 87, 107-115, 123, 215, 318, 325
Adelphi 7, **114**
Admiralty Arch 7, 320, **325**
Admiralty House 7, 320, **325**
Admiralty Screen 7, 320, **325**
Albert Memorial **146**
All Hallows by the Tower 9, 14, 20, **29**
All Hallows Church 9, **118**
All Saints (Chelsea Old Church) **54**
All Saints Church, Margaret Street 5, **144**
All Souls Church 5, 116, 285, 292-**293**, 297
Alsop, Will 1, 204, 250
Anchor, The 298, **305**, 311
Apsley House 89, **114**
Aquatics Centre (Olympic) **253**
Archer, Thomas 88, 100-101, 326, 336
Arnos Grove **191**
Art Deco 1, 39, 172, 186-187, 192-195, 259,
    268, 308, 339, 341-342, 350, 359, 363
Athenaeum 7, 285, **294**
Australia House 7, 312, 317

B

Babylon Restaurant & Roof Garden **342**
Baker, Sir Herbert 189, 318, 325
Banco Commerciale Italiana 9, **143**
Bank of England 9, **121**, **189**
Banqueting House 7, 23, 47, 86, 89, 106,
    320, 326, **327**, 331
Barkers 342, 354, 362, **363**
Baroque 61, 72, 86, 94-95, 98, 100-101,
    182, 190, 325, 336

Barry, Charles 141-143, 322, 328
Bazalgette, Sir Joseph 136, 151
BBC Broadcasting House 5, 285, **292**
Bentley, John Francis 162, 174
Bibendum Oyster Bar **339**
Bishopsgate Institute 9, **163**
Black Friar Public House 9, 337
Blackfriars Bridge 192, 298, **308**, 341
Blueprint Café 9, **344**
Borough Market 298, **304**, 311
Britannic House 9, **185**
British Library 3, 125, **226**, 232, **345**
British Museum 3, **17**, 20, 124, **125**, 159, 161,
    179, 187, 204, **232**, 233, 345
B T Tower 3, **209**
Buckingham Palace 7, 285, 286, **295**, 297
Burlington, Lord 87, 98, 104-106
Burlington Arcade 7, **357**
Burne-Jones, Edward 149, 163
Bush House 7, 312, 317
Butterfield, William 71, 144

C

Cabinet War Rooms 7, 329, 331
Cadogan Hall **181**
Café Below **334**
Canada House 7, 320, **323**
Canary Wharf 274, 277, **281**, 282, 283
Carlton House Terrace 7, 285, **295**
Carreras Cigarette Factory **186**
Central Criminal Court, Old Bailey 9, **178**
Centre Point 3, **210**
Chambers, Sir William **107**
Channel 4 Headquarters 7, **225**
Charlton House **43**
Cheshire Cheese Public House 9, 266, **268**
Chester Gate 5, 284, **289**
Chester Terrace 5, 284, **288**
Chiswick House 84, 89, **104**-106, 353
Christ Church, Newgate 9, **64**

Christ Church, Spitalfields 9, **95**
Circle, The 9, **216**
City Hall 9, **236**, 237, 239, 298, **300**, 311
City of London Information Centre 9, **245**
Cloth Fair 9, 257, **259**, 264
Coliseum Theatre 7, **176**
Commonwealth Institute **208**
Conran, Terence 339, 344
Cornwall Terrace 5, 284, **289**
Country Life Offices 7, **177**
County Hall (Former) 7, **182**, 310
Courtauld Gallery 316, **319**
Courtauld Institute of Art 110, 312, **316**
Cremorne Riverside Centre **247**
The Crescent, City of London 9, **119**
Crosby Hall **54**
Crossness Pumping Station **151**
Cumberland Terrace 5, 116, 284, 287, **288**, 297
CZWG Architects 216, 307

D

Daily Express building 9, 266, **268**
Daily Telegraph building 7, 266
Daimler Car Hire Garage 3, **193**
George Dance the Elder **117**
George Dance the Younger **117**
Danish Embassy **213**
Darwin Centre, Natural History Museum 161, **248**, 249
Dean Rees House 257, **259**
Dennis Severs' House 9, **131**
Duke of York's Column 7, 285, **295**
Dulwich Picture Gallery **121**

E

Economist Building 7, **208**
Edward VII Galleries (British Museum) **179**
Eltham Palace **39**
Embankment Place 7, **225**, 318
Euston Fire Station 3, **173**

F

Farrell, Terry 202, 224-225, 318, 345
Fitzroy Square 3, **115**
Flamsteed House 274, **277**, 283
Florin Court 9, 257, **259**
Foreign & Commonwealth Office 7, 320, **328**
Former Lex Garage 7, **190**
Fortnum & Mason 7, **360**
Foster, Norman 184, 204, 221-222, 232, 239, 282, 300, 307
Foster & Partners 232, 236, 239, 244, 300, 369
Foyer Bar, Claridge's **342**
Frederick Place 9, 115
Freemasons' Hall 3, **187**
Fulham Palace **49**
Future Systems 218

G

Geffrye Museum **128**
Gehry, Frank 200, 246
George Inn 9, 298, 304, 311, **335**
German Gymnasium **152**, 153
Gibbs, James **102**, 261-262, 276, 314, 323
Gilbert Scott, George 26, 41, 52, 78, 137, 138, 146, 154, 191, 328
Gilbert Scott, Giles 37, 40, 191, 231, 307, 348
Globe Theatre 298, **306**, 311
Gloucester Gate 5, 284, **286**
Gloucester Lodge 5, 284, **286**
Golden Hinde 298, **304**, 311
Goldfinger, Erno 171, 197, 200, 210
Gothic 7, 9, 21, 25, 26, 28, 32, 40, 41, 52, 53, 55, 60, 65, 70, 71, 76, 78, 89, 94, 97, 98, 123, 134, 137, 138, 141, 142, 144, 146, 155, 168, 174, 180, 269, 295, 313, 328, 374
Graduate Centre, London Metropolitan University **241**
Greenwich Foot Tunnel 274, **275**, 283
Guildhall, The 9, **16**, 40

H

Haberdashers' Hall 9, 257, **262**, 264
Hadid, Zaha 1, 204, 246, 253
Handel House **131**
Hanover Gate 5, 284, **289**
Hanover Terrace 5, 284, **289**
Harrods 169, **359**
Hawksmoor, Nicholas 7, 26, 71, 74, 78, 88, 93, **94**, 95-97, 275, 276, 280
Hay's Wharf 298, **300**, 301
Hayward Gallery 7, 206, 207
Herzog & de Meuron 203, 231, 348
HMS Belfast 298, **300**, 311
Hoare's Bank 7, 266, **269**
Holborn Viaduct **147**
Holden, Charles 172, 179, 189, 191, 196
Holy Trinity Church, Chelsea **163**
Holy Trinity Church, Marylebone 5, **123**
Home House 5, **110**
Hooke, Robert 58, 60, 64, 67, 68, 71, 73, 75, 81, 277, 367
Horniman Museum **164**
Horse Guards Parade 320, 322, 325, 327
Houses of Parliament 7, 33, 134, 136, **141**, 320, 329, **330**, 331
Hungerford Bridge 225

I

Imagination 3, 215, **220**, 221, 222
India House 7, 312, **318**
Inn the Park 7, 321, 331, **349**
Institute of Directors, The 7, 285, **294**

J

Jacobsen, Arne 213
Jewel Tower 7, **33**, 141
Dr Johnson's House 9, **127**, 266, **269**, 273
Jones, Inigo 14, 23, 43, 44, 47, 48, 59, 68, 86, 89, 104, 105, 261, 279, 327
Jones, Sir Horace 139, 265, 272, 356, 359, 367

K

Keats House 128
Kensington Palace **93**
Kent, William 93, 105, **106**, 322, 326
Kenwood **112**
King's College 7, 312, **316**
The King's Observatory, Richmond **107**

L

Lambeth Palace 7, **55**
Langham Hotel 5, 138, 284, 290, **292**
Lansdowne House **110**
Leadenhall Market 9, 265, 356, **359**
Leighton, Lord Frederick 148, 149, 358
Leighton House 148, **149**
Liberty's 5
Libeskind, Daniel 204, 241
Lloyd's of London 9, 201, **214**, 215
London Bridge 204, 251, 298, 300-303
London Central Mosque 5, 284, **289**, 297
London Eye 7, 182, 198, 244, 310, 364, **371**
London Oratory Church of the Immaculate Heart of Mary **158**
London Transport Headquarters 7, 188, **189**
Lord's Cricket Ground **217**, 218, 219
Lutyens, Sir Edwin 168, 177, 185, 267, 289, 328

M

Maggie's Centre **246**
Make Architects 245
Mansion House 9, 117, **118**
Marble Arch 5
Marylebone Parish Church 284, 289
Methodist Central Hall 7, 169, **180**, 321, **340**
Middle Temple 266, **270**, 273
Midland Grand Hotel 3, 146, **154**, 157, 226
Millennium Bridge 9, 298, **307**, 349, **369**
Modernist 208, 213
Monument, The 9, 366, **367**
More, Thomas 20, 54, 158

Morris, William 12, 139, 147, 163, 171, 177
Museum of London 9, **17**, 282, 283

N

Nash, John 42, **116**, 284-297, 322
National Gallery 7, 202, 320, **321**, **322**, 331
National Maritime Museum 44, 274, **279**, 283
National Portrait Gallery 7, **346**
National Theatre 298, **308**, 309, 310, 311
Natural History Museum **159**, **248**
Nelson's Column 320, **321**, 346
New Government Offices 7, 320, **329**
No1 Canada Square 274, **282**
No1 Poultry 202

O

O2 Arena 274, **282**
Octagon of Orleans House **103**
Odeon Cinema 7, **195**
The Orangery, Kensington Palace 92, **335**
Osterley Park **111**
Oxo Tower 298, **308**, 311, **341**

P

Palace of Westminster 7, 25-26, 33, **140-142**
Palestra 9, 204, **250**
Palladianism 87, **89**, 107, 108
Palladio, Andrea 89
Park Crescent 5, 284, 288, **290**
Peter Jones **362**
Phoenix Theatre 7, **191**
Renzo Piano 1, 201, 204, 214, 251
Piazza, Covent Garden 7, **48**
Piccadilly Circus 285, **294**
Pizza Express, Alban Gate 9, **345**
Portcullis House 7, 198, 320, **329**, 330
Portland Place 5, 284, **290**
Port of London Authority 9, **184**, 187
Portrait Restaurant & Bar, National Portrait
    Gallery **346**

Prince Henry's Room 7, 266, **270**, 273
Privy Council Chambers 7, 320, **328**
Pugin, A W 141, 162

Q

Queen Elizabeth Hall 7, 207
Queen's House 23, 43, **44-45**, 47, 89,
    274, **279**, 283

R

Ranger's House 274, **276**, 283
Regent's Park Zoo 5, 286
Renaissance 22, 23, 58, 61, 89, 94, 176, 323
Renaissance London, Chancery Court
    Hotel 3, **341**
Reuters Building 9, **267**
Rex Whistler Restaurant, Tate Britain **336**
RIBA Stirling Prize 32, 218, 239, 242, 246, 250
Ritz, The 7, 169, **340**
Richard Rogers 201, 204, 214, 225, 246, 251, 282
Rogers Stirk Harbour & Partners 246
Roman Bath 7, 312, **314**
Rotunda Bar & Restaurant, King's Place **351**
Roundhouse, The **143**
Royal Academy of Arts 7, 89, **222**, 223
Royal Albert Hall **150**
Royal Arsenal, Woolwich **99**
Royal Courts of Justice 7, 312, **313**, 319
Royal Exchange 9, 60, **358**
Royal Festival Hall 7, 200, **205**, 310, **343**
Royal Hospital Chelsea **91**
Royal Institute of British Architects (RIBA)
    5, 221, 284, **292**, 297, 377
Royal Naval College 274, **279**, 280, 283
Royal Observatory 274, **276**, 277, 283
Royal Opera House 7, 20, **235**
Royal Society of Arts (RSA) 7, 114, 312, **318**
Russell House 7, **101**

S

St Alban 9, **65**
St Alfege Church 274, **275**, 283
St Andrew by the Wardrobe 9, **66**
St Andrew, Holborn 3, 9, **66**
St Anne, Limehouse **96**
St Anne and St Agnes 9, **67**
St Bartholomew's Hospital 9, 34, 257, **261**, 262, 265
St Bartholomew the Great 9, **34-35**, 257, 258, **261**, 265
St Bartholomew the Less 9, 257, **261**, 265
St Benet, Paul's Wharf 9, **68**
St Bride, Fleet St 9, **69**, 266, **267**
St Clement Danes 7, 312, **314**, 319
St Clement Eastcheap 9, **70**
St Dunstan in the East 9, **70**
St Dunstan in the West 7, 266, **269**, 273
St Edmund the King & Martyr 9, **71**
St Ethelburga's 9, **50**
St George's, Bloomsbury 3, **95**
St Helen's Bishopsgate 9, **38**
St James Garlickhithe 9, **71**
St James's Palace 7, **42**
St James's, Piccadilly 7, **90**
St John's Priory 9, **36**
St John's, Smith Square 7, 95, **336**
St Lawrence Jewry 9, **72**
St Magnus the Martyr 9, **72**
St Margaret Lothbury 9, **73**
St Margaret Pattens 9, **74**
St Margaret's Church, Westminster 7, **41**, 320, **330**, 331
St Martin-in-the-Fields 7, 103, 320, 321, **323**, 331
St Martin within Ludgate 9, **75**
St Mary Abchurch 9, **75**
St Mary Aldermary 9, **76**
St Mary at Hill 9, 77, 78
St Mary-le-Bow 9, 64, **77**, 334
St Mary-le-Strand 7, **102**, 312, **314**, 319
St Mary's Church **162**
St Mary Woolnoth 9, 88, **96**
St Michael Cornhill 9, **78**
St Michael Paternoster Royal 9, **79**
St Nicholas Cole Abbey 9, **80**
St Olaf House 9, **195**, 298, **301**
St Pancras Grand Champagne Bar **350**
St Pancras Old Church **37**
St Pancras Station 3, 132, 138, **154**, **350**
St Paul's Cathedral 9, 56, 59, 60, **61-63**, 83, 192, 245, 307, 349, 366
St Paul's Church 7, **48**
St Pauls's Deptford **101**
St Peter upon Cornhill 9, **81**
St Peter, Vere Street 5, **103**
St Stephen Walbrook 9, 64, **83**
Saatchi Gallery 247
Sackler Galleries, Royal Academy of Arts 7, **222**
Sadler's Wells Theatre 3, **229**
Linley Sambourne House 147
Savoy Chapel 7, 312, **318**, 319
Savoy Hotel 7
Scotland Yard 7, 320, 325, **330**
Selfridges 5, 171, **360**
Senate House 3, 166, 179, **196**
Shard, The 9, **251**
Shri Swaminarayan Mandir **228**
Skylon Restaurant, Grill & Bar 7, **343**
Smirke, Sir Robert 42, 52, **124**, 125, 179, 226, 232, 316, 323
Smithfield Market 9, 139, 257, **264**, 265
Soane, Sir John 3, 37, 47, 108, 117, 118, **120**, 121, 122, 123, 124, 189, 276
Soane's Museum, Sir John 3, 120, **123**
Somerset House 7, 88, 312, 316, 319
South Africa House 7, 320, **325**
Southwark Bridge 298, **305**, 306
Southwark Cathedral 9, **32**, 298, **303**, 304, 311
Spanish & Portuguese Synagogue 9, **51**
Staple Inn 3, **43**

Steiner House, Rudolf 5, **190**
Stirling, James 202, 336
Sussex Place 5, 284, **289**
Swiss Re Headquarters 9, 238, **239**
Syon House **109**

T

Tate Modern 9, 203, 230, **231**, 245, 298, 307, 311, **348**, 349
Temple Bar 7, **272**, 313
Temple Church 7, **52**, 53, 266, **270**, 273
Tomkins, Haworth 242
Tower Bridge 9, 272, 298, **300**, **367**
Tower of London 9, 30, **31**
Townsend, Charles Harrison 163, 164, 165
Trellick Tower 197, **210**, 211, 212

U

Ulster Place 5, 284, **290**
Unilever House 9, **192**

V

Vanbrugh, Sir John 86, 89, 94, **98**, 99, 168, 178, 180, 280
Vanbrugh Castle **98**
Vauxhall Cross **224**
Vertigo, Tower 42 9, **344**

W

Wallace Collection 5, **234**
Waterhouse, Alfred 137, 159, 161
Waterloo Bridge 192, 310, 316, **368**
Waterstone's, Piccadilly 7, **361**
Wembley Stadium **244**
Wesley's Café at the Methodist Central Hall **340**
Wesley's House, John **130**
Westminster Abbey 7, 18, 21, **24-28**, 33, 41, **97**, 258, 320, **330**, 331
Westminster Cathedral 7, 162, **174**, 175
Westminster Hall 7, **33**, 141, 327

Whitechapel Art Gallery **165**
Whitefriars Monastery 266, **269**
Wigglesworth, Sarah 247
Winchester House 9, 298, **304**
Wren, Sir Christopher 26, 52, **58-83**, 88, 89, **90**, 91, 93, 94, 123, 168, 177, 178, 180, 267, 272, 277, 279, 280, 295, 314, 334, 367

Y

Young Vic Theatre **242**

Z

Zimbabwe House 7, **179**